Lighting the Fire

A Cherokee Journey
from Dropout to Professor

Steve Russell

Library of Congress Cataloging-in-Publication Data

Russell, Steve, Lighting Fire: A Cherokee Journey from Dropout to Professor

Summary: A Cherokee dropout abandoned by his father finds a way to graduate college and law school and become a judge and a professor.

Songs referenced in this book include:

Page 1: "Never Been to Spain" © Hoyt Axton

Page 42: "Little Egypt" © Jerry Leiber and Mike Stoller

Page 44: "I Guess I Owe it all to Pamela Brown" © Sony//ATV Music Publishing LLC

Page 60: "I Can't Stop Loving You" © Don Gibson

Pages 61 and 271: "This Land is Yor Land" © 1956 (renewed), 1958 (renewed), 1970 and 1972 by Woody Guthrie Publications, Inc. & TRO-Ludlow Music, Inc. (BMI).

Page 206: "Hey, That's No Way to Say Goodbye" © 1967 Leonard Gohen; © 2009–2020 Sony Music Entertainment Canada Inc.

Page 319 "You Only Live Twice," © Leslie Bricusse and John Barry

ISBN: 978-1-939282-44-6

Published by Miniver Press, LLC, McLean Virginia
Copyright 2020 Steve Russell

First edition June 2020

DEDICATION

When I took the name "Russell," I dedicated my life to my maternal grandparents, Judson George and Bessie Lois Russell, who took me in, gave me a Cherokee role model, Will Rogers, and lit the fire.

When I was born with the name "Teehee," my life was dedicated to a community of survivors of the great North American Holocaust. I hope the life represented in these essays is worthy of the Cherokee people.

"If this were play'd upon a stage now, I could condemn it as an improbable fiction."

Twelfth Night, Act III, Scene 4

"The secret of our success is that we never, *never* give up."

Chief Wilma Mankiller

CONTENTS

ACKNOWLEDGMENTS

Parts of this book were first published by the Indian Country Today Media Network, owned by the Oneida Nation, one of the *Haudenosaunee*, the modern Six Nations—linguistic relatives of the Cherokee. This Cherokee is grateful to the Oneida Nation for publication opportunities that allowed writers to keep their copyrights.

Bob Roe edited some of my best work for *Indian Country Today* and for *Newsweek*. He got paid for that, but I benefitted from his insights on this book because we are friends. Miniver Press editor Mira Singer substantially improved the original manuscript.

Chris Napolitano hung in there with me through the hardest part of the cancer situation and helped get this book jump-started.

I hesitate to begin listing people who were continual inspirations because there would be no practical end, but I should mention people who put their hands on the manuscript or parts of it and made it better with edits or technical expertise or both. In addition to Napolitano and Roe, these dear people contributed their talents for the sake of the story: Ray Cook, Mary Mobley, Martha Ture, and Sara M. Walsh.

This is my story, but in several instances, I found documents that showed my memory to be faulty. I've done my best to tell the truth, but I own any errors that remain.

All of my girlfriends mentioned in this book are given fake names. I have tried to take care that nothing embarrassing can be reliably attributed to any person outside my family. My wives are stuck with me. There is no way to ignore them and no way to disguise them.

~1~

WHAT IS NEEDED FOR SCHOOL

Hoyt Axton left us a song that said he'd never been to heaven. Perhaps he has now, and that would be our loss. Most of us have never been to heaven, but some of us have been to Oklahoma. They tell me I was born there, but that's hearsay, as far as I'm concerned. That puts me in a tough position because I'm told a memoir has to be told from memory. I'll do the best I can.

My earliest memory not aided by a folk song was a sojourn to the oil patch in Pampa, Texas, where my mother made a futile effort to mother me. I was about 3 years old. I remember snowdrifts in Pampa taller than me, and traffic signals of such bright reds and greens I could not look away from them. Bristow had no traffic signals at the time. I remember visiting a doctor. I remember my mother beating me with a belt on several occasions, and, when I cried, telling me that if I did not shut up she would "give me something to cry about."

My mother's attempt to play mother did not work out. Aside from the beating and the illness, I don't remember the details. She left me with her parents back in Bristow, Oklahoma, where I became a major disruption of their golden years. In my first memory after being returned to Bristow, I'm harassing my grandmother: "Wake up, Granma! I need you to read it to me."

"It" was the word balloons in the *Tulsa World* comics.

That obnoxious Indian toddler was lucky I can't time travel back to 1951 and grab my younger self's attention for a talk about how children should treat elders. "Granma" was Bessie Russell, my mother's mother. I could not see beyond the entertainment I wanted right then to understand she was nodding off because she had washed dishes all night at one of the cafes on Route 66, or "Main Street," as we called the Mother Road in Bristow.

With superhuman patience, she would shake off the fatigue and pronounce each word in the cartoon strip as she related it to something in the drawing. And she would always remind me: "This is something you need to learn to do for yourself. You're a smart boy and you don't need somebody reading to you."

Sure enough, if the *World* hit the front porch before Granma got home, I was moved to pull off the rubber band that held the newspaper together, dig out the funnies, and I would be making my best 4-year-old effort to learn the words. Easy ones first, like "Pow!"

I didn't care much for *Mary Worth*, but I would sometimes get into *Steve Canyon* or *Little Orphan Annie* and be in an unseemly hurry to catch the next six inches of the story. I lacked the insight to see myself in *Dennis the Menace* or *The Katzenjammer Kids*, but I did place myself in *The Lone Ranger*, at least when I caught the story when the comic strip moved to live action on the radio. That series contained the only Indian character I remember from those times who had a name. In my imagination I rode with the Lone Ranger's "faithful Indian companion, Tonto," the sidekick's sidekick, and we were much more practical than that white dude with the funny-looking mask that was supposed to be a disguise.

I slowly learned to read the funnies, and then Granma started pushing me to read the front-page news, headlines first. That was not as hard as reading the funnies because we listened to the news on the radio several times a day. I knew the president was named "Truman" and there was trouble in a place called "Korea." It would be a while before I learned to recognize a word longer than "Eisenhower."

I knew the sounds of the letters from reading the funnies and I knew the major news stories from listening to the radio every evening before *The Lone Ranger*. I confess I got more upset when *The Adventures of Superman* went off the air than I did about the bad stuff on the evening news. They were all stories to me, and I did not give any thought to whether they were true in the same sense the live music broadcasts were true: "This is KVOO, the Voice of Oklahoma, bringing you, live from the Cain's Ballroom in Tulsa, Oklahoma, Leon McAuliffe and the Cimarron Boys. Take it away, Leon..."

McAuliffe would take it away with pedal steel guitar licks he had perfected with Bob Wills and his Texas Playboys. Wills still toured up and down the Mother Road, and he would stop in Bristow to eat at a restaurant called Hamburger King, a choice dictated by a dirt and gravel parking lot big enough for the tour bus. The radio news and the radio stories were roughly equal to 5-year-old ears, but the music was as real as Bob Wills' tour bus.

The school year I was to turn 6, Granma tried to enroll me in Edison Elementary, the closest to my home of three grammar schools in Bristow. I did not understand one of the three was for black kids only. Edison would not take me because my sixth birthday did not come until February and the argument that I already knew how to read was fruitless. Granma briefly got me in a kindergarten run by the Catholic Church, but I got kicked out for treating those Bible stories the nuns claimed were true as just like other stories, and therefore up for debate. I had apparently given some thought to the story of Jesus, and my expression of skepticism about how the story ended was the last straw.

A year later, I finally got admitted to Edison. When I showed up in that Oklahoma public school, I was fresh off years of being told by my grandparents that I was smart, a mantra that would soon be replaced by regular reminders that I should go to college.

Author's First Grade Photo, Edison Elementary School,
Bristow, Oklahoma. Copyright expired.

Being ahead of my classmates in reading felt good, but there
was one downside. I was in love with my first-grade teacher, Miss
Daniels. Her long, shiny black hair reminded me of my mother,
and she shared my mother's first name, Wanda. I would see my
mother twice or maybe three times a year. I considered her
wealthy because she always had a car—always a Ford until she got
really prosperous and acquired a Mercury—and she always
seemed to have important things to do where they had more oil
than was left in Bristow. I'm not sure I would have recognized
my mother if I met her on the street, but I always remembered
her beautiful hair, black like Miss Daniels'. I very much wanted
to impress Miss Daniels.

The major group reading exercise was called "reading circle."
The teacher would call on a student to start reading and that
student would go until they made a mistake, which the teacher
would correct and then pick somebody else to continue the
story. Early in the year, Miss Daniels quit calling on me. I was
crushed. Also bored, since there is just not that much story for
listening pleasure in *Fun with Dick and Jane*. All there was to do

while other kids read was to imagine Puff and Spot getting into a big fight. Like cats and dogs.

Miss Daniels did not appreciate it when I would whisper to others what I imagined was going on with Puff and Spot. I later saw her reasoning—calling on me would break the reading circle because I would not make a mistake. But, placed outside the circle, I lost the opportunity to impress Miss Daniels.

In spite of my conduct, I did pretty well in the first grade, and even better in the second, but I got knocked off the public school rails in the third grade, when we were assigned to copy whole pages of one cursive letter.

I would copy the letter until I could make it to my satisfaction and then I was done. No further copying interested me, and I've never been willing to do tasks that did not interest me. This trait steered me toward eventually becoming the typical Indian public school student: a dropout. The third grade was when I became no longer the hotshot but just another troublesome kid who would not take orders.

Indians were not just the most numerous minority at Edison—about 20%—we were the *only* minority, because black kids were still segregated in Oklahoma schools and the folks from the Middle East (Lebanese and Syrian people) were Christian and capitalist and so did not stand out. Most of the Indian kids would peel off from the public schools before high school graduation to become part of those dismal Indian dropout rates that persist to this day. In the third grade, I entered on the statistical path Indian students were expected to follow, but I physically remained in dear old Edison long after my brain checked out.

The teacher was ordering me to waste my time making many copies of letters I knew how to make and I was determined not to obey that order. It was a simple contest of wills, and I quickly learned that after a certain amount of arguing with the teacher, I would get kicked out of class. That was more than just tolerable, because wherever they put me, there always seemed to be a book nearby aimed at a higher grade level than the one I was supposed to be studying.

Books were the kindling for the fire lit by my grandparents, a secret entrance to a world that, unlike rural Indian Territory after it became Oklahoma, knew no boundaries for Indian kids. Reading could take me places I had never even heard rumors about and confer powers to fly over, under, or through the many constraints of my mundane life.

My childhood was generally defined by the limitations on what Indians could become and things I could not have, but there was one big exception. Very early, I learned the magic words that would always open the money spigot and even cause my grandparents to borrow if the cistern was dry:

"I need it for school."

The other kids got the cardboard folder; I got a faux leather briefcase.

The other kids got a box of eight or maybe sixteen Crayolas; I got sixty-four.

The other kids got ballpoint pens; I got a fountain pen.

My clothes may have been second-hand, my shoes often fell apart while I was wearing them, buttons were missing on my shirts—I could have answered a casting call for *Oliver Twist*. But if I could utter the magic words to my grandparents, all things seemed possible.

They paid too much for a *Funk & Wagnall's Standard Encyclopedia* because the fellow selling it door to door claimed I would "need it for school."

When I wanted to play in the band, my grandparents signed a note to buy a clarinet on time. I really wanted to play in a rock 'n' roll band. The band director sold me on the clarinet by claiming that if I learned clarinet I could play saxophone as well.

The sax was too expensive, even if I did "need it for school." Most of the hit records in those days contained a raucous sax solo and Elvis had only begun to pare records down to guitars and a drum.

The clarinet, like the encyclopedia, cost far more than my grandparents could rationally afford, but that was the magic of the claim it was "for school." I did not lie, but I stretched my school supplies list so thinly that my grandparents must have understood I was dashing to the end of the leash.

My grandparents made every effort to feed the fire of curiosity. Their two most effective measures cost nothing. One was that we had no television until the fourth grade and the other was that they told me regularly I was smart.

I'm ashamed of sitting at the feet of one grandparent or the other whining, "Read it to me...read it..."

The money disappeared by my broad definition of "school supplies" does not fill me with similar shame. They made a judgment about how to light a fire in me, to keep my attention on education if not on schooling. Like most of my peers, I would drop out—the first time in the sixth grade—but unlike most of my peers, I still made it to college.

My opinion of my grandparents' judgment now is reflected in my conduct. I have nine grandkids, and if they want anything from me all they need to do is repeat the magic words: "I need it for school."

STEVE RUSSELL

BORN CHEROKEE

At the time of my birth, where I was at the center of attention but which I really don't remember, the Cherokee Sacred Fire had been burning from time immemorial, or so those of us born Cherokee are told by our elders. We know it is so from times memorialized in history because those of us born Cherokee are told by our writers.

We know the Fire burned in the early 19th century when a Cherokee man of no schooling but great learning invented a method to put the Cherokee language on talking leaves. The Cherokee villages scattered in and around the Smoky Mountains united to form a constitutional republic, and the citizens of that republic had a higher literacy rate than the United States of America did when the young settler nation deigned to begin calling the Cherokees "civilized."

We know that in 1838 the Fire lit the last council before the Removal in Red Clay, Tennessee. It was brought on the Trail Where They Cried to Indian Territory, a journey that is part of the blood memory of modern Cherokees. The Fire was not extinguished by the tears, and the embers survived to light ceremonial fires in Indian Territory as it became Oklahoma in 1907.

The Sacred Fire was returned to the homelands in 1951, and embers from it were used to light the Council Fire when the elected leadership of the Cherokee Nation of Oklahoma and the

Eastern Band of Cherokees held a joint council on April 3, 1984, back in Red Clay, Tennessee.

The Cherokee Sacred Fire that had turned seven woods to ashes from time immemorial in the Smoky Mountains did the same in Oklahoma as a Cherokee man named Haney Walter Teehee crossed from the Cherokee Nation to the Muscogee (Creek) Nation to seek work in the oil fields.

The Fire burned on impassively as Haney Teehee searched on a cold and wet day and returned without a job but with a bad cold that did not go away. Haney, like his father Henry, had married a white woman, and his death left her with their 2-year-old son, Clifford Wayne Teehee.

Cliff Teehee grew up in the Muscogee (Creek) Nation without the Cherokee language and became the third generation of male exogamy when he married a beautiful and headstrong child of a driller and a housekeeper. Wanda Lucille Russell came within one semester of graduating from Bristow High School, which was closer than her husband got before she watched him ship out with the U.S. Navy in 1944, an enlistment rendered less hazardous when WWII in the Pacific formally ended on September 2, 1945. My father would end his Navy service as part of the occupying force in Sasebo, Japan.

I was born part of the baby boom on the day the Paris treaties formally ended WWII in Europe. I share my birth year with the AK-47 assault rifle, the U.S. Air Force, NASCAR, the Voice of America, *Meet the Press*, the International Monetary Fund, India as an independent nation, Pakistan, and the Stigler Act.

The Stigler Act joined the Dawes Act and the Curtis Act on a roster of infamy for all American Indians: laws passed to separate us from the reservations we got in an involuntary exchange for our homelands. The designation "Indian Territory" had already become a cruel irony, but Stigler was aimed at the tiny slivers of property still held in trust for citizens of the Five Tribes: Muscogee (Creek), Seminole, Choctaw, Chickasaw, and Cherokee.

The Sacred Fire burned as this additional barrier to Indians retaining their property went up and other barriers fell in 1947. Jackie Robinson became the first African-American to play major league baseball, suiting up for the Brooklyn Dodgers and going on to become Rookie of the Year. Chuck Yeager broke the sound barrier when he flew Mach 1.015.

The Fire burned as, in Cleveland, the American League baseball team adopted what *The Chicago Tribune* called "the most offensive image in sports," Chief Wahoo, a caricature that resembles the way Nazi propagandists had represented Jews but one that is only now being phased out by the Cleveland Indians.

The Fire burned as the NAACP presented a petition for relief from racism to the United Nations, stating in part, "No nation is so great that the world can afford to let it continue to be deliberately unjust, cruel and unfair toward its own citizens."

The Fire was a long burning backdrop to Indian relations when, in Richmond, Virginia, Dr. Walter Ashby Plecker walked in front of a speeding car and departed the world he had altered for thousands of people with his authorship and enforcement of the Racial Integrity Act of 1924. That law recognized only two "races" in the Commonwealth of Virginia, "white" and "colored," effectively legislating American Indians out of existence. From his post as Registrar for the Virginia Bureau of Vital Statistics, he enforced the "one drop rule" against African-Americans and Indians alike, and no "colored" person like my father could lawfully marry a white person like my mother until the U.S. Supreme Court struck down the law in 1967.

In Oklahoma City, the state legislature authorized building the Turner Turnpike, a construction that would bisect the Creek Nation immediately and become part of a system that would bisect the Cherokee Nation where the Sacred Fire was burning and seal the economic fate of the town where I was born.

In Bristow, Oklahoma, formerly the Muscogee (Creek) Nation, I was born with a Cherokee blood quantum of one-eighth and an opportunity to keep the Fire burning.

Or not.

STEVE RUSSELL

~3~

BESSIE AND JUD

I had no father and then no mother present for my growing up, and I would not have chosen that, but it did not take me long to understand that not everybody who had parents was better off. I can't say I never got beaten bloody but that never happened at home, the home provided by Bessie and Jud Russell. Mostly Bessie, because Jud was older and sicker.

Bessie Lois Van Hooser Russell in the backyard of her home in Bristow, Oklahoma, with grandson Stephen Teehee. Family photo.

Granma kept her composure in the face of broken bones, gunshot wounds, snakes, electrical fires, spiders larger than my young fist, and scorpions likewise. Even missionaries did not scare her. Having lived her life close to the bone, she did not scare easily.

I'd like to think I don't scare easily, either, but the truth of it is more complicated. Many years later, when the doc brought my cancer diagnosis in December of 2016, my external reaction was to turn to my wife (who had been watching my health go downhill for months with no idea of why) and say, "You know, we had a helluva run, didn't we?"

That remark—a genuine sentiment delivered with a genuine grin—brushed back her tears. While my external reaction was real and heartfelt, I was having a no-less-real internal reaction that pulled me back to the day in the '50s when my grandmother got the same diagnosis.

Granma was coming home from downtown Bristow, a city founded in Indian Territory in 1898 when a stop on the Frisco line between Sapulpa and Oklahoma City got its own post office. To be more exact, Bristow came to be in the Muscogee (Creek) Nation. By the time I was born, the federal government had trampled all the Indian removal treaties that promised Indian Territory would never be part of a state without tribal consent, so Bristow was in Oklahoma.

Walks to town involved no hills and no great distances. Route 66 (Main Street) and 6th was the center of metropolitan Bristow, but now Granma came tottering up the alley behind our house at 210 W. 12th. She always used the alley because it was closer to downtown and because 12th Street was a sea of red, sticky mud every time it rained.

It was also one border of "Niggertown," as most white folks called the area beyond paved streets. There were white families, mostly poor white families, on the same side of the street as us, and they, too, came and went by the alley when on foot. One family had plenty of money to live elsewhere but they were bootleggers and had professional needs for not just speedy ingress and egress but also access to both white and black communities. Indian residences were scattered around Bristow more by economics than by race. My presence did not identify the Russell home as Indian.

Granma had gone to the doctor for a lingering stomachache that had me thinking she was incredibly brave to have waited so long, but I was still learning about being poor. She carried an X-ray, the address of the University of Oklahoma charity hospital in Oklahoma City, and a bill that would be paid the way the cat ate the grindstone. Because I knew Granma didn't scare easily, one look at her face told me all I needed to know about cancer and how my elders judged the danger of it.

There was no Medicare and no Medicaid then, and if Franklin D. Roosevelt had not passed Social Security, the Russells would have had nothing but Grampa's pension from the Spanish-American War and Granma's wages from menial labor. Impecunious white elders died in dire circumstances during the Great Depression and Social Security was FDR's attempt to institutionalize people taking care of each other. Granma might have gotten quicker help (if not more help) if she and her husband had stayed near the Sac & Fox Agency, where they met.

The Sac & Fox wound up in Stroud, Oklahoma—less than 5 miles from Bristow—when the Bureau of Indian Affairs split Sac & Fox off a collective federal administration with some other small tribes (Kickapoo, Potawatomi, Shawnee, Iowa). In the reservation days, Indian agencies were distribution points for commodities, post offices, and usually a trading post. The agency was the center of commerce on most reservations and the first stop for honest visitors. Agency sites picked by the U.S. government became centers of Indian communities and later small towns in rural Oklahoma.

The differences among the small towns mirrored the travel of the oil boom and therefore the jobs. Grampa's job as first a roughneck and then a driller brought him to Bristow, where my grandparents came to own the house where we lived. It was bought by a settlement for injuries that ended Grampa's work in the oil fields, a settlement generous enough to fund two water faucets, a flush toilet, and one electrical circuit on each side of the house, serving an outlet in the middle of the ceiling of each of the seven rooms. The house was originally a duplex, and the two circuits for the entire house would prove inadequate for the load.

Grampa had gotten a pension for having followed Theodore Roosevelt to Cuba to steal an empire from Spain, and both grandparents got small checks from Social Security. Granma washed dishes in restaurants on Route 66 and she cleaned the swell folks' houses and minded their children.

Both Russell grandparents were pure settler stock with typical settler stories of grit in the service of greed. Granma's father, a Dutchman named Samuel Van Hooser, was by all accounts not a pleasant man. It was rumored in the family that he had killed his wife. Indians considered Van Hooser to be typical of the white persons lured to Indian Territory by the Homestead Act's promise of "free land."

"Free land" signified a giveaway of Indian property, but the terms were not for the lazy or the timid. To claim land, you either had to be the first to drive a stake in it and register your accomplishment or you had to eliminate competitors by trickery or by main force and then live on the empty land for five years minus your years of military service, breaking soil and making crops and dealing with the occasional Indian rendered "hostile" by his eviction.

Sam Van Hooser had gotten himself eighty acres of "free" land in McDonald County, Missouri. It was hilly and rocky soil hard by the Indian Territory border, but it had a sweet spring bubbling clear and cold out of a limestone aquifer. From the people I got to know as an adult, I came to understand the last Indian owners were probably Old Settler Cherokees who came west before forced removal from the homelands. When Granma died in 1972, I came to own that eighty acres, forty clear with unlimited use and first refusal on the other forty, until a few years ago, when the descendants of my mother's sister swindled family in favor of a real estate speculator. I deeded the remaining forty acres to my youngest son.

After perfecting the Missouri title, Van Hooser turned his attention to the great land rushes that led to the Oklahoma mascot becoming the thief who did not get the memo about why thieves needed honor. These Oklahoma settlers, known as "Sooners," cheated on the rules of land rushes and drove their stakes in advance. Sam was a Sooner but not sooner enough, and got no land despite being part of the thousands of itinerant thieves lured by pre-stolen "free" land that collectively made Indian Territory a land that could have inspired Obi-Wan Kenobi's literary description of the Mos Eisley Spaceport, "a wretched hive of scum and villainy."

This villain abandoned my grandmother Bessie and her mentally challenged little sister, Mabel, at the Sac & Fox Agency. If Bessie Van Hooser Russell's later cancer had gone untreated, like Mabel Van Hooser's earlier scarlet fever, my life would have been very different as a ward of the government.

Bessie took whatever work she could find among the Sac & Fox. Cleaning up after a drilling crew at a boarding house near Prague, she met Judson George Russell, a man as worldly as she was unsophisticated.

I'm not sure if Jud Russell was a driller by then or still roughnecking. He was from a big family of Scots and English Russells in Sandusky, Ohio. While Granma was practically Sac & Fox, Grampa had merely come to work in the oil patch. Neither expected to lord it over Indians. In the Cherokee Nation, both would have been "white intruders," but low on the Cherokee government's priority list for deportation...if the Cherokee government had a list.

The Ohioan oil worker and the rural housekeeper had no assets other than grit. They clung together through the Great Depression, squatting in a condemned building, raised two daughters, acquired a home, and just when it appeared that the hardest times were over, along came another mouth to feed, the child of their youngest daughter's marriage to a Cherokee named Teehee. Wanda Teehee née Russell was on the run, convinced that Clifford Teehee intended to kill her. That gave the elder Russells the choice to put me off on the government or to have their only grandchild child some tiny tot version of couch-surfing.

Wanda Lucille Russell, family photo approximately 1943.

My grandmother's decision to take me in had personified her strength and duty, more likely to charge than to totter. The pain would break her later, as it has broken me, but the wild fear on her face when she heard the diagnosis was nothing I'd ever seen. Whatever cancer was, it had to be horrible.

~4~

THE LETTER JACKET

Granma's fearsome X-ray set up the first of many excursions to The City. The docs wanted her accompanied but Grampa was not able, so Granma and I would rise before the sun and walk across town to the Greyhound station. I was not qualified to be her escort for many reasons, but what were we going to do?

Being big for my age—barely in double digits then—got to be an advantage, and the med students showed me how to maximize leverage if I had to try to pick her up. In an age before 911 and free long-distance calls, they gave me a list of numbers I could call in case of emergency in all of the towns on Route 66 between The City and Bristow.

I was scared for her but happy to go to Oklahoma City, both for adventure's sake and because Bristow was not safe for me at the time.

Since I was, as I said, big for my age—Granma said "husky" and the kids said "fat"—ordering clothes out of the Sears wish book had become difficult. The many categories and possible ways to measure were daunting when my body transgressed age brackets, but I had to wear the mistakes. At one of the two secondhand clothing stores in town, Grampa bought me a jacket. I was pleased to be wearing the purple and gold colors of the local high school while I was still in grammar school—it seemed much more fashionable than my other clothes. I did not understand what a "letter jacket" was. I soon found out.

"Hey, Chief Ha-Ha, where'd you get the letter jacket?"

The high school kids congregated across the street from the school near some trashcans where they could toss their cigarettes if any teachers decided to notice they were smoking. I was too young to attract their attention normally.

"I'm talking to you, fat boy."

"My Grampa gave it to me."

"So, where'd he steal it? He ain't no letterman."

"My Grampa doesn't steal!"

"Then it musta been you..." The speaking went on as a foot contacted my backside, sending me up on my toes. As I collapsed, a set of hands grabbed me from each side and I was being bum-rushed into an empty alley. One more heave and they let go.

Now I was on my knees in the gravel, surrounded by high school boys. I knew several by sight but none by name.

"OK, Chief Ha-Ha, do you want to be whipped for it or do you want to pay for it?"

I was crying. "I didn't steal anything!" I wailed.

One said, "I'm sure he wants to pay for it," as he unbuttoned his jeans and pulled out his penis. Several others had already removed their belts. "Indians always pay up. You just gotta catch 'em young and make sure they understand why we let a few live—to suck white dick."

"C'mere and show us your place, Chief. Pay your bills."

As I was looking up at that huge penis, I felt something warm and wet running down my neck. I was being pissed on, but it was soon coming from all sides and all of it aimed at my face. I was crying and yelling for help and at some point one of my tormentors said, "Here comes Fusco."

Joe Fusco, I learned later, was the high school band director. They all took off, but one grabbed me by the collar of my letter jacket and started dragging me. There was a loud rip and then he gave up.

Before that lesson in the gravel alley, I hadn't given much thought to "our place" or even "Indians." I knew about the Trail of Tears, but I did not know how any of the tribes with which I was not involved came to Oklahoma.

I was not critically injured in the physical sense and neither was the letter jacket—the rip turned out to be in the lining—and so I wore it on my grandmother's next excursion to the University of Oklahoma teaching hospital in Oklahoma City.

The first of our many cancer pilgrimages—the one for my grandmother's surgery—was my second encounter with a magical device called an elevator. I had seen one in the Roland Hotel in Bristow that changed locations at a glacial pace but the one in the University Hospital was so speedy that I could sit in the general waiting area on the first floor and if they announced Bessie Russell, I could jump on that sucker and be upstairs before Granma got her wheelchair ride to the front.

The smaller waiting rooms on the treatment floors were reserved for family members of patients in immediate danger. We (myself, my mother, my aunt, and even Grampa) waited in one of those rooms the day of Granma's surgery.

The general waiting area was louder and looser and where most of the kids got stashed. I would normally stash myself there when I had escort duty. The last time I expected to have that duty, she was not to return for several months and I would not be coming on account of school. I left the letter jacket folded neatly on a chair in the back of the waiting room.

I thought that was the end of my relationship with my grandmother's cancer and the University Hospital in Oklahoma City. Granma always spoke highly of the medical students and faculty who managed her care. I never heard anyone belittle her for not knowing medicalese, and one day, when some jerk started a public oration in the indigent care waiting room about what "bums" we were, the OU guys showed him the door *tout suite*. Everything had worked out as well as could be expected, but it turned out that a loved one in mortal danger leaves memories in a 10-year-old that do not go away so easily.

21

My grandmother's stricken look when she got her diagnosis was the first image that would sit still in my head sixty years later when I got mine. What followed within the hour of mine was a cascade of comparisons between my own situation and hers. When my eyes started tearing up, I was shocked that the comparisons had made my sorrow about her situation rather than my own.

By the time of my diagnosis, my health had been on a slide for a good long time. I can't say the diagnosis made me want to throw a cancer party, but it gave me some place to direct what is, compared to Granma's situation, substantial firepower. With my disability rating, I'm entitled to any kind of care the Department of Veterans Affairs offers. I have Medicare. And I have the group health insurance from my first career as a judge. I also have a family situation as warm as hers was cold, and concentric circles of dear friends all over the world.

We both got one thing with the cancer diagnosis that has not changed in the intervening sixty years: a list of foods we ought to eat and others we ought to leave alone. The difference? I shop where I please, but her choices were limited to the government commodities run.

The kind and decent Okies frosted a cake different than what they planned when Granma returned from her next appointment carrying a package she had not had when she left. She was "cured," meaning that appointments were down to only one a year and she could do whatever she felt good enough to do.

Smiling broadly after that good medical report, she pulled out the mystery package. "You will never guess what those medical students found that they knew belonged to you."

Unfortunately, I could guess. At least, it no longer smelled like urine.

~5~

MY INNER NET OF THINGS

I was born a writer, and so I must identify and respect matters of universal curiosity. It's reasonable to be curious about the poor in ways not at all patronizing. After all, "poor" is always a relative term. We are continually reminded that the United States is the best place to be poor.

Despite my best efforts to interrogate my seventy-three years of memory, I cannot see back in time to when I did not have the urge to put words on paper, which is where we put words in those primitive times. I can date my first publications to 1962, a piece of fiction in a Bristow High School literary magazine, and a piece of nonfiction in the *Tulsa World* about a tour of the Tulsa International Airport with the Civil Air Patrol.

The fire to be a reader, lit by my grandparents, spread to become an urge to produce writings of my own. I considered the people who produced the writings I wanted to read to be doing noble and noteworthy work, important work. I thought if I could do what they did I would be important. It didn't take long to feel the power flowing down my arm through my pen, sometimes from my heart and sometimes from my brain.

There! I've solved it, almost. I was not using a number two pencil and a Big Chief tablet when I was first writing. I was using a fountain pen that had to be fed little plastic ink cartridges, and a spiral notebook. That puts the time as late as 1957, because that would be the approximate time when I acquired those tools. It also explains why I have no recollection of taking notes in Oklahoma City in spite of all the time spent waiting in the room of that name. I had just turned 11, and I would write for over four years before I published anything.

That's as close as I can come to the "when" of it, but it seems to me now that the "how" of it is more important, and the "how" was a feedback loop from reading. If the written word was magic, I wanted to be a magician. Poor people can't be anything, so anything they become is magic. If I was a magician, whether I was born or made so is important to me, but also to anyone else born without significant assets in this land of the wealthy poor.

I remember reading somewhere that people in Guatemala would flatten cans for roofing shingles, the same kinds of cans we threw away, the kinds of cans dog food came in when we could afford it. In India, an electric motor on an appliance would be rewound with new copper wire, but here, in the land of the wealthy poor, the old appliance would be sold for scrap or thrown away and a used one purchased.

It was all true. I took out the trash and saw the empty cans. And I remember when the refrigerator we called the "ice box" out of habit—because it had replaced a real ice box—quit working. There were some inconvenient days until my grandfather managed to swing another one. His credit was good because his word was good, in spite of not having a job.

We, the lucky poor, may or may not be aware of our luck, but we do think about how we could tell if we became not poor. How would we use money to change things? It was, by and large, about things.

I wanted a car that started every time and a place to live with light switches on the walls rather than chains dangling from the incandescent bulb in the middle of each room. A bathroom with no holes in the floor and reliable hot water completed my fantasy abode, and I never even considered location, location, or location.

The toy section of my fantasy world contained a typewriter, a guitar, and clothes that fit me.

My goals sound modest now. Then, I might as well have been considering intergalactic travel. I'd given some thought to whether my abode or my means of transportation should get the top spot on the wish list and I decided the latter. This is because my ride went where I chose to go (when I had a ride) and abodes stayed put. I never thought of owning a house but rather of what I would like to rent.

First, the ride. I was as car crazy as any teenager, and every dealership in town (both of them) had my nose prints on the glass. *Route 66* was a great TV show on many levels, but two things sucked me in before I noticed the quality of the stories: the fact that I lived on Route 66...and the Corvette.

I should make that "Corvettes," plural. The story was about a well-to-do and college-educated guy (Todd Stiles, played by Martin Milner) and a working-class guy (Buz Murdock, played by George Maharis) who roamed up and down the Mother Road having adventures. An early episode accounted for the Corvette when Tod's dad suddenly died, leaving his son surprised that there was no money. Tod's inheritance was a new Corvette, free and clear, and he had his education. He hit the road with his best friend, Buz. That was the set-up for writing as complex as I've seen before or since for television, but the writing did not account for how, every year, the Corvette became the latest model. Those guys changed jobs so often there's no way they could afford a yearly trade, and this was long before automobile leasing was a thing. So, there was that loose end. I don't remember if General Motors was a sponsor or just a purchaser of product placement, but that Corvette stayed magically new.

In my memory, the Corvette is red. I don't know how that could be, because the series was shot in black and white. Maybe sports cars were just supposed to be red and so I willed it red. Whatever color that baby was, I was not the only person snapping at the consumer bait.

Every year, the Bristow Chevy dealer got the loan of a Corvette for an open house to introduce the year's new models. Free popcorn and peanuts and soda pop and a Corvette up close and personal—the whole town would show up for that. But after the open house, the Corvette would go back on a truck and head off down the Mother Road until General Motors was ready to bait the hook for the next model year. Nobody in Bristow ever bought a Corvette.

I've explained my best recollection of the net of things it would take to make me feel prosperous. I will say it flat out, embarrassed as I am now to have thought that way. A list of things added up would equal happiness, according to the values I had absorbed.

Grampa went down to Oklahoma Tire & Supply in 1959 and bought a new power lawnmower on time to replace the reel mower I had pushed in our back yard, the front yard being too completely covered with shade to support much grass. I was allowed to make my own money rolling it door to door. Having my own money at age 12, what did I buy? I bought a quart of Meadow Gold chocolate milk and drank it from the carton right outside a little neighborhood grocery store. I poured it too quickly and it ran down the front of my shirt and I just kept chugging. I chugged the entire quart. It was mine and I could do what I wanted with it, smart or dumb.

The pleasure of being able to afford chocolate milk and to waste it was ephemeral, but it might help explain how I became morbidly obese.

The first toy, the first gadget, the first *thing* I would buy from my mental net of things that would equal happiness was a portable typewriter when I enlisted in 1964. I don't remember the brand, but I did not pay much, and it was not worth much. Three years later, I was able to replace it with a typewriter made by my favorite high school teachers, Mr. Smith and Mr. Corona. The Smith-Corona was still manual, but it was heavier, better made, and more able to stand up to the pounding I gave it regularly.

I was a 17-year-old high school dropout when I bought the first typewriter and 20 years old with only some military technical training when I bought the Smith-Corona. What did I need with a typewriter? I was a writer. I knew it then as certainly as I know it now.

I might publish and I might not.

I might be destined for fame and fortune or obscurity and poverty. My life might turn out full of companionship and excitement or of loneliness and boredom.

None of that mattered to the fact that I would be writing.

It's what writers do.

STEVE RUSSELL

~6~

SILVER PIGEONS AND COPPER PENNIES

My first real job in Bristow did not work out for lack of adult supervision. Not because I was lazy or needed directions but because I needed protection.

I was supposed to deliver *The Daily Oklahoman* in the morning and *Times* in the evening. These papers competed with the ones I had always read—the *Tulsa World* in the morning and the *Tribune* in the evening. The Oklahoma City papers had less circulation in Bristow than the Tulsa papers and the morning papers were far more popular than the afternoon versions.

There were older boys in Bristow who ran together regularly. I would call them "packs" rather than "gangs" because gangsters conduct themselves like human beings and you can figure them out by adopting their point of view. I cannot ascribe motives to my tormentors in Bristow, but I do not remember a time when I was not their prey. My elderly grandparents couldn't do anything about it, so all I could do was try to stay within sight of adults likely to break up a fight.

I had a way of walking home dating from my time at Edison Elementary and it worked even when I was playing hooky in the public library. Edison, the junior high school, the high school, and the library were all in one big city block. The buildings were close enough together that there was always a line of sight to windows where adults might notice what was going on.

There was an alley across 10ᵗʰ Street from Edison that ran parallel to Main Street. The house facing the school was where my Creek classmate, Joy Parkinson, lived. Her dad was legendary for his knowledge of Fords because he worked in the maintenance department of the Ford dealer that faced Main Street.

I felt safe when there were people in the Parkinson home. Her dad never heard me called "Chief Ha-Ha," but I always figured he would not appreciate slurs against Indians because I took him to be full blood. Whether or not he was what we called 4/4, his blood quantum plainly exceeded mine. He was a big man whose knowledge of Fords gave him an enhanced status among boys.

Farther up the alley, facing 11ᵗʰ Street, was even safer territory. Billye Newton was another classmate and I had become friendly with her parents, particularly her mother Wanda, who was the only adult who ever looked at my report card other than Granma. I knew the Newtons well enough that I could cut though their property if there was any danger of ambush in the alley.

I was not welcome in the yard of the Jones' mansion across 11ᵗʰ Street from the Newtons, but I would rather be yelled at than beaten, so if I was being stalked, I would run up the driveway and right past the house, break though the hedge in the back yard, and I would be on the dirt road where I lived, 12ᵗʰ Street, too close to "Niggertown" for the all-white predators to come. There was animosity between blacks and whites but, on the black side, the animosity did not extend to Indians. I was experiencing the white side.

My encounters with thugs doomed my attempt to make money delivering the Oklahoma City papers when I was barely a teenager, 13 years old in 1960. The job involved meeting a delivery truck early in the morning at a loading dock near the railroad tracks, cutting the bundles open, and folding the papers individually for delivery.

The thugs took to meeting the deliveries every couple of days and heaving the newspaper bundles to the roof of the building. I walked all the way around the building and could find no way to climb to the roof. No papers meant no deliveries.

I quickly discovered that racing my adversaries to the newspapers got me beaten and the newspapers still wound up on the roof. Call the police, you say? The only time the police showed face on my side of town was to answer a disturbance call or arrest somebody. The only words I ever heard from a policeman were barked orders. In my world, involving the police was a recipe for making things worse.

When I witnessed a shooting across 12th Street one day, I called the WKY radio newsline because there was a reward if they used the tip on the air, but I didn't call the police. Nobody else did, either.

I did enjoy delivering the Oklahoma City papers because my grandparents still got the *Tulsa World* and I still retained the habit from when I was 4 years old of reading the whole thing, but I no longer started with the funnies.

I started with the front page. I had quit the habit of radio news but television news never captured my interest, so I gleaned what was happening in the world from the newspapers. The Tulsa and Oklahoma City papers did not choose exactly the same wire service copy to reproduce, and the slight differences gave me the illusion of another dimension. The printed word was to me the halidom of news. Spoken words were cheap, but to lie in print would be sacrilege.

My principal recollection of the news in those times was not from the U.S. I followed the Algerian War tearing apart France's Fourth Republic as if it were a soap opera. In my limited understanding of history at the time, France was a major, modern nation. Modern nations were not supposed to fall apart so completely, and I had never heard the term "constitutional crisis." I remember Charles de Gaulle came riding to the rescue and founded the Fifth Republic. Because de Gaulle had been a war hero, I understood him as France's Dwight Eisenhower. The United States required a general to stop the war in Korea and France required a general to stop the war in Algeria. That was my somewhat cockeyed view of how to end a war, but I had no clue why France was at war in Algeria in the first place and I could not have found Algeria on a map. Why, I wonder now, did I swallow the Vietnam War as being like Korea rather than like Algeria, when we were stepping into the shoes of the same colonial power?

Oklahoma newspapers were too provincial to offer any analysis that competed with the government's point of view. They did not deserve my reverence, but they formed my opinions when I was too young to wonder what was over the horizon. I would have been 7 years old during the Battle of Dien Bien Phu and there are limits to precociousness. One limit was the Oklahoma newspapers and another was lack of anybody with whom to argue.

As much as I enjoyed the free reading material and the ink on my hands, I would need some kind of transportation to deliver newspapers through the Bristow gauntlet. A car was out of the question. I was too young at 12 or 13 and even my grandparents had no car.

It was about 1960 that the motor scooter craze hit Bristow among my peers. Scooters were magical devices, offering mobility without the expense of a car while remaining slow enough that parents could be persuaded they were not motorcycles.

The Cushman Eagle was king of the small-town roads. If parents needed to be assured the boy was not riding a motorcycle, the boy wanted to pretend that he was. The Cushman Eagle was straddled like a motorcycle and it had a manual transmission with the shift lever up by the gas tank.

Running a distant second was transportation that remained common in Europe before and after the scooter craze in rural Oklahoma, the Vespa. The Italian machine was most commonly sold at Sears under the Allstate badge, a house brand that also included Puch motorcycles.

The Vespa was a classic step-through scooter and had a two-cycle engine, requiring oil to be mixed in the gasoline. The shifter was built into the left handle grip, which was probably safer than taking one hand off the handlebars to shift the

Cushman. The Vespa did not seriously challenge the Eagle, though. Pulling the baffles out of the Eagle tail pipes produced a satisfying racket and Cushmans were made in the USA. The Vespas just buzzed loudly, like their name translated from Italian, "wasps."

I begged and wheedled my grandparents into borrowing to put me up on two wheels with a motor. I had owned two bicycles in Bristow and both were stolen, so I'm not sure why I thought I could have a scooter and keep it.

Delivering newspapers on foot was possible in Bristow when the newspapers did not get stolen and I did a lot of it after Neel Griffith hired me to deliver the Tulsa papers. Mr. Griffith's red GMC pickup with a camper shell on the back to keep the papers dry patrolled the whole town every morning supervising his crew of teenagers. In addition, the Tulsa papers for the whole city came to a one-room building where the Mother Road took a hard right toward Stroud. In that building rented for the purpose, we all folded our papers for throwing and then headed out to our respective routes. Those of us on foot could often catch a lift to the starting point from Mr. Griffith.

My route covered the west side of Main Street from 6th to 12th. The residential part of those numbered streets was only four or five blocks. It was walkable except on Sunday, when I had to borrow a scooter or get somebody to stash another bag of folded newspapers at a point where I would have gotten rid of enough of the first bag to lift a second. I used canvas bags designed like saddlebags for a bicycle or a scooter. There was a hole between the two sides for my head and, with that setup, I could lift a lot of newspapers.

I had done this for part of the summer of 1961, until my grandparents were able to buy me a brand-new scooter at a little over half the price of a Cushman Eagle. It was a Mitsubishi Silver Pigeon, and its status mirrored my own. It did not fit in and would never be cool, but it got the job done.

The scooters all had locking ignitions. I relied on the need for a key and the fact that there would be nowhere to hide it if stolen to keep the Pigeon in my possession. My experience with bicycles caused me to consider the possibility of theft, but I had not considered the possibility of vandalism.

Within the month, mysterious dents started showing up in the sheet metal when I had it parked in a public place. It got more serious one night when I was attending a meeting of a Boy Scout troop at the Methodist Church.

It was dark when I kick-started the Pigeon to head home. I was talking to somebody and so I sat on it at idle. Before we quit talking, the engine sputtered and died. The Pigeon—fairly new at the time—refused to crank up, and the refusal combined with my mechanical incompetence struck fear into my heart.

I pulled the wire off the spark plug, held it near the plug, and kicked over the engine. The Pigeon had spark. I opened up the fuel filter and there was a mere drip where there should have been a flow.

I borrowed a flashlight from George Back, the scoutmaster, and shined it into the gas tank. I could see sticks and leaves. Back down at the filter, I poked a stick up the fuel line. That coaxed out a little more gasoline and a lot of dirt. Mystery solved.

I could not imagine how to get all that crap out of the gas tank. The opening on the engine side was too small and the opening on the filler cap side was too far from the stuff that needed to be removed. It was like a ship-in-a-bottle puzzle.

Mr. Back offered me a ride home. He told me not to worry about the Pigeon, that he would borrow a truck and pick it up the next day.

The Methodist Church was on the east side of town and I was walking a grid of half of the west side to deliver newspapers, so I was not in a position to check the whereabouts and condition of the Pigeon, but in the middle of the next week Mr. Back called my grandparents' house late to say I should come down to the machine shop where he worked.

The next day I got the newspapers delivered and then I either went to school or played hooky—I don't remember. While I was inclined to the latter, I might have met my classes that day so as to not put my truancy in Mr. Back's face.

Whichever, when I arrived at Standard Auto on foot, Mr. Back pointed out the Pigeon sitting in the shop on its kickstand. He told me to turn it over, and when I did, it cranked right up.

When my emotions allowed me to speak, I asked him what I owed. He demurred on getting paid, and by his act of grace the most serious vandalism against the Pigeon was neutralized. I bought a locking gas cap to avoid a repeat.

I learned over time that I could not protect the Pigeon. My grandparents had a garage but it was full of junk and it would not lock anyway. Both of my bicycles had been stolen from my grandparents' back yard and that was where I had to keep the Pigeon.

Damage to the Pigeon progressed from cosmetic to something I cannot explain to this day. I would come out to crank it up in the morning and there would be a rattling noise. A close inspection would reveal some bolt or screw visible from the outside was loose. In the case of bolts, this was odd because the Pigeon required metric tools, which did not grow on trees in Bristow.

The closest these nocturnal visitations ever came to danger was the time the brake was loosened and I did not notice it until I was at the end of the alley about to turn onto Elm Street and I only had rear brakes. The front brake cable had been disconnected but left in place. It was an easy fix that even I could handle, but the discovery of the problem was a bit scary.

Like a Vespa, most of the Pigeon's mechanicals were hidden behind sheet metal. It was easy to open and impossible to lock, so I tried to never open it when in a public place so as to keep the ease of access as secret as possible and confine the vandalism to external parts.

There was no place to put the anger and frustration at not being able to just go to work and then to school like a normal person. I parked the Pigeon as close to the back door as I could get it and wished we had lights outside, but we barely had lights inside—just the one bare 60-watt light bulb hanging from a cord in the middle of the ceiling in each room.

I could not roll the Pigeon inside because the house was up on cement blocks. In the world I inhabit now, there are slab foundations or pier and beam foundations. My grandparents' home had no piers. It sat directly on cement blocks. It also had no beams, although there were additional supporting towers of cement blocks under the house. Every winter I would have to crawl through the mud between those cement blocks with a propane torch to unfreeze the water pipes.

The step up to get in the back door was almost a foot. On the front, there was a porch that stepped up about a foot and a half at one end and five feet at the other. Because the house was originally intended to be a duplex, there were two doors at each end and one door on the west side, but none of the five doors offered a sill even close to ground level. There was no way to push a motor scooter inside.

Another result of this peculiar setup was that the floors were not level and there were sometimes gaps between the floors and the walls in addition to the holes in the floors here and there that spewed an icy breeze in the winter. Grampa would poke rags in the cracks around windows and doors in an attempt to help out the natural gas space heaters, a big one in the living room and a small one in the bedroom we all shared.

When I got old enough to demand my own bedroom, my grandparents acquiesced readily. They had two available, one used for storage and one kept relatively neat for guests. I could have my own bedroom, but it did not come with an additional space heater. If I had bought a heater with my newspaper money, there was no gas connection to hook it up.

An electric heater was out of the question because the only place to plug it in would be the wire hanging from the ceiling. All the rooms had the sort of light fixture that offered a couple of plugs above the light bulb. In the room where we plugged in the refrigerator with an extension cord. the cord was usually hot to the touch and we were always blowing fuses. These were the old-style fuses designed as threaded plugs with a little window in the top that showed you a strip of metal burned in half if the fuse blew.

In addition to being able to identify a blown fuse by looking, since the fuses screwed into a hole exactly the size of a penny, when we had no fuses, I would cut the power at the meter and insert pennies where the fuses should go. In those days, the pennies were made of copper. Since 1982, pennies have been zinc with a copper coating. I'm not sure the new pennies would replace a fuse, but when they came along, the house had passed out of my family's ownership and burned down.

I suspect an electrical fire.

STEVE RUSSELL

BIBLE BELT SEX EDUCATION

Bristow would have been a lonely place for me if I had not found a way out. I have never to this day had sex with a woman in Bristow who did not come there with me. I never had a girlfriend in Bristow understood as an intimate friendship that stopped short of physical intimacy.

Bible notwithstanding, there was plenty of sex around, straight and gay. My attitude towards gay people was off the beaten path in that I did not hate them. That might have been because there was a high school teacher who was out in the '50s, over ten years before the Stonewall Rebellion kicked the doors off the closets in New York City. There was also a gay Indian kid who was not out to everybody, but many of us knew. Hate is easy in the abstract but gets harder up close and personal, and so any inclination towards hate I might have absorbed from the background thump of Bibles was nipped in the bud.

Some of my teenage friends made merciless fun of the gay teacher, including in his presence, but there was no violence or, as far as I know, tattling. The Indian kid made a pass at me when we were both 17 and his method was a bit crude. We were in a car cruising down Main Street when he reached over and put his hand on my crotch. While I knew I was supposed to do him violence in response, I could not. I actually apologized to him while he had my penis in his hand.

I meant it, too. I was sorry I could not accommodate him. I never could connect sex with right and wrong and still can't. It's the lying and the coercion and other obviously bad behaviors that seem to go with restless hormones that justify the moral shorthand that sex is bad, if a moral shorthand with such import can be justified.

My clearest memories of sexual activity in Bristow took place in the Princess, the more upscale of the two movie theaters. I associate it with Cinemascope and color; the Walmur had a square screen and the films were black and white, usually westerns where the Indians were the evildoers chased by the cowboys in the white hats when there were no guys in black hats to chase.

Yes, it was confusing to a youngster, but the Indians on the screen seemed to be objectively bad because of the way they were acting, so I wondered, where were the Indians who were not bad? This might be why Indian kids of my generation admired Tonto.

Admiration turned to hero-worship for some of us when we found out Jay Silverheels was really Mohawk and he picked his own screen name from what teammates called him when he was a Hall of Fame lacrosse player. Silverheels was the first in a long line of typecast actors who were dispatched when a casting director called the Screen Actors Guild office and asked for "the Indian."

It would be the 21st century before Hollywood was able to accommodate more than one Indian actor, so it was necessary that most Indian roles went to non-Indians. In the '50s, Indian children took it as our lack of talent rather than Hollywood's lack of commitment. Sometimes Indian extras would be clustered as a "war party" and allowed to "speak Indian," Navajos playing Comanches and Cherokees playing Apaches and everybody playing Sioux.

The extras, knowing that was as close as they'd ever get to a credited part, would say some pretty raw things while "speaking Indian," commenting on everything from the intelligence of the director to the size of his genitalia. Things are not perfect now, but they are much better. Indian actors are sometimes cast in roles that do not call for an Indian.

Talking Indian has changed as well. Wes Studi, raised with Cherokee as his first language, delivered his lines in Cherokee when he played an Apache, but in more recent times he played Cheyenne Chief Yellow Hawk in the correct language. Canadian Saulteaux actor Adam Beach learned enough of the Navajo language to deliver messages in Navajo-as-code in *Windtalkers*. He did get some ridicule from Navajos over his pronunciation, but it was good-natured.

The Princess was the site of movies that seemed more serious, whether they were or not. At a young age, I knew the name Cecil B. DeMille. John Ford westerns introduced me to Monument Valley and made it deservedly an iconic representation of the west. As an adult, I came to Monument Valley as a Navajo Tribal Park and it felt like a place I had always known.

I remember getting scared by films twice. One was a western where a man was shot in the leg and emptied a bottle of whiskey into the open wound. The other was a film called *Elephant Walk*, which left me looking over my shoulder for Oklahoma elephants that might step on me. I don't remember where that awful gunshot wound happened, but the elephants were in Technicolor at the Princess.

Sex at the movies was usually in the many films loosely based on Biblical stories. The first female nipple I ever saw on the screen was on one of those dancing girls who always managed to show up in Biblical epics. The Princess showed the Brigitte Bardot vehicle, *And God Created Woman*, from which the kids of my age only heard whispered rumors about Bardot's backside because we were not allowed to buy tickets for secular nudity.

There was more sex education in the theater than on the screen. I remember sitting down close to the front once and hearing some stir behind me. I turned about to see the scion of one of the swell Bristow families applying himself vigorously to giving a blow job to one of his equals. As his head bobbed up and down, I overheard something about his having lost a bet.

41

Another time, in the balcony, I chanced to see one of the high school seniors with a date, his hand deeply down the back of her pants. Attention gotten, I sat down and watched him unhook her bra. I wondered if such wonders would be in store for me some day.

It seemed so unlikely at the time. My only lesson in post-pubescent female anatomy came as I left the octopus ride brought by one of the traveling carnivals that did a stand in Bristow every year and caught the bally. Or, I should say the bally caught me.

The sun had been down a while but it was hard to tell in the garish light of the midway. I was part of the tip before I knew what a tip was—the gaggle of marks who were attracted to the bally and found themselves hemmed in by the sudden crowd, not noticing that the people the back were carnies, not locals, whose job was to make leaving the tip seem rude.

The talker was skilled. He started on a loudspeaker but, once the tip was formed, he put the electronics aside and spoke in a clear, strong voice that needed no amplification.

He had the talent that makes a great stage actor or politician. He spoke to the crowd in a manner that convinced every man and boy in the tip that the spiel was for him, personally. The tip was all male because the bally was about a girl show. I don't remember the specifics but I'm sure it was something like the subject of a popular song, "Little Egypt," who "came a struttin' wearing nothin' but a button and a bow."

Even at my age—about 14, but I looked older—I knew how unlikely naked ladies were in Oklahoma. But it was only a couple of bucks, and I thought, *close counts in horseshoes, hand grenades, and naked ladies.* So, I parted with a couple of greenbacks and shuffled into a tent with the rest of the tip.

In was dark inside but for a spotlight on the "stage," which consisted of a roped off area level with the panting audience. She danced to recorded music at what seemed like arm's length in a costume that revealed about as much as what the ladies in the cities near military installations wore at the beginning of a show. She was certainly naked under the costume because each time the light hit her at a certain angle, we could see nipples and pubic hair. I guess I date myself when I say this was before the influence of porn stars and so ladies had pubic hair, something I had never seen before.

In the blowoff, she removed her top and strutted slowly around the edge of her performance area before skipping out the way she had come. She was a white woman with long dark hair who appeared to be middle aged, but she had no stretch marks (which I could not have identified anyway). I have no more detail to report because, honestly, I was not looking at her face.

Before the tip dispersed, the talker was back at the edge of the "stage," adopting a low, confidential tone. Because it was the last show of the evening, there would be a special opportunity just for us and for just another buck. The rest of the show, he stated matter-of-factly, "would be fully nude, of course."

A dollar lighter, I found myself within a few feet of an adult woman doing her best impression of Lady Godiva. I'm glad the only light was on her and not on me because I probably look pretty foolish when slack-jawed and cross-eyed at the same time.

After getting everybody's attention (no great trick while naked), she spoke for the first time and rendered what I now know as a classic blowoff story. Her tips, she explained, were the only money she did not have to split with somebody else. It's entirely possible that was true, but it was probably more significant to the response that she promised "something special" for those who dropped something in this last pass of the hat.

I was hoping it was the last pass of the hat, because I was done. Carnies used to say of their marks, "Leave him a dollar for gas." Just because the world is divided into carnies and rubes does not mean they have to be enemies. On this night, they did not leave me a dollar for gas. I was not angry, but it was a good thing I was close to home.

What in the world could be more "special" than being within a couple of feet of a naked adult woman when you've never seen one? The first thing she did has a name now. It's called "twerking," if I understand the term correctly.

Lying on her stomach, she repeatedly clenched her glutes and let them go until her round, white buttocks were trembling in the carny spotlight.

When she rolled over, I became acquainted with female masturbation. Laugh if you wish, but that is valuable information for an inexperienced young man to have—a first clue how to rub a woman the right way.

The blowoff that finally ended the show introduced me to what was probably the first of many simulated female orgasms. Or maybe not. If you could reliably tell before being intimate with the same woman for a long time, I was not informed and would not become so for many years.

There's a black pit of despair that causes a woman to masturbate in a carny tent in front of a bunch of strange men every night. Or perhaps there is. We are certainly invested in thinking so.

I am better equipped to be certain of the black pit of despair that put me in the audience. Despair began arraying itself around me as quickly as my erection disappeared. To write about it stirs those feelings, but now that I've seen the entire arc of my life, the spectator sex and later prostitutes do not seem such a tragedy from my side of the transaction.

I'm old enough now to recognize my debt to the archetypal Pamela Brown in Tom T. Hall's song. ("I Guess I Owe it all to Pamela Brown.") There was no Pamela Brown to break my heart. I did not offer a woman everything only to see her run off with some other picker who had a cool truck.

Tom T's song stands in for the story that might have been if I'd had a girlfriend in Bristow, Oklahoma. I was primed to fall in love but I could not offer a girl everything when I had nothing and was very aware of it.

Also, I had no social skills. I remember in the latter part of elementary school, at age 10 or 11, they were trying to teach us to dance. I was OK until I was expected to put my arm around a girl's waist. I was attracted to the partner I drew, but I was embarrassed beyond belief. I kept dropping my arm to my side to avoid touching her, and my face felt bright red as I stumbled around the room, putting my feet in all the wrong places and wishing the torture would end.

Bristow has much to answer for, but not this. It comes from being raised by elderly people who were not in touch with how modern young folks roll. I had been in the fourth grade, about 9 years old, when we got a television. The delay in having access to a TV was good for my attention span but not so much for my socialization.

It was not terribly long after my humiliating encounter with dance lessons that I began to see people in pairs, but I despaired of ever being a part of that. Who would pair off with a fat and ugly Indian kid whose one skill—fluency in the written form of my native language—had little use in Bristow?

When I found situations where writing counted for something, I began to believe in myself, and that made it easier to imagine a woman believing in me. Finding those situations took a long time.

STEVE RUSSELL

~8~

TOOLS OF THE TRADE

Dropout rates to the contrary, Indians did not appear to be purposely squeezed out of the public schools of any of the three cities in three states where I failed. Instead, they were offered material appropriate to their (presumed) abilities, and this is where the 20th century status of Indians—all stereotype, all the time—did harm. For me, the stereotype meant I had to fast-talk my way out of "shop" classes. To the teachers advising me, I was being offered a chance to graduate with a marketable skill. I must have appeared ungrateful.

They had no way of knowing that the danger level any time I put my hand in a toolbox was much higher than for normal people. The most probable outcome was that the task would eventually be left to be done by somebody competent and I would have injured myself or an innocent bystander. My idea of skill was being able to withdraw from the attempt to repair having caused no further damage. My way with tools made placing me as an apprentice only possible if a master of a trade were willing to risk both his reputation as an instructor and his physical safety.

There was one other lawful way for a young Indian to make his way in the world: it is a well-known fact that all Indians excel in the visual arts. Even without that stereotype, my mother and my aunt, who had preceded me through the Bristow schools, were both excellent artists, which was taken to be evidence I had some talent in my genes.

The truth of it was that I could not draw straight lines or color within them. I had no sense of what colors served which emotional function or which colors looked good with other colors. Not only could I not create visual art, I could barely understand enough about it to watch it go by.

The one course with vocational implications was one I picked for myself, and the skill I acquired in that one course has almost made up for the misery of high school in general. I signed up for a typing class because I fancied myself a writer and found myself in a class with only one other male. He claimed he was there to meet girls and his cover story worked well enough that I adopted it. I cared enough about that typing class to return to the lab and practice at hours when it was just me and a dozen or so manual typewriters.

If my favorite high school instructors became Mr. Smith and Mr. Corona, nobody seemed to notice except the kids who made fun of my choice. The cover story came in handy. No teacher, including the typing teacher, ever asked why I was trying to acquire the skill or suggested any practical use a male might have for typing.

These fruitless attempts to identify some future for me that would define what I needed from the public schools did not fit well with the continuing admonition from Granma that I needed to "go to college." One problem with the admonition was that nobody in the school system saw college in my future, and a related problem was that Granma, and Grampa before he died, had no clue what "go to college" meant and neither did I.

At one time, I thought my Aunt Eleanor had been to college because she became a registered nurse. That turned out not to be so. The government had been short of nurses during WWII and had extended grants to people willing to learn the trade and practice it while the shortage persisted. The grants did not involve a general college education, just enough instruction to pass the pertinent exams. Discovering that left me back to not knowing anybody who had been to college.

I presume all my teachers were college graduates, but I did not think to ask for guidance and they did not offer. None of them seemed to think I was college material, either because they did not observe me to be studious or because I had no money.

Getting into college, rumor had it, required an examination of some kind and better than average high school grades. Once admitted, you had to support yourself in addition to coming up with whatever the costs were.

The absurdity is clear in the rearview mirror, but at the time it made perfect sense that my two major challenges were getting to college and avoiding the public schools. I had no sense of the public schools being a stepping-stone to college, let alone a necessary one.

From the third grade, when my heart was no longer in school, I had practiced the fine art of skipping classes. I discovered the perfect place to hide, the last place anybody would look for a truant: the public library, a small building in the same city block as the public schools.

I thought I was being clever, but now it's clear that the librarian knew who I was from the time Granma brought me in to get a library card, and she knew what time it was and therefore where I was supposed to be.

With some collusion from adults, I spent a lot of time in the library reading books based on their physical location. I learned the Dewey Decimal System, but for some reason I did not start at the beginning of a classification, but rather at the end of a shelf. At first, I was trying to put books between where I was sitting and the librarian, but I kept it up long after I knew she was not going to turn me in as a truant. Sixty years later, I remember a shelf about Indians and some shelves about history and biology, but I remember even less from regular classes.

As I got older, I ventured off the school grounds during the day, and once I got picked up for truancy by a Creek County deputy sheriff. My first ride in a police car was to the county seat in Sapulpa, where he sat me down in front of a county judge.

The judge proceeded to explain what he would have to do to me if I would not go to school. He would have to commit me to a "juvenile facility," which did not sound like a very nice place. I was scared and I only spoke when he required me to speak.

At the end of his peroration about the evils of truancy, he asked me: did I understand what was going to happen to me if I didn't go back to school and stay there?

"Yes, sir."

The deputy took me back to his cruiser and we headed toward Bristow.

"So," he said, "I expect you're going back to school now?"

"No."

He looked poleaxed by my response but I had felt poleaxed from the moment that judge issued his threat. The "juvenile facility" he threatened sounded much worse than the threat my grandparents used to hold over my head—that if I didn't quit ditching classes they would pack me off to Chilocco, the Indian boarding school.

I didn't see that I had a choice. I lacked the imagination to think of anything worse than failing in school and being ridiculed nonstop by my peers. Had it not been for playing in the Bristow High School performing band and typing as fast as some of the girls, there would have been nothing that allowed me to experience competence or the promise of competence. There was a brief flicker of hope when, because of my size, I got looked over as a potential football player. If I had known that playing high school football could lead to a scholarship to play college football, I would have been even more excited.

I was happy to be invited to football practice, partially because football is the established religion of Oklahoma and Texas and partially because the only colleges I could name were the ones that fielded competitive football teams. When the big day came for the coach to look me over, he naturally took me for a potential lineman.

I don't remember whether I was lined up offensively or defensively, but I do remember the fellow on the other side of the line of scrimmage was a bit smaller and so I thought I could block him. Then the ball was snapped and the next thing I remember I was sitting on my butt trying to catch my breath and experiencing an exquisite wave of pain washing over my entire body.

I got up slowly and walked to the sidelines, shedding gear as I went. The coach wanted to know where I was going and I responded that if that other fellow wanted to go in the direction I was defending badly enough to make me hurt that much, I was happy to let him do it. There was nothing happening on the football field worth having my bell rung repeatedly, so my high school football career ended after one play and in circumstances that would have damaged my reputation if I had a reputation to damage.

My one play on the practice field was a perfect metaphor for my entire relationship with the public schools. There was nothing for me there but failure and humiliation.

Pushing against my flight instincts, there was plenty of apparent coercion that I took to be more real than it was. I realize now that my grandparents could never have navigated the bureaucracy to ship me off to Chilocco—I wasn't even tribally enrolled and my enrolled father was not around to help. The judge was probably not going to ship me off to a "juvenile facility" unless I committed a real crime. When I became a judge, I reasoned that putting truants in with burglars would create more burglars while keeping the same number of truants.

I couldn't stay in school but it appeared somebody would likely try to make me regret it if I left school. This was not a small problem unless compared to how to get to college, an aspiration that in my mind had nothing to do with high school or with employment.

The purpose was to become educated, a transformation I thought would show me what I wanted to do for a living. I was a writer, but I could not imagine getting paid for it. Once I could see some way to earn a salary, I would know how to seek out the tools of the trade.

STEVE RUSSELL

~9~

THE DROPOUT CHRONOLOGY

My first attempt to physically drop out was in the sixth grade, and that was behavior outrageous enough to come to my mother's attention. My truancy made my grandparents miserable that I would not attend and it made me miserable that I was disappointing them—but not as miserable as wasting my days on pointless repetition from teachers and ridicule from other students.

In the middle of the sixth grade, my mother took me into custody and hauled me away to Odessa. This was only the second time I spent time with her, the first being the early disaster in Pampa. I was anxious about how Odessa would work out but curious what it would be like to live with people who had a normal income.

My second experience of living with my mother gave me the opportunity to finish elementary school at Dowling—like many other schools in Odessa and in Texas, named after a Confederate States of America war hero. Dick Dowling's derring-do at the Battle of Sabine Pass—something I only learned about when assigned to his eponymous school—made his story exciting to sixth graders—sort of like Davy Crockett minus Crockett's appeal to principles greater than self-interest.

The Confederacy, I was beginning to notice, produced more colorful characters than the Union. But I thought then and now that treason is treason, and it's not the kind of thing that should get schools named after the perpetrators.

I have two recollections of Dowling, the school. First, my fighting got much better there. I gave as much as I got, for a change. The other memory is a fad of the sixth-grade boys: everybody had a switchblade knife. They were cheaply made but they were real. I can't think of any reason for the fad except that the knives were easy to acquire and preteen fashion was influenced by James Dean in *Rebel Without a Cause* and Marlon Brando in *The Wild One*. I'm happy to report that I never saw a switchblade used in a fight.

In Odessa, a two-income family could do well, and my mother kept books for small businesses while her husband fixed and reconditioned magnetos, which were necessary to the ignition system of the pumpjacks that dotted the landscape of the Permian Basin. With its dual income, my stepfamily was able to afford a home on the side of the highway with no honky-tonks and less crime. It even tried to capture one of the two major status symbols for people living in and around the Chihuahuan Desert.

My mother and her husband did not have a boat parked on a trailer in their driveway. Boats were commonly kept for show, even though there was no place to put a boat in the water for 100 miles in any direction.

They did attempt the other evidence of prosperity in the desert: a green lawn. A green yard without resorting to dye is a serious challenge where the native vegetation is creosote bushes, prickly pear cactus, tumbleweeds, and stunted mesquite trees. They kept up the pretense in the front yard by wasting prodigious amounts of water, but the back yard was a lost cause.

In Odessa, I naturally read the newspaper, the *Odessa American*. It was there I first encountered the idea that men could, in a sense, own women. Lots of men subjected "their" women to physical discipline with little interference from law enforcement. That was the light end of tolerating violence, but there was a heavy end that made periodic appearance in the *American*. It was reading news reports of spousal killings that taught me all unlawful homicides were not murders. If a man had been cuckolded, jury verdicts made prosecution for murder futile, with some murder cases ending with a conviction for manslaughter and some with complete acquittals in the face of what sounded like overwhelming evidence. The same privilege of killing the paramour of a spouse and the spouse did not extend to women.

I was not put off by the ramped-up violence of Odessa. It was fascinating to read a newspaper where gunplay did not always rate the front page like it did in Tulsa and Oklahoma City. I never got any closer to the rowdy part of Odessa than reading about it and driving past on the way somewhere else.

Odessa became a serious punishment for ditching school in Bristow both because Odessa offered nowhere to go with books and because the desert was not my natural habitat. I missed green things.

I don't remember anything about my grades at Dowling, but I was allowed to enroll in seventh grade the next school year, which means I broke even in spite of playing hooky and I was still on track to graduate in 1965. In my mind, the immediate problem was not when I graduated or even if I graduated but rather how to get home.

The experience of being taken against your will is not improved by a blood relationship to the perpetrator. I managed to make enough earnest promises to my mother that I would shape up and at least attend school that she was willing to let me get back to Bristow and blessed greenery. I think she figured that if I just showed up, I would pass.

My begging and wheedling were done with all the good faith I could summon at that age. I was making promises about high school on the cusp of entering the *junior* high school (as they called middle school then), specifically the seventh grade.

My promise to improve my attendance did have some shelf life. Memory may be failing at my age, but the worst seventh grade conduct I can recall was going to class with a hamster in my pocket. My sense of shame over that, alas, is not about disrupting the class but rather about scaring the hamster. That confession shows my good behavior was purely instrumental. The only value I had internalized was the felicity of keeping clear of the Permian Basin.

Race as a value, positive or negative, had to come up in those years. The kids in Odessa did not understand me to be Indian, but just that I had a weird name, and adults did not try to steer me away from the college track until I first provoked them by disinterest in school. Still, Odessa would never be home.

Back in Bristow, the integration mandated by *Brown v. Board of Education* was not without friction among the students and there was a bit of sparring with words and with fists between whites and blacks. Like the rest of the Indian kids, I stayed clear of those disagreements. We had always been allowed to use the white facilities, with the possible exception of the country club (about which I am not informed). Only those of us who paid attention to national news understood what a big deal integration was in some places.

The disconnect between integration as I understood it by reading the news and integration in my daily life is my dominant public policy memory of that time. Other than that, I have a few vignettes that take up more space in my long-term memory than anything in the curriculum.

There was a seventh grade teacher who had been persuaded by the eugenics movement at its apogee before WWII and was still preaching it. While the text of his sermon was about IQ, there was a racist undercurrent. It was not hard to apprehend the unspoken assumption that low IQ traveled in the genetic heritage of nonwhite people. I didn't know the history of eugenics and so I didn't know that the racism did not start out hidden. We—the Indians and the blacks—got the message when he spoke about the dangers to the gene pool in interracial marriage, even though he said it without a claim of white superiority. I was the product of an interracial marriage and I had never before thought of myself as a pollutant in the gene pool.

Another memory involved a seventh grade English class, the only time I remember passing one. I was naturally headed for a failing grade because I would not do homework, when the teacher fell ill and withdrew for the rest of the year. She was replaced by the mother of one of the kids who had been a classmate since first grade. She took me aside and made an offer that if I would read books on at least grade level and write book reports, she would restore some of the points I had lost for not turning in homework. That bargain zipped me right to the top of the class.

She may have figured in my third memory of that year, unless I am mistaken and this happened at the beginning of the eighth grade or even the ninth grade, both of which I started in Bristow. The location of the classroom I know, and that says middle school. I promised to do the best I can and that's all I can do.

We had elections for student "offices" that had the names of real offices but there were no real institutions to go with them, so it was hard to take the exercise seriously.

One of the new classmates we acquired when the black school shut down was being passed through the system by social promotions. He appeared to be mentally challenged at a time when there was no special education for black kids—I'm sure the teachers would point out we barely had anything for white kids. There was a special education house, but it was either segregated because it was private and *Brown* did not apply or the black kids' parents could not afford it. He was a good-natured fellow, but he could not read or write or do simple arithmetic.

We elected him class secretary. He would be responsible for writing down the minutes of our meetings, if we ever had any meetings. The teacher kept us after class and began to scold us for making fun of him.

I raised my hand and she paused her tirade.

"We weren't making fun of him, ma'am. We were making fun of you."

To her credit, she seemed to grasp the absurdity of competing for imaginary offices in a nonexistent organization.

She let us go and I don't recall there being any more nonsense about student government. The kid we had elected secretary never had to take any notes and he was tickled plumb to death at the positive attention he got.

The seventh grade was my last clean finish of a full grade in the Bristow schools. From there, I would attend two eighth grade schools and three high schools before finally putting an end to my war with public education.

All of my failures were not about teaching styles or the stereotyping of Indians. There were some important things I was just not learning, either because I did not grasp the importance or I did not grasp the subject matter itself.

I would later tell university admissions officers that I had no high school records to offer because I don't think I ever passed an algebra class or an English class on the high school level. To say I was able to finesse these gaps in my knowledge is not to say having the gaps was a good thing.

Arithmetic did not come easily to me. I have never learned the multiplication tables even now. I multiply by performing multiple additions in my head. The woman who would become my law partner, Vivian Mahlab, eventually taught me some long division in the third year of law school to enable me to figure estate taxes. I had survived dividing smaller numbers with hacks like visualizing the units I was adding in my head to fake multiplying and counting them.

My university degree plan required only three hours of math, and I was able to find a course in number theory, which taught me why my arithmetic hacks worked. Most problems were stated in words rather than equations, and my Air Force computer experience was useful when I got thrown into the deep end. My time on the consoles of various Air Force computers had left me able to read registers displayed in binary-coded octal, and in my Air Force days I could do calculations more easily in octal (base eight) than in decimal (base ten). When I left the computer field for good at the end of my freshman year, programmers were working almost exclusively in hexadecimal (base sixteen). The nerds often refer to hexadecimal as "hex," which seems to me an appropriate description. These skills have atrophied now from many years of disuse, but they enabled me to pull an A in a freshman level math course because I was lucky enough to find one that focused on the narrow niche where I had been working.

My failings in the other fundamental academic skill, English, are more complicated. In middle school and high school, I simply refused to study grammar, because, I would haughtily proclaim, I was born a writer, and we writers don't stoop to that level.

The writer's method is to read lots of excellent writing, fiction and nonfiction. From that experience, you understand the sound of correct writing. Poorly constructed writing offends your ear like fingernails on a chalkboard.

Two of the times I was sent away from an English class and "to the office" during my first attempt at Bristow High School in 1961, I was unknowingly practicing the writer's method. In one case, I got caught ignoring the lesson of the day just as I did most days. I was in the back of the room, hunched over a textbook for a higher grade level and so immersed in one of Shakespeare's tragedies (it was either *Hamlet* or *Macbeth*) I did not notice the teacher walking to the back of the room to investigate my inattention.

The other time, I was in the throes of my romantic period when we were assigned a quiz over some grammatical nonsense the teacher had explained the day before. I dashed out answers— probably incorrect answers, but I shall never know—and proceeded to address my fixation on romantic poetry by testing my memory.

I would have gotten away with that had I not, when she asked for our quiz answers, handed in the wrong piece of paper. Because I was in the back of the room, my paper was on top of the stack. She looked down at what was supposed to be my quiz and read:

She walks in beauty
Like the night of cloudless climes and starry skies...

My attempt to render Lord Byron from memory got me another trip to the office.

One point of these stories is that I share the blame for my miserable high school record. The teachers lacked the authority to deviate from the approved curriculum and I lacked the inclination—some would say, the common courtesy—to apply myself to somebody else's priorities.

I must also admit that I despised Bristow High School so much it made me crazy at times. Finding a place to hide where I could curl up with a book had been easy at Edison Elementary but as I got to higher grade levels it became nearly impossible. It was as if I could not breathe within the building and I would start to hyperventilate half a block away to maximize how long I could hold my breath.

During my abortive run at the ninth grade in Bristow, I did a particularly useless bit of truancy when I put a few possessions in a box, tied it to my Silver Pigeon motor scooter, and left town on a school day.

I know this happened after February of 1962, when I had just turned 15, because the fandango had a sound track that was released in that month of that year: Ray Charles's seminal crossover, *Modern Sounds in Country and Western Music*. "I Can't Stop Loving You" was a big hit for Charles and it became an earworm I could hear in my head with or without a radio. I discovered I could sing anything out loud when the Pigeon was at highway speed. It lacked the decibels of a Vespa or a Cushman Eagle but it was loud enough to cover up lots of vocal sins.

I steered the Pigeon south on Chestnut Street, which became Oklahoma 48 at the city limits. The highway was straight enough that I was not driving the scooter as much as I was hanging on and impersonating Ray Charles at the top of my lungs. It was amazing how that act unwound my anger.

Along with the anger subsiding came a realization of the utter silliness of my pretend escape. Where did I think I was going and how would it be better than Bristow? By the time Oklahoma 48 intersected with U.S. Highway 62 near Castle, I was seeing the choices at that intersection as symbolic of the life choices facing me.

A right turn on 62 would take me to the Sac and Fox Nation, already significant in my life as the place where my grandparents met. A left turn—naturally, it had to be a *left* turn—would take me to Okemah, the boyhood home of Woody Guthrie, Dust Bowl Troubadour and author of the song that should have been the national anthem, "This Land is Your Land." Either way, I knew I would be doin' some hard travelin'.

I turned right on U.S. 62, but all of that singing at highway speed dried out my throat and all that thinking made me thirsty anyway, so I stopped at a small grocery store in Boley, Oklahoma, to drink a soda pop and soak up some history.

Boley was established in 1903 as one of many "Negro towns" where black people lived after the Civil War. Boley differed in that it was established not just by freedmen but by Creek freedmen, former slaves of the Muscogee (Creek) Nation, many of whom had Creek blood and all of whom had a treaty right to enroll in the Creek Nation if they chose

The population of Boley was claimed by the Census to be about half black and under ten percent Indian, mostly Creeks. That last is according to the locals, since the Census follows the laughable conceit of "race" which holds a Creek to be like a Tonkawa who is like a Hopi who is like a Makah, ad infinitum.

When I started college, some anthropology texts still taught "race" as if it were a meaningful and objective way to classify human beings. The so-called Five Civilized Tribes all practiced chattel slavery, and to support the morality of it they caught the disease of racism from the white settlers. The settlers had started out enslaving the indigenous people, but Indians made poor slaves because, when they escaped, they had somewhere to go.

Settler plantation owners shopped in Atlantic seaports for African slaves, a practice the Five Tribes aped when they formed their own plantations. Only one of the Five Tribes, the Seminoles, caught on to escaped Africans as potential warriors highly motivated to fight the settlers.

The Seminoles fought the Spanish and then disappeared into the Everglades to fight again when a suitable target presented itself. They did the same against the British, and finally the Americans. Escaped slaves formed their own communities among the Seminoles and made common cause with the Seminoles against whichever colonial power was threatening. Those communities were not unlike the "Negro towns" in population if not in armament.

Looking back on my visit to Boley, there's a lot of absurdity packed into the Indian kid surrounded by Indians who think he looks white in racial terms while he is thinking they look Negro by the same myths.

That day, I cranked up the Pigeon, which appeared to be the only motor scooter in Boley, and roared off toward Prague, a city in the Sac and Fox Nation where Granma still seemed to know lots of people. She and the locals said "PRAYgue." It was only when a Czech professor at the University of Texas, Eduard Taborsky, hired me as a grading assistant ten years later that I learned that the namesake city in Europe is pronounced "PRAHgue."

From Prague, I turned right on Oklahoma 99 and headed back north to Stroud, home of the Rock Café, a fixture on the Mother Road since 1939. When I was on the run from school, it was still open twenty-four hours and was the home of coffee that would remind you why you drink coffee.

Route 66, the Mother Road from Chicago to Santa Monica, was also called "the Main Street of America" by some. Others called it after my favorite Cherokee, Will Rogers Highway. Will Rogers, the Indian Territory cowpuncher, claimed Claremore, on the Oklahoma section of Route 66, as his hometown. His first stage success in the U.S. was at the Louisiana Purchase Exposition in St. Louis, also on Route 66. From St. Louis, he became Will Rogers, the touring vaudeville entertainer who hit the beginning of Route 66 in Chicago regularly and finally, as Will Rogers the movie star, he bought a ranch in the Santa Monica Mountains. Route 66 was his life on a highway map.

In 1962, I ended my 85-mile rectangle by scooting from Stroud to Bristow on a remnant of the Mother Road that had been re-designated as Oklahoma 66. Looking back, I played a spectacular and pointless game of hooky that day, starting to escape and quickly realizing I had nowhere to go.

I had long resolved to never let my schooling interfere with my education, a sentiment I thought was original to me until I saw it misattributed to Mark Twain, as so many witticisms are. As best I can tell, Grant Allen got to it first in 1894.

I was so fond of the quotation that I stuck it on my email signature line and attributed it to Mark Twain in 1995. Somebody called BS on the attribution to Mark Twain and I was unable to prove it to be correct, so I quit using it.

With or without Mark Twain, I declared war on the Bristow school system for wasting my time. I had to give up my claim to be the author of the sentiment, but I never gave up the sentiment itself. The public schools were designed like a roach motel. You are supposed to enter at age 6 and you can't leave until they stick a fork in you and proclaim that you are done.

I did not wait for the proclamation. I knew when I was done.

The final battlefront, high school, got inextricably linked to my effort to learn the mysteries of my missing birth family. Of course, I was curious. I loved my grandparents but I was always aware of the abstract cloud of human life cycles that decreed I would lose them before I was fully grown. That abstraction became cruel reality when my grandfather died on November 11, 1961.

My school attendance—never anything to brag about—became mythical for the end of the semester of Grampa's death—my first semester of high school—and did not improve the next semester. The next school year would bring high schools numbers two and three. Mysteries would be solved, if not exactly in a manner that improved my life prospects.

STEVE RUSSELL

~10~

PUTATIVE FATHER

My grandparents had given up the battle to keep me in school, resulting in my exile to Odessa, Texas to finish the sixth grade and the eighth grade. The ninth grade—my freshman year—was 1961–1962, and I didn't exactly finish. At least I was playing hooky for money, delivering the *Tulsa World*, rather than just trying to avoid school.

My mother knew how miserable Bristow High School was because she had not finished it, and she also knew I hated Odessa because I said so at every opportunity, so she determined that it was time I got to know my father. Looking at it as an adult, I have to admit the logic of her idea. It had to happen someday, and I was old enough to process the downside if he had not improved.

I knew next to nothing of my father. My grandparents did not tell stories about him, although when the subject came up, I would catch Granma making faces. She would then deny having done it. All I had were some pictures of a big Indian in a Navy uniform.

I had not seen my father since I was no more than 5 years old, but I recalled him driving a 1950 or 1951 Ford like Robert Mitchum in *Thunder Road*. He drove it fast like Mitchum and it had a radio blaring Hank Williams tunes. He used to take me to Beggs in it to visit relatives and there was a playground at a school along the way with a corkscrew slide that was very high,

Clifford Wayne Teehee, family photo approximately 1945.

with metal sidewalls to keep kids from falling off. I remember seeing that slide from a distance and wanting to try it, but when my father stopped and let me run over and look up the ladder, the height scared me, and I thought better of it. I was 3 or 4 years old at the time. He was offended that I had wasted his time, so he picked me up and climbed the ladder with me under his arm. I was terrified. At the top, he sat me down with my feet pointing into the first curve. I begged him not to, but he shoved me off, and I slid around and around, screaming, until the thing spat me out at the bottom. My legs were too short to break my fall and I landed flat on my back. The hard landing knocked the wind out of me, so I quit screaming. My father thought that was hilarious and threatened to haul me back up the ladder for another go. Several other childhood memories suggested scaring me entertained him. He held me out over the Deep Fork River and threatened to throw me in. He spun me around by one arm and one leg until I was so dizzy I puked.

My only memory of him that was not scary was that he had among his possessions a button accordion. That instrument fascinated me even though my arms were not long enough to open it all the way. It had several broken reeds and I kept trying to find a tune that would work without them. He seemed impressed by how long I could occupy myself with a broken accordion. When he told me he had to leave Bristow for a job, he added that he would be back, and promised he would leave the accordion with me.

He did not leave the accordion and he did not come back.

That had been the last contact until my mother's decision. It wasn't much basis for a relationship, but maybe my memories had become jumbled over ten years later. Maybe I had it all wrong or, even if I had it right, maybe he had changed. So, I agreed to the plan, and in the summer of 1962, at the ripe age of 15, I got on The Dog with a ticket to Beaverton, Oregon, and three pieces of luggage riding under the Greyhound—my clarinet, my record player, and a cardboard suitcase containing clothes and writing materials.

I got a window seat and spent a lot of travel time acquainting myself with the Chihuahuan, Sonoran, and Mojave deserts. In California, we turned north on the 101. At every rest stop, I would get off the bus and walk around the terminal, trying to soak up some feeling for each place.

All in all, it was a fine adventure for a boy of my age. Then, in Fresno, disaster struck. I got back on the bus and discovered, as it rolled away from the terminal, that I did not have my wallet. I lost all my money and the portion of my bus ticket I would need to get from Portland to Beaverton.

I got off The Dog in Portland in a bus station of an intimidating size and wandered around until I found a kiosk that said, "Travelers Aid Society." Figuring that I was a traveler and in serious need of aid, I told my tale of woe to the person at the kiosk, who apparently thought I was trying to scam a free ticket to Beaverton.

Sent away with no aid and no suggestions, I wandered around the terminal until I discovered a huge map on the wall that showed the entire vicinity. For the first time, I could see the relationship between Portland and Beaverton. The scale of the map told me it could not be more than 10 miles, so I memorized the streets and started walking.

If this had been, say, Bristow to Tulsa, I would have stuck out my thumb, but I knew the rules. You needed to be outside the urban area and you needed to be in a place where a motorist could safely pull over and pick you up. I never found such a place. Much of the twisty road outside Portland was not even safe for walking, but I had no choice.

When the road came down from the dangerous curves, a sign told me I was coming into Beaverton. I was feeling thirst as if all those deserts I crossed caught up with me and settled in my mouth. I spotted a Shell station with a soda machine in front that had a water fountain attached.

I made for the water fountain, only to be met by a man in a uniform with that familiar yellow shell on it who told me the water fountain was "for customers only." After walking several more blocks, I found another service station with a similar setup. I waited until the attendant was pumping gas for somebody and dashed up to the water fountain.

The city water in Beaverton was much better than the city water in Odessa—not that I was in a position to be choosey. Energized by the cool water, I walked on into town and found the bus station, where somebody was supposed to meet me, but I knew I had missed that connection.

A schedule posted above the ticket window told me that there were several buses from Portland every day, so I sat down to wait. I was tired anyway and grateful for the chance to sit in a place where nobody was likely to run me off. A couple of Portland arrivals later, I began to despair of being met.

In those days, there were public telephone books and how many Teehees could there be? I found Clifford easily enough, on SW 167th. A look at the numbered streets near the bus station showed single digits. I had about 4 more miles to walk and it was getting dark.

Once more consulting a map in the bus station, I started walking out Farmington Road. By the time I found 167th, it was dark and I was tired. Some numbers I could read in the dark and some I could not.

Not long after I lost sight of the lights on Farmington, I saw a street number that told me I had gone too far. Looking back to the last mailbox where the number said I had not gone far enough, it appeared that there were three houses that were likely candidates for my destination. Because of vacant lots and darkness, I was uncertain. All the houses on the street were set back pretty far and none of the three had a light showing or a car in the driveway. I had no idea of the time, but the sparse traffic indicated it was late.

I was sleepy as well as tired and hungry and I expect my judgment was even worse than that of the average 15-year-old. I determined to lie down in the ditch between the mailboxes and the yards and try to sleep. I stumbled upon a cardboard box in the ditch that I thought would be handy to insulate me from the ground. That was too optimistic. Cold just became colder. I was shivering and my teeth were chattering.

I had heard that if you were about to freeze to death it was easy to sleep, so I guessed I was in no danger of freezing to death. When sleep proved impossible, I trudged back toward Beaverton.

At the edge of town, I saw a dumpster full of broken-down cardboard boxes that looked like a place to sleep, but as I stumbled toward it, a police car started heading in my direction with red lights flashing.

I briefly broke into a run but quickly realized how silly that was and stopped. The officers either invited or ordered me to sit in the back seat of their cruiser. It was soft and it was warm and staying awake became a major effort.

When they heard the name "Teehee," they looked at each other in an odd way. I was so zoned out that it was much later when I put together the quiet back and forth that translated to "Should we tell him?"

They gave me the short version, that "the last time" Cliff Teehee was arrested, it took a dozen officers to subdue him and several of them were injured.

They also gave me a ride back to the bus station and bought me a sweet roll and a cup of coffee—the first food I had since Fresno. I spiked the coffee with lots of sugar and cream to jack up the calories because I did not know when I would eat again. The cops left me there with a quarter to make a phone call, which I did every now and then. Nobody answered.

It was past noon the next day when my stepmother, Barbara Teehee, showed up. She walked directly to me as if we had met before, a woman with dark hair, about a head shorter than me, with no makeup and sensible shoes and a baby on her hip. We collected my three pieces of luggage, and as we pulled away from the bus station in an elderly DeSoto sedan, she explained that the family was not home that week because they were at a "camp meeting."

Having been raised in the Bible Belt, I knew the phrase and I was dismayed but too zonked by hunger and fatigue to say anything.

I don't remember if they were staying in a tent or a small cabin, but it was in some kind of park. Barbara showed me a cot and I was instantly asleep. I slept all the way around the clock, waking up late the following morning.

It seems curious to say this now, but I don't recall when my father showed up—I just recall being told that he was working and had asked Barbara to collect me while still riding herd on the little kids—Eddie, Walter, and Ladonna. My sister was just growing from toddler to walker and the two boys were grammar school age. Barbara had been able to get friends to watch the older three while she took baby John and went hunting me.

When I woke up, she fed me. This was when I first learned I would be living with vegetarians. I could make a wisecrack about how my immediate hunger made anything sound good, but the truth is that for much of my childhood I was a sort of involuntary vegetarian in that we could not afford much meat. I say "sort of" because Granma cooked just about everything in bacon grease.

The two things I remember about the vegetarian meals the first day are that I made my peace with potato chips—something I had never liked before, but I guess I had not been hungry enough—and that Barbara had many kinds of fake meat that came in cans labeled "Loma Linda." From the first taste, I decided Loma Linda was good stuff but calling it meat had to be a joke. There was no resemblance to meat in taste or texture, so I figured it was concocted by a vegetarian who was working like a blind person picking colors.

No longer sleepy or hungry, I began to wonder about my father. Questions that had always been with me were about to be answered, or at least begin to be revealed. In the pictures I had seen of my father, he was in his Navy uniform. My great-grandmother on my father's side, who lived on the other side of Bristow from where I grew up, had pictures on her wall of every ship on which he had served.

These Navy-blue traces of my father led me to root for Navy in the Army-Navy game and, briefly, to fantasize about "college" meaning the Naval Academy at Annapolis. That lasted until I understood you have to be recommended by somebody important to get into a military academy. I didn't know anybody important.

He was not dressed like a sailor when he showed up to the camp meeting, but I still could have picked him out of a lineup from those old photos. He was tall like me, toothy like me, but much more muscular. I had understood him to be roughnecking when he left Bristow, but in Oregon he was working construction. When asked, he gave his occupation as "hod carrier." I had to be told what that meant—the main support worker for bricklayers and cement finishers. It was not considered unskilled, but it was hard labor. He took pride in his work. Driving around Portland, he would point out the projects he helped build.

All was not hunky-dory in the building trades, though, and his complaints spilled out over months. He told me he had trained to be a heavy equipment operator, but he never practiced the skill because he would not join the union.

I never understood his beef with the Operating Engineers. It could not have been unions generally, because he carried a card from the Laborers' International Union of North America. So why not the Operating Engineers?

I think it was something about the hiring hall. If your number came up you had to take the gig or go to the bottom of the list. Cliff Teehee had become, off and on, a Seventh-day Adventist, which was Barbara's faith. If he was having a religious day, he could not take a gig offered on Saturday. If he was not feeling religious, then he enjoyed the pay premium for working on the weekend.

I say his religion came and went because, in the six months or so I was there, he would be harassing Barbara for observing her faith part of the time and harassing me for not observing her faith the rest of the time.

I had never heard of a Seventh-day Adventist, but I cracked a book right away—there was plenty of reading material about the faith in the Teehee home, although I never saw him read any of it.

In addition to the Catholic Church, I had in Bristow attended several flavors of Protestant churches, none of which ever passed the giggle test. My attitude towards monotheistic patriarchal desert cults was pretty well set in stone by age 15, and it only shook loose when I rubbed up against liberation theology while working for the United Farm Workers Union, which would not happen for another ten years. Depending on who was asking, I was either an atheist or an agnostic. The latter was the truth, but the former was sometimes amusing to claim.

From readings in the Teehee household, I quickly learned that I had grown up with a limited notion of bizarre. Adventists are the most robust of a number of sects that arose after the movement led by William Miller came a cropper in the "Great Disappointment." Miller had persuaded himself and lots of followers to divest themselves from worldly attachments in preparation for the Second Coming. According to what his Bible study informed him, Jesus would arrive on October 22, 1844.

I later learned in the study of social psychology that when a prophecy fails to pan out, the faithful will double down in proportion to how much inconvenience the belief has already caused them. The Great Disappointment was an early case study leading to this conclusion.

As far as I know in my old age, there are only three ways to discover the truth: deduction, induction, and revelation. Two of the three are infallible. A deduction has to be correct if the major and minor premises are correct and a revelation has to be correct because the correctness is inherent in the definition.

Historically, the problem with revelation has been that if something different has been revealed to somebody else, the competing purveyors of truth tend to settle the dispute with a fight to the death. I only speak of the historical record. With the sole exception of Cliff Teehee, I've never seen a violent Adventist.

In addition to having services on Saturday rather than Sunday, Adventists are dunkers rather than sprinklers and they believe in the inerrancy of a text that no Adventist I ever met could translate and which didn't exist for over three hundred years after the Christian Church was rolling along without it.

I did learn one more detail about Adventist beliefs at the camp meeting on my first day fully awake in Oregon. The campground was located on a river, and there was a beautiful swimming hole with clear water like in the Cherokee Nation. The bank was lined with tall rocks, but because the water was so clear it was easy to see that diving would be perfectly safe. I changed into my bathing suit.

Returning to the swimming hole, I climbed up on the tallest rock. As I looked around at the other kids, I thought it was odd that I could only see females. Of course, I couldn't see the entire place, so I shrugged and took my dive into the clean, beautiful river. When I surfaced, girls were bailing out of the swimming hole in every direction and running back toward the camp yelling something I could not make out.

When adults came running to evict me from the swimming hole, I came to understand that Adventist teenagers did not swim in mixed company. I suppose I should have been embarrassed at not knowing the rules, because I was on their turf. Honestly, though, I just found the whole contretemps to be puzzling, sort of like some of the fundamentalists back in Bristow who thought it sinful to dance.

It seemed to be a warning that I had fallen down some kind of rabbit hole. Cherokees dance in our most sacred ceremonies; men and women may enter a river in each other's presence in our purification ceremony.

I found myself surrounded by absurdity, and my putative father claimed absurdity as a justification for his often-expressed anti-Catholic opinions. When I wanted to know why the Pope and not the Patriarch was correct in the Great Schism, he inquired why I was asking. I had to explain to him that the Adventist family tree comes down through the Pope. He was shocked, but not shocked enough to ease up on Catholics.

His complete ignorance of Cherokee customs, spiritual and otherwise, was heartbreaking to me, but I don't think he noticed. At that age, I had not yet worked out the politics of blood quantum and I knew nothing about its science. There are many Teehees on the Dawes Roll (the master roll for the Cherokee Nation) but it is my father's quarter blood that qualifies him for enrollment in the United Keetoowah Band.

The Keetoowahs represent traditional purity to people who buy into the foolhardy blood quantum nonsense that the settlers have sold to so many Indians. I had not bought it, but I had not rejected it either. It seemed to me that he didn't care about his Cherokee identity, except when he complained about the amount of a per capita payment declared by tribal government when a lawsuit settled.

I wish my father had taken me to a stomp ground, but plainly that was too much to expect. I don't think he knew the protocols or cared to know. Raised in the Muscogee (Creek)

Nation, I have no stomp ground where I am responsible for either the upkeep or parts of the ceremony. For me, attending a Cherokee stomp ground requires an invitation like the invitation I needed to attend a Creek stomp ground.

One of the questions I had come to Oregon to answer was whether my father could teach me enough to make me feel less Creek and more Cherokee. I had no interest in giving up my Indian identity entirely even if that were possible, but he seemed to be doing his best to accomplish that very thing. I knew the history of the violent encounters between Indians and Christianity, but I thought that was a long time ago. Adventists appeared harmless to me—with one exception.

I had the bad luck to be related to the only violent Seventh-day Adventist I've ever known. I often showed evidence in the forms of a black eye or a bloody lip of my father's penchant for arguing theology with his fists. His theology was hazardous to my health, but only as he practiced it.

I did not have the ability to defend myself. The only time he got injured trying to do me injury was luck. He threw me into a hedge in the back yard, but when he cocked his fist and dived in after me, one of the branches my backward fall had broken stabbed him in the eye. He screamed that I had blinded him. Barbara did her first aid duties but, having seen the whole thing, did not blame me.

When he would turn his aggression on her, she did a better job of defending herself than I did defending myself. I remember one time he hauled her out of the Adventist Church on a Saturday to go on some family outing he had decided was more important than what was going on in the church. In the abstract, I would agree, but that's because I see no value in an institutional church. Barbara did, and it seemed to me that if they were going to be married, something so fundamental should have been negotiated long before I showed up. Instead, he told her in a threatening tone of voice that she "had better get on the stick." I had never heard an adult address another adult in that tone that seemed to carry an implicit "or else."

I was just outside the kitchen once when he was talking to her that way, but when he approached her to apply the "or else," Barbara picked up an iron skillet off the stove and swung it hard with both hands, hitting him flush on the side of his head with a satisfying (to me) thump.

It sure sounded like he had gotten his bell rung, but he did not go down. He gave her a quizzical look and started laughing.

I was just outside the doorway, frantically looking for something that would work as a weapon, but I didn't need one, because his laugh turned out to be a signal that his impulse to "discipline" his wife was over. He retreated and left Barbara, a registered nurse with a full-time job, in the kitchen where she did all the work.

Her creativity with vegetables and the Loma Linda stuff (then owned by the Adventist Church, I learned) was impressive, but I was afraid that asking her to teach me her skill would give my father another reason to ridicule my masculinity.

His little kids got hit regularly for failing to obey or more often failing to obey quickly enough. The middle son, Walter Dale Teehee, didn't get hit more than Eddie or Ladonna (John being too small and Bonnie not yet born when I was there), but they usually were hit somewhere on the body. Walter, for no reason I could see, was a magnet for headshots. Only slaps with an open hand—but hard and almost always on the head.

Ladonna was under grammar school age, so she had to be 5 years old or less, and I was appalled that our father thought he needed to use a belt on a child of that age. Since he aimed at her bottom and usually hit her legs, the issues were her pain and his stupidity rather than the safety problem in the blows to the head that seemed to have Walter Dale's name on them.

No one was seriously injured by the violence permeating the Teehee household, at least in the physical sense. My own physical injuries never lasted long, but my dreams of Clifford Wayne Teehee, the quarter blood Cherokee and Navy veteran of World War Two who could teach me about the ways of Cherokees and the ways of war, were fractured beyond healing.

~11~

THE TEATS ON A BOAR HOG

My father's absence had made him a blank slate on which I had written what I wanted to be true. The rest of my family had either engaged in a conspiracy of silence or decided to err on the side of caution because he had been gone for so long. I was 15 years old and nobody was mean enough to set me up purposely to expect the worst—but instead I was set up for a major disappointment because of what I did not know and was not told.

Barbara Teehee, my stepmother, not only had nothing to do with my disappointment, she became my friend for life. She later visited me when she took a road trip in a camper with another elderly lady long after Barbara (who did not believe in divorce) had gotten a divorce. I spoke to her on the telephone when she was dying of cancer and we both knew it. Her crazy beliefs did not put me off because she was not demanding that I believe them and I was not peddling what little I knew of the ceremonial life of Cherokees to non-Cherokees either.

While Barbara was consistent in not pushing, my father was inconsistent in pushing. I realize now the reason was probably brain chemistry; then I thought it was because he could not match a 15-year-old in a theology debate. I must admit the possibility that he could not understand his own inconsistencies.

We were once visiting the Devil's Punchbowl State Natural Area on the Pacific Coast. His religious principles, when they were switched on, were clear and unforgiving in the matter of extramarital sex. However, that day on the beach, some teenage girls were lounging on a blanket near us wearing bikinis and I was enjoying the view when my father said in a confidential tone of voice:

"You want some of that?"

He went on to use the bodies of the anonymous girls as a reason why I needed to lose weight, as if I were fat on purpose and as if I could relate to a girl I did not know in terms of "wanting some of that." Both of his assumptions were wrong, but I had learned that stating the facts could be hazardous to my health.

On the way from the Portland area to the spectacular scenery of the Oregon Coast, we sometimes passed though land named after the Tillamook people, a Salish-speaking tribe with a Chinook name. I was interested to know on whose bones we were walking; my father was not.

About 40 miles south of Tillamook, Barbara's parents operated a dairy farm. Visits there backed up the opinion I was forming that my father's hard salesmanship was not characteristic of Seventh-Day Adventists. One day I asked Barbara's father whether his vegetarianism was motivated by his health or his faith. I had learned that a dairy farm is not an appropriate undertaking for someone unable to work hard every day.

He thought about my question before answering, and finally said, "I think that whatever makes your health stronger makes your faith stronger."

It was a good answer because it set me to thinking, but it was also a good answer because it contained no trace of the religious hard sell, no threat of dire consequences in this world or the next. His thoughtfulness and gentle demeanor reminded me of his daughter's willingness to tolerate my beliefs or lack of them.

My father's violence obstructed coming to any similar understanding with him. There were two more issues peculiar to me that obstructed forming a warm relationship with my father in addition to his sporadic attempts to make religion mandatory and his habit of hitting the little kids and his wife.

The first was his continuing attempt to teach me the uses of hand tools and small power tools. In those efforts, I was on his side and I was doing my best. I could see then and now the value in being handy with tools, which my father certainly was. Unfortunately, his pedagogy was no match for my incompetence. His principal method was ridicule, and he seemed to think that the louder he said something, the more likely I would understand and remember it. The Teehee house was heated by a wood stove, so I did manage to learn how to use a chain saw and how to chop kindling with an axe, holding a foot or so of 2x4 in one hand and an axe gripped just behind head in the other and slicing as I moved my fingers out of the way. It looked way more dangerous than it was, or I think so because I never hit a finger. In home repairs and construction, I gave up and just tried to avoid his explosions after he taught me a phrase I had never heard before: "useless as the teats on a boar hog." He was commenting on my clumsy efforts to place terrazzo correctly before the cement began to set. That comment was his general opinion of my worth, not just my aptitude for tile setting. I carried it to his death and will carry it to my own.

The second issue that caused trouble between us in addition to what I could not do was what I could do. I had played clarinet in the performing bands in Bristow and Odessa. When I went to audition for the performing band in Beaverton, I ran into a scheduling conflict. As a result, I fell into an acting class that quickly captured the energy I had put into the band.

I never understood my father's philosophical objection to acting—something about adopting a false identity—but I remember he was really put off when I had to learn some fundamentals of applying makeup. Real men, he told me, don't use makeup.

I did not want to lose my embouchure, so I had to sneak around to practice on my clarinet because, he told me, a clarinet was not a fit instrument for a man. When I explained how I took up clarinet as a cheap way to learn saxophone and invited him to buy me a sax, he was not amused.

My interests in music and acting lubricated the friction caused by my general lack of social skills, and before long I had more Oregon friends than I ever had in Odessa. I was not used to having lots of friends and I liked the experience. The bad news was that all of my friends were musicians or actors or both. My father did not approve of musicians or actors. He thought both endeavors were threats to my masculinity, a subject he visited often enough that I reinterpreted something odd that had happened on the first day I met him at the camp meeting.

We both had headed for the latrine at the same time to take a leak and I noticed him staring at my penis. At the time, I thought maybe he could not remember whether he had me circumcised and I was uncertain of the Adventist position on male genital mutilation. The third or fourth time he expressed concern about my masculinity, I decided he was just trying to see how long it was.

A related issue made all the scandal about musicians and actors worse because it cut to the heart of an identity I had already adopted. Remember, in the cardboard suitcase riding under the Greyhound I had clothes...and writing materials? I *was* a writer. Full stop. Even then, I could not remember a time when I did not think of myself as a writer. My one suitcase contained spiral notebooks with short stories in various stages of completion and swatches of poetry, which at that age I thought needed to rhyme. I had begun to question the necessity but had not quite broken free.

A man who writes poetry is, my father held, "a pussy." The bottom line for my status in my father's eyes was that the activities closest to my heart were not worthy and those that were fit for a man were beyond my abilities. I lacked my father's talent for building anything well designed and sturdy. I had some talent for performance, but my father's attitude toward it limited my opportunities to perform.

The all-school plays, presented in an auditorium better than I was used to both in capacity and in presence of technical gadgets, were to be *Diary of Anne Frank* and *My Three Angels*. I had my eye on the part of Putti Van Daan in *Anne Frank*, who seemed to me the most disturbed and therefore the most challenging character. I backed away from the urge to go for the juiciest role when it dawned on me that my father would have kittens over the rehearsal schedule even if he didn't try to forbid the entire endeavor when he learned I would have to be aged with makeup. Reading for Van Daan would have cost me at least a bloody nose, so I opted for working on the stage crew. The time commitment was much less and so allowed me to hide my involvement from my father until the dress rehearsal.

My father's contempt for acting had an even more direct impact on my social life when I read for the lead in a play produced by my drama class and written by a classmate, Tori Motte. While I did not yet dare to even think the word "girlfriend," I was mightily attracted by her talent as both an actor and a playwright and her ready acceptance of the outlandish notion that I, too, was talented. The fact that the playwright was a girl reinforced my father's view that theater was not an interest fit for a man.

I spared my father the ignominy of my leading role until the week we offered the public performances. At that point, I could no longer come up with a cover story to explain the time I was about to spend at school. Just writing the previous sentence brought home to me how inverted my school problems had become. In Oklahoma, I would be trolling for a cover story to explain not being on the high school campus. In Oregon, I needed to explain why I was on the campus rather than learning to do something useful.

The useful thing I was doing outside of school was a yard work gig for an elderly couple, Mr. and Mrs. Gay—I don't remember their first names, but I remember their faces and a few of their idiosyncrasies. For example, Mr. Gay felt foolish whenever he had to say the name of a certain supermarket. Forced to mention the supermarket, he would purposely butcher it as "Poogly-Woogly."

I did the mowing and trimming and weeding of the Gay property. They lived in an even more rural area in a house on two lots with a small orchard in back. The task I remember most fondly was picking cherries—big black ones, sweet beyond my experience—an experience limited by the fact that cherries are not grown in Oklahoma or Texas and they are pricey at the supermarket. My idea of cherries was limited to Maraschinos.

If I spent the entire day at work, they would provide my lunch, and we would sit and talk. Mr. Gay would sometimes be preparing his shopping list for "Poogly-Woogly." The Gays wanted to know where I was getting my frequent black eyes and fat lips and defensive marks on my forearms.

I told the Gays the truth, straight truth with no bobbing and weaving. When they expressed concern, I blurted out my escape plan. I was saving over half of what they paid me, and I was trying to sell my transistor radio and record player by taking them to school and asking for offers. I didn't tell them that I had also stolen some money from my father's wallet, something that caused me no guilt then or now.

I expected to save enough money for a bus ticket across the state line into Idaho. Boise was the destination I had in mind. Early one morning I would get one of my friends to give me a lift to the Portland bus terminal. I would say I had something happening after school and hope that I would be in Idaho before I was missed.

From Boise, I planned to hitch back to Oklahoma.

They were impressed by my gumption and Mr. Gay offered to be my ride to the Portland bus station when the day came. I accepted and thanked him profusely. I was anxious to be off before the weather got much colder, but I had to put together some money to eat on when hitching. My experience with that mode of travel was that the speed of it was a matter of luck, not planning.

I think it was early December when I acted with less money than I had hoped because the weather was getting scary cold. My transistor radio had been stolen by a classmate who claimed he would sell it for me, and I could do nothing without the risk of being found out. I left my record player in my locker at school because it had no takers and I was traveling light.

I had stashed my clarinet in the locker but had not tried to sell it. I told myself that if I ran out of money I could try busking. The truth was I did not want to give up the horn my grandparents had sacrificed to buy for me, and, in spite of the alleged threat to my sperm count, I liked playing clarinet.

The morning I left, I wore an extra layer of clothes. In the storage areas of my clarinet case for sheet music and extra reeds, I had packed as many Slo Poke suckers as I could. The object was energy, not nutrition.

Mr. Gay met me when I got off the school bus in Beaverton. When we got to the bus station, he went in with me and we stood in the ticket line together making small talk. At the front of the line, he stepped in front of me and purchased a ticket all the way to Bristow. His generosity made me so emotional I was embarrassed. I would not be getting off the bus in Boise and the money I had saved for the bus ticket had become my traveling money.

I was rolling on the Greyhound and still contemplating my good luck when I began to see another Oregon, not so green as either the Portland area or the Pacific Coast. I had not known that the other side of the Cascades was high desert, important knowledge had I been traveling without the protective shell of the bus. The Dog took what I thought was an odd route but, in my mind, I was on the run, so odd suited my purpose. Cheyenne to Denver made sense, but then instead of heading for Kansas, the route dropped down though the Raton Pass to hit I-40, which goes all the way to Oklahoma City.

There was a long rest stop in Raton, New Mexico, where I dug into my money stash to buy some real food. I was not out of Slo Pokes, but I sure was tired of them. Sipping coffee, I started trying to make a plan. Up to that point, my only plan was escape. Successful escape was looking like a done deal.

I resolved not to contact my mother. I had told her about my situation, but she just reminded me that I had agreed to be in Oregon. So I had, and I liked Oregon just fine. I even discovered I did not consider Beaverton High School an imposition on my time. My anxiety at having to swap out the performing band for a drama class had not lasted a week.

However, my agreement to relocate did not anticipate that my father would find me lacking in the skills suitable for a man while the skills I was beginning to develop—all of them—were effeminate. A real man played guitar rather than clarinet, a real man did not write prose or, worse, poetry, and a real man needed Jesus to protect him from an angry Christian God.

His fists would never make me a Christian or teach me the building trades, but it was clearer every day that both of us would not survive his attempt. Retreat, however difficult, was my only other option. Had he known that distaste for patricide was driving my escape plan, he would have processed my decision as cowardice. It would be one more proof of my unfitness for manhood.

I understood that my presence at that bus station café in Raton, New Mexico, added cowardice to my general lack of manly virtues, but the irony escaped me as I worried over taking up the role of "the man of the house" for my widowed grandmother.

Back in Bristow, it would make sense to look up Neel Griffith and see if he would give me back my job delivering the *Tulsa World*. I had left him in the lurch when my mother plucked me out of Bristow, but surely he could see that was not my fault. That would bring in enough money to ease the burden on my grandmother while I figured out my next move.

Sated by the greasy and warm bus terminal food, I dozed as the Dog rumbled out of metropolitan Raton. My sleep was troubled as it usually was, but with a different kind of trouble.

Finding work and then figuring out how to launch myself out of Bristow were hard and familiar questions, but they were of a different order than trying to be ready at every moment for fight or flight. Oregon signified imminent danger that could not easily be managed. New Mexico was feeling like home free, and I was even glad when the bus shook me awake to see the most boring scenery in Texas as we came to the vicinity of Amarillo, located on the northern edge of the *Llano Estacado*, the "staked plains," a land so flat that if you needed a landmark, you had best bring your own.

Technically, we joined the Mother Road—old Route 66—at Amarillo, but I felt it acutely starting in Oklahoma City. All of those small towns that had their economies smothered by the Turner Turnpike were my home turf, with memories attached to each one, from the Creek stomp ground near Kellyville to the gooseberry pie in the café next to the bus station in Chandler.

I had been gone less than a year but my life had changed far out of proportion to the time. The rumor that had been my father was a violent reality and the hope that he would teach me anything about Cherokee reality was dashed. My losses in making the journey felt substantial, but I'm not sure that losing illusions ought to count as losses.

Losses or not, the ledger of my life had another side.

I made sure I got Tori Motte's mailing address before I left. The play she wrote and her satisfaction with my performance were glue that led me to pursue her for years. I wrote to her as soon as I could and explained my disappearance—right after my thank you letter to the Gays.

Being accepted among a group of talented people had made me feel useful and competent, as did the audaciousness of my escape. Disappearing in Oregon and showing up in Oklahoma was a dire necessity, but also a pretty nifty piece of work.

All this rebutted my father's teaching that I was useless as the teats on a boar hog.

STEVE RUSSELL

THE LAST WEST TEXAS WALTZ

My grandmother, Bessie Lois Russell, still lived in the Bristow, Oklahoma house where I grew up, the house she shared with Grampa until he died, the year before my mother shipped me to Oregon to meet my Cherokee father. I never doubted that Granma would take me in again. I never told her what I had endured. The telling would have caused her pain, and it was not necessary.

My mother knew where I would go to ground. I have never learned how or when my absence was discovered. When I put the question to her in the nursing home where I have placed her, she claimed to have gotten a phone call from my father's father. That is not possible.

Haney Teehee was the half-blood Cherokee who left the Cherokee Nation to seek work in the oil fields. He died in 1928, when he was 20 years old and my father was 2. Family legend claimed his death was a result of going out in bad weather to seek work. Whatever the cause of his demise, it happened in 1928, so he did not make a telephone call to my mother in 1962.

The only explanation I can offer is that Mr. Gay somehow hunted down her phone number and made the call. He was elderly and male, so she must have misunderstood his connection to me. The bus ride Mr. Gay had engineered was a bit more than two days and the drive from Odessa to Bristow is one long day. There might have been enough time for my mother to meet the bus in Bristow and I was relieved that she did not. I held out hope that my father was too embarrassed by my escape to tell her I was missing and too contemptuous of my abilities to believe that I could get farther than Portland.

The relief was short lived. From the bus station, I was walking down Main Street towards 12th when a familiar red Falcon Futura pulled up beside me. I did not get the impression she was pissed off, at least not in proportion to what I had just done.

I had not made plans for a return to her custody even though I knew it might happen. What does somebody in custody need with plans beyond the one that counts—a plan for no longer being in custody? This applies to children in a loving two-parent home as much as it applies to prisoners in a maximum-security prison. It is in the nature of custody that your decisions are limited. When I saw her car, I knew I was headed back to Odessa, Texas, that God-forsaken hellhole just outside the eastern edge of the Chihuahuan Desert. We departed greenery for sand the next morning.

Reappearing in Odessa when I did gave me a ringside seat for the demise of my mother's penultimate marriage that I only learned years later was not a ceremonial marriage. As I understand it, my mother had been shacked up with a young rake by the name of Leonard Paul Prescott. When that relationship tanked—just before he went to prison—she took up with his father, Paul Leonard Prescott. It was the older Prescott to whom I thought she was married, and she was by the common law of Texas at the time.

Genetic science to the contrary, my mother was somehow wired to produce sons regardless of the father's identity. I was the firstborn. She had another son a year later by a one-night stand on the shores of Lake Pontchartrain while she was fleeing death at the hands of my father. His name was Douglas. She gave him up in an open adoption, so I was able to meet him soon after I learned of his existence in 2011. With Paul Leonard

Prescott, she had two more sons. Robert is six years my junior and Paul was born a year after Robert and became the youngest, unless there is something else she did not tell me.

The ostensibly married couple lived in the part of Odessa that allowed my enrollment in Permian High School—later of *Friday Night Lights* fame. It was my third high school. My freshman year in Bristow was complicated by my urge to be employed and my lack of patience. I did not graduate as a Beaverton High School beaver because my father made it impossible. If college was the promised land, I knew there had better be more than one way to get there because four years of high school was three and a half more than I could handle.

I would not finish at Permian, either, as things fell apart for my mother. I finished the fall semester that was in progress when I escaped Oregon, but the classes Permian offered did not match my Beaverton schedule very well. Right after the spring semester of 1963 got started, Leonard Paul got out of prison and his father agreed to put him up until he could get on his feet. That was just as weird as it sounds.

Being a thoughtful dad, Paul Leonard's first order of business upon his son's release from prison was to get him laid. Therefore, there would be a father and son road trip to Ciudad Juárez. I am not sure what my mother was told about the road trip, but I would not be surprised if she was told the purpose was to get Leonard Paul laid. I was invited "to help with the driving."

I do not remember if this was just before or just after my 16th birthday, and therefore whether I had a license. The reason they needed a third driver would become apparent. Somebody had to stay sober.

We started out around midday in the "family car," a pink 1958 Mercury station wagon with fake wood panels. It was about 300 miles west to Ciudad Juárez, over roads lonely enough that most traffic and even some highway patrolmen winked at speed limits.

After spending the night in Pecos—of Judge Roy Bean fame— we were in Mexico by late afternoon of the next day, having passed the border with zero formalities, strolling through a market where Mexicans did the selling and Americans did the buying. When the shadows began to get long, we drove out of the downtown area to a place that appeared to be block after block of nightclubs like those on the rowdy side of Odessa.

We parked the Mercury about a block into the district and entered one of the establishments. It was not a totally foreign experience to me only because I had been in a "private club" outside of Bristow where there was an open bar even before Oklahoma gave up prohibiting alcohol. Since the very existence of the club was illegal, they would serve anybody who could look the part of a customer. I was always big for my age.

While I had seen a bar before, I had never seen one with so many bottles, so many mirrors, and so much exotic lighting. It was a bit disorienting. The two Prescotts seemed amused and I took that to mean they expected I would be ill at ease. I was determined to defeat that expectation.

They went to the bar and ordered. The music was so loud I did not hear what they ordered, but Paul Leonard invited me to order a drink. My face must have given away my confusion, because I noticed him exchange another amused glance with Leonard Paul. They were both chuckling quietly and that lit the afterburners on my determination to appear suave and sophisticated.

My alcohol consumption in Bristow had been limited to fruity wines and an occasional beer, but in Mexico I ordered the only mixed drink I knew by name: a martini.

By the time it showed up, I could see they were drinking American beer in Mexico. That seemed odd to me then and now that I know about Mexican beers it only seems odder.

I picked up my icy cold stemmed glass and took a sip. Gin has never passed my lips since that moment. It felt as if I had been siphoning gasoline and sucked on the hose too long. I can't even remember if I swallowed it or spit it out, but whatever I did was entertaining to the two adults. Their quiet chuckles had dialed up to laughing out loud, and I was mortified.

Paul Leonard showed some mercy and ordered me a Coke. He finished the martini, and before he had done so, Leonard Paul wandered off with one of the garishly dressed ladies at the bar.

When Leonard Paul came back looking like a satisfied customer, Paul Leonard had one lady on each arm, both substantially younger than his 50-ish. By the time Paul Leonard got back, Leonard Paul was shopping again, and Paul Leonard told me I could "Pick one. Pick a clean one."

That was the first time anyone had ever said a word to me about sexually transmitted diseases. Picking a clean one sounded like a good idea, but how was I supposed to tell? I was suddenly surrounded by females rubbing on me from all sides. This was a new sensation, but not exactly erotic. They had my complete attention, but I had no erection.

There was quite a range of ages and, looking back, what I did was about as bright as ordering a martini. I picked the one who appeared to be closest to my age. I was still smarting from my last attempt to appear sophisticated and a young girl was less threatening. Some of the older women were already laughing, and that was no way to influence my decision unless they did not want to go with me.

After a sum of money changed hands, the young one took my hand and led me through a beaded curtain doorway. On the other side were several doors. She went directly to one, opened it, and pulled me into a room lit by a lamp on a small table next to a double bed. There was just enough room to walk between the bed and the wall.

I sat on the bed. She started getting undressed and motioned for me to do the same. She spoke as much English as I spoke Spanish: *de ningún modo*.

When the front of her dress came down, the visual effect was that her breasts came off with the dress. I was aware that some girls padded their chests. Boys of a certain age go out of their way to peek down there, and it's easy from my height. I had seen plenty of padding when trying to see what was being padded.

This girl, though, was not merely padded. She appeared to have no breasts at all. I could only have guessed her sex above the waist by the size of her nipples, which were as large as any I had ever seen and looked odd on her flat chest. Her pubic hair was sparse, and her legs were short.

I was still not erect and being naked alone with a naked girl did not do the job. Once she was out of her clothes, I was no longer thinking of her as a woman, but as a girl. Since nobody, including me, considered me a man yet, having sex with a girl did not seem wrong unless I thought prostitution was wrong, and I had not developed an opinion about prostitution.

I did not foresee I would need to have an opinion about prostitution as quickly as I did. Anything I decided would be too late for the circumstance I was facing. At that moment, face to face with a naked girl who had been paid to have sex with me, I was incapable of abstract thought.

I regretted the language barrier and attempting to obtain some Spanish was another immediate upshot of my adventure. She taught me by gesture and by example that there is no foreplay with a prostitute. Without the language barrier, I think I would have come clean about my inexperience and tried to negotiate for some kissing and touching. I did not know that most professional ladies do not kiss.

I used to find it strange that a woman would accept a man's penis inside her but not touch lips with him, but now it seems no odder than my university students being convinced that oral sex is less intimate than vaginal penetration.

Oral sex, I understand now, would have been the answer to my erection problem, but it was not necessary. When she took my penis in her hand, it finally rose to the occasion. She pulled my foreskin back and inspected me closely...apparently, I was not the only one who'd been admonished to "pick a clean one."

With some difficulty, she pulled me into the missionary position. She giggled as I experimented with where my elbows could go. I was thinking, "Girl, I'm trying to avoid hurting you and you're laughing at me."

My self-esteem had been getting more fragile all evening, so naturally any laughter from her was processed as ridicule. Even I, though, had to suppress amusement from my perch on my knees and elbows over this girl who I could not look in the eye because she was so short. It was just as well, because I still wanted a kiss.

She gripped my penis again and rubbed it around her labia. She was so well lubricated I know now she had a stash of K-Y somewhere. I had no clue what was natural, but what she was doing felt delightful.

I floated on the cloud designated in folklore as number nine, until she apparently got tired of transporting me to bliss or impatient to get the business transaction over. Since I was not thrusting, she planted her heels on the bed and moved her pelvis upward, taking me about half way into her. I took the hint and started thrusting.

I squirmed between her legs for what began to be an unseemly amount of time to me and probably already was to her. She had to know that I faked finishing, but when I indicated my satisfaction, we both quickly dressed and returned to the bar area. The two adults were all grins and wanted to know how I felt.

I represented as the King Hell Stud that I certainly was not. The girl did not care to make eye contact with me after the transaction was done, and that shot down my feeling that we had shared something special. I had another cold Coke and sat at the bar as the two adults went and came until they were ready to leave.

When we walked outside, evenfall was over. The sun had set, and we had that wave of coolness that the night brings on in the Chihuahuan Desert. When we got back to the parking space, the car was surrounded by four young men. One was seated on each front fender and the one closest to the curb had an open switchblade knife with which he was cleaning his fingernails. He had enough English to explain that he and his friends had been "guarding" the car and expected to be paid for their trouble. Paul Leonard found that to be absurd and said so.

This alerted the others and at least one more produced a switchblade and pressed the button to open it.

All I could think to do was get my back against the nearest wall so at least I only had to deal with one attacker at a time. I did not understand why Paul Leonard and Leonard Paul did not stand back-to-back for the same reason.

Leonard Paul suggested a negotiation over the "fee" the Mexicans were trying to collect and I understood for the first time that he was sloppy drunk. He was in the best shape for a fight of the three of us, but his intoxication destroyed any advantage his age and fitness might have offered. I thought of the tire iron in the back of the Mercury, but I was pretty sure the car was locked. I stayed with my back to the wall.

Leonard Paul, speech very slurred, offered our opponents a buck each. The guy who had been cleaning his fingernails turned from Paul Leonard and said to Leonard Paul, "*Cinco.*"

"What did he say?" Leonard Paul asked his father.

"Do I speak Spanish?"

Clean Fingernails rolled his eyes. "Five. Five dollars. Each."

"To drive away in my own car?" When Paul Leonard yelled this, his speech displayed almost as much intoxication as his son's.

Still, introducing actual sums of money had changed the interaction. We were still menaced, but the danger felt less immediate.

Some kind of negotiation took place in spite of the fact that neither Prescott spoke a word of Spanish and the Mexicans spoke only a little English. Nobody paid any attention to me.

Leonard Paul seemed to share my distaste for a fight and he managed to cut a deal for two bucks each. There was a tense moment when he told his dad to pay them, but Paul Leonard fished out his wallet and did the deal.

Paul Leonard then put away his wallet and got behind the wheel; Leonard Paul went high-stepping past the car guardians and grabbed the shotgun seat. I was still invisible to all, but I dived into the back seat. We rode in silence until we crossed the international bridge.

Once we'd crossed the border with the minimal formalities of the time, we pulled over to get gas. While the attendant was pumping, Paul Leonard turned and addressed me over his shoulder, asking if I felt "OK to drive?"

I had taken one sip of a martini. Assuming I swallowed it, I followed it up with two Cokes. Most important, the adrenaline was still pumping from the almost-rumble. I got behind the wheel.

I pulled out of El Paso with a full tank of gas on the route that would become I-10 in a few years. Both of my passengers were snoring before I passed the city limits. The time was early evening. That thirsty V-8 got a little bit better than 10 miles on a gallon of premium, so I had to wake Paul Leonard up once to pay for gas. With that one stop, I made it straight through, due east, and the sun was a penumbral glow over the horizon when I pulled into Odessa.

Further Mexico excursions were not necessary, because a couple of weeks later Ginny showed up. She was introduced as Leonard Paul's girlfriend, and she moved into the guest bedroom with Leonard Paul. She had no visible means of support. Neither did her boyfriend, but he had an excuse, and he did move right along on looking for a job.

Ginny did not get out of her pajamas most days except to have sex. I seldom saw her in street clothes and it did not take long to figure out she was doing the deed with every male in the house except the two little kids. Her pajamas were tight and near transparent. Being a teenager, I never tired of looking at her nipples and her public hair—both plainly visible.

It was only a matter of time until she caught me looking and invited me into her bedroom to look without the gauzy cloth in the way. And to touch.

My mother did not find out Ginny had seduced me until after Ginny had blown up her marriage—which made my corruption the least of Ginny's sins. When my mother found out Ginny had been getting horizontal with both Prescotts, there was one quick shouting match with Paul Leonard and she told me and the other two kids to pack our stuff.

As I'd had to do when I quit delivering the *Tulsa World* in Bristow, I had to quit the job delivering the *Odessa American* I had gotten with such ease after arriving back in Odessa in December of 1962. My mother was moving me again. This time, at least, she was blowing off her own job with zero notice as well.

Property of the common law marriage between my mother and Paul Leonard included two Ford Falcons in addition to the 1958 Mercury that had taken us to Mexico, of 1961 and 1962 vintage. The older Falcon was a light blue, four-door sedan with a 3 on the tree. The newer one was a bright red coupe with a 4 on the floor. I had been using the coupe to deliver the Odessa newspaper and naturally I hoped she would take it.

She took the blue sedan. In spite of its age, it had fewer miles. I understood but I was still disappointed.

As I was loading my belongings into the blue Falcon, Paul Leonard walked up to me with a stricken look and asked me to "talk some sense to her."

As much as I despised Odessa, I had made my peace with it, and so I was not hostile to what my stepfather wanted. I was back in the performing band. I had a job for walking around money and access to a car. Having just gotten my life leveled out after all the Oregon uproar, I did not particularly want to leave.

What I wanted had never mattered, and why would she listen to me when she was in the process of ripping apart the only life my half-brothers Robert and Paul had ever known? They were wandering around in the foot traffic between the house and the blue Falcon looking confused and very unhappy. Paul Leonard had lived with her for enough years to know I was right, but his desperation was showing.

She was so pissed off she didn't even ask me to drive until we stopped in Wichita Falls—a bit over 300 miles—for waffles. We had made this drive often enough to build a routine. The Toddle House was a twenty-four-hour joint in Wichita Falls where we always stopped. Normally, we changed drivers once on the first leg. The second leg was a little over 200 miles and the coffee at the Toddle House might take one driver all the way to Bristow regardless of the hour.

Within hours of her decision to leave, we rolled into Bristow in that blue Falcon stuffed with, mostly, clothing. The two younger boys were sacked out on top of the clothes that covered the back seat. My Silver Pigeon stayed in Odessa and I never saw it again. Once more, I saved my clarinet.

Naturally, Granma took us all in—my mother and the three sons she acknowledged at the time, one by Clifford Teehee and two by Paul Leonard Prescott. The calendar read 1963, and I would not learn of a fourth son until 2011.

I re-enrolled in Bristow High School, home of the Purple Pirates, taking my fourth and last run at high school back where I started. BHS was the same high school from which I had a letter jacket that had complicated my life years before, the same high school my mother had tolerated within one semester of graduating.

The boys and girls I had known all my life were going to be the Bristow High School Class of 1965. They were juniors. If I could have somehow pulled all my credits from three high schools together, I might have been in the middle of my sophomore year. But everything had a catch. The drama class I loved in Beaverton did not exist at Permian. The typing class I found so useful was not on my schedule for a full year. I may have had some credits, but I was not sure where to find them.

I had an agenda in my head. I wanted to find a job, get a pilot's license, learn some Spanish, go to college. I was so far behind that catching up to the class of 1965 was the only thing that did not get on my agenda because I deemed it impossible.

STEVE RUSSELL

~13~

AIR FORCE EDUCATION

My last run at Bristow High School ended in the semester when I arrived in 1963. My mother finally threw up her hands and let me goof off for a couple of months when I promised to go in the military just as soon as I had my 17th birthday. When she signed off on my enlistment in advance, I tried to use that completed and slightly altered form to get in at age 16, but the Air Force caught me and I had to wait.

During my wait time, I took the Armed Forces Qualification Test. Right after the calendar rolled over to February of 1964, I caught a ride to Tulsa with my mother and walked from her job over to the recruiting center. I had 25¢ in my pocket. Thinking I might as well go whole hog on starting from nothing, I gave the quarter to a panhandler during the walk. The recruiter pulled my paperwork together and put me on a chartered bus with approximately thirty teenage boys.

The romance of leaving home with no money came a cropper when somebody noticed that all of my paperwork did not show the same birth date. When they asked me my real birthday, I told them. That's when I learned the government would put me up in an Oklahoma City hotel until I turned 17. They gave me three vouchers a day good for meals at the restaurant in the hotel, which was just a tiny cut above going hungry. I bummed a phone call from the Air Force and persuaded my mother to send me twenty bucks, which would go pretty far in those days. So much for the romance of starting with nothing.

I had to wait about a week. I remember going to several movies, but the only one that planted any memories that remain was *The Apartment*. Of course, the gang physical was memorable for how long we were lined up naked. And we got some shots without needles. Pistol-like gizmos were pressed against our arms and apparently shot the vaccine in with compressed air. Some people learned the hard way that if you moved as the technician pulled the trigger you would be rewarded with a streak of blood across your arm—in addition to getting yelled at again.

After we were poked and prodded and shot in the arm, I had to go back to the hotel while everybody else got on a bus headed to the airport. In about a week, my turn came to get on a gooney bird (AKA DC3) and head south. There was one stop in southern Oklahoma to add a few bodies and then we flew to Dallas, where they fed us in a restaurant in the airport that was several steps up from the one in the hotel. After that meal, I got my first ride on a jet aircraft from Dallas to San Antonio.

The last leg of the flight seemed very short. In San Antonio, uniformed non-commissioned officers herded us off the airplane and on to dark blue school buses. It was dark when we arrived at Lackland Air Force Base and got assigned to barracks. We would be awakened at the crack of dawn by a drill sergeant banging on the metal bed frames, awakened to a state of anxiety that would not end for eight weeks.

When my classmates walked across the stage in 1965 to accept their diplomas, I was well into the second year of my hitch in the Air Force, and more concerned about a different war than the one I had fought with the public schools.

I've often wondered whether recruiters for the U.S. armed forces fight over who gets to be assigned near big Indian communities. Indians have always lined up to join the military services. That history makes quotas easier to meet, but recruiters still need to know what moves young Indians in order to craft a credible sales pitch.

From the French and Indian War, fought before the United States existed, Indians fought in pursuit of their own interests. There were Indians on both sides, but they had their own reasons for supporting either the French or the English.

In modern times, the U.S. has faced existential threats that threatened Indian nations as well, principal among them the last unambiguously "good war" to contain Adolf Hitler's Germany. It was plain from Hitler's writings that a Nazi victory meant either servitude or extinction for Indians.

For Indians who did not feel threatened by the Nazis, there was another self-interest: military service has always been a reliable ticket out of reservations, where unemployment is high and wages are low. Because Indians are the least successful ethnicity in U.S. public schools, education has not always been the key to a better future. Many of us also view military service as a rite of passage to manhood. Counting coup on an enemy or stealing his horses is out of fashion.

Whether the ultimate motivation was perceived threat or personal advancement, military service has been such a reliable way forward that most Indian boys pulled a hitch. However, since my war—the Vietnam War—the presumption that any U.S. war is justified is gone.

Vietnam was different enough from the existential threat of WWII and even the U.N. police action in Korea to change attitudes about U.S. military interventions. In Vietnam, the U.S. stepped into the boots of France, the defeated colonial power, and sent troops to help a Francophile and Roman Catholic minority—quislings, from an indigenous perspective—hold power over a Buddhist majority.

When U.S. public opinion split over whether we were opposing Communist aggression or putting down a national liberation movement, the same split showed up in Indian country among a generation just beginning to understand themselves as colonized peoples. Since Vietnam, the questions are asked out loud. Which nation is right and which nation is wrong? The only Indian boys I knew who did not serve during the Vietnam War had volunteered and been rejected.

With the all-volunteer military today, more Indians are getting rejected because a high school diploma is required. The USAF was an early adopter of the diploma requirement, but my Air Force recruiter had made me a high school graduate with a stroke of his pen after I refused to be passed off to the Marine Corps recruiter, who was not yet looking for graduates.

The USAF guy had also massaged my scores on the Armed Forces Qualification Test, raising my awful score on mechanical aptitude and lowering the other scores, because I was supposed to pass all sections of the test and had not. The non-mechanical scores were extremely high, and when he lowered them to make it more credible that I had barely passed the mechanical section, he was kind enough to maintain the relationships among the scores so there would be a fair picture of my aptitudes.

I did not find out about my recruiter's shenanigans until after I had served four years of active duty. It took me a long time to decide if he had done me a favor or merely done himself a favor. I decided that while he may have been just reaching to make his quota, the military was my ticket out of Oklahoma and the Air Force was where I wanted to be in 1964.

I've often wondered whether every Air Force recruit who claims he does not want to be a fighter pilot is a liar or whether that's just me. There's something about being in a cockpit with dual controls even flying low and slow that sucked me right in. My first rides in commercial airplanes had been on my way to Air Force boot camp and those passenger aircraft were not exciting or even very interesting compared to a two-seater.

Since my son Paul finished Marine Corps boot camp many years later, I am not allowed to whine about Air Force boot camp. The major things I learned were the value of specialization—we would have guys shining boots, making beds, waxing floors, who were quick and good—and the necessity of teamwork. We may have been randomly selected to live together, but we learned to function as a unit.

I was greatly tempted to start smoking cigarettes, something I had not done except for some teenage experimentation. In USAF boot camp, the reward for doing good work was a smoke break. Those of us who did not smoke got to stand at ease and wait for those who did.

While in boot camp, we got tested and tested again so the Air Force could decide what to do with us. I gathered that the technical training bases had schools for troops with similar aptitudes, because when the assignments were posted there would be more than one specialty per base and no apparent pattern to the assignments.

Naturally, I was hoping for an assignment that involved flying. When the lists went up, I missed training to be a loadmaster on cargo planes by just a couple of names. The field I drew was data processing machine operator. I had no clue what that meant and therefore no opinion beyond disappointment at not flying—but what would be the point of having an opinion? It's not like I had a choice.

Tech school training happened in "cycles," meaning that you would get your orders and then have to wait for the next round to start. This is how I came to be killing several weeks of time at Sheppard Air Force Base, just outside of Wichita Falls, Texas. During the wait, we were assigned all kinds of busy work until it was plain that all the busy work was done.

How do I know that? I witnessed the quintessential make-work project and I would not believe it existed had I not seen it with my own eyes: there was a crew of trainees digging a ditch around a rather large building. On the other side of the building, there was another crew filling it in.

One day in spring of 1964, I was assigned to a work detail that involved moving cases of canned goods by truck from a warehouse to the commissary (the base grocery store). As we were loading the truck, the weather got weird—kind of a strange light not exactly coming from above and the wind picking up suddenly. Then the sirens went off.

Several of us ran up the hill across from the warehouse, which was the only direction we couldn't see from where we were. About the time we topped the hill, the hail started falling and we were looking at a big black funnel cloud in the distance but not far enough in the distance to suit me.

In the service, you are thrown together with guys from all over the country, so some of us knew a tornado when we saw one and some didn't. I paused to try to convince myself it was not headed our way but it was. We ran down the hill shouting for the rest of our crew to take cover.

The sky got darker as we ran and the hail got bigger. At first it was the size of peas but it quickly grew to be dangerous. A golf-ball-sized hailstone smacked me in the mouth and I could taste blood. I could also see that was not the largest hailstone. I heard a thump and the guy next to me yelled.

We needed to take cover, but take cover where? I noticed a dumpster full of cardboard and had the thought that burrowing into the cardboard might be safe as being an egg in a carton. The civilian who was bossing the work detail yelled at us to go into a particular warehouse made of concrete blocks rather than into the ones next to it, which were somewhat rundown wooden buildings that matched others on Sheppard AFB and were said to be from WWII.

Inside the warehouse, the safest place seemed to be against the wall on the windward side. I looked up at the top of the wall and saw that every twenty feet or so there were connecting beams that held up the roof. I stood there trying to decide if being under one of the connections was safer, because the wall would be less likely to collapse, or more dangerous, because, if it did collapse, the beam would certainly kill anybody it hit.

While I was trying to make up my mind, the lights went out and I dived down against the wall at a point I thought was under a connecting beam. The building began to shake and the blood on my mouth trapped a layer of dirt that was falling from the ceiling. I had a sharp pain in both of my ears and the place sounded like a train was about to come through the wall. The warehouse roared and shook and I closed my eyes because the dirt that was falling had gone horizontal and was stinging them.

Suddenly, the roaring stopped and there was light. It was not the building lights coming back on. It was daylight coming from where the roof had been. I was able to stand up easily because the debris was shallower next to the overhead beams.

Most of the guys who were buried in between the beams easily dug themselves out; one had heavier stuff pinning his leg down and we quickly dug him out. His pants leg was ripped. There was not much blood and the bleeding had stopped, but he could not walk unassisted. Because I was better suited by size, I took on helping him limp out on his good leg.

We started moving back toward the road. The dumpster I had contemplated hiding in was gone. The flatbed truck our work detail had been loading was gone. The wooden warehouses nearby were bare concrete slabs, buildings and contents blown away. The concrete block warehouse that had sheltered us was a pile of rubble with the roof missing.

I noticed the metal overhead door from our shelter looked like it had been hit by a load of birdshot. Gravel from the driveway had been picked up by the tornado and driven into the metal door. It did not penetrate but it was embedded deeply enough to raise the thought of how that gravel would have attacked flesh.

About the time we got back to the road, an Air Force staff car with little flags over each wheel well came down the road and stopped, allowing me to make a fool of myself at age 17 in a manner that still makes me blush. An officer got out of the car, a Very Important Dude with bird shit all over his hat bill, and I dropped the guy I was supporting so I could snap to and salute.

He was not hurt as badly as I was embarrassed. Nobody said anything to me and Very Important Dude got back in and told his driver to move on as soon as he found out nobody was seriously injured. The tornado had cut a swath of destruction though the base, but you could see buildings still standing in the distance. We learned later only one person was killed.

Those of us who lived in Tornado Alley considered ourselves lucky. People from other parts of the country started counting the days until they could finish training and go someplace safer, like Vietnam.

The tornado strike ended made up work for trainees waiting for their schools to cycle by creating plenty of real work, some of which was pretty unpleasant, like picking up tiny bits of trash embedded wherever the wind took them. I remember paper woven together with plants so firmly that picking it out was like untying a tight shoelace.

Mercifully, my data processing class cycled before we were reduced to using tweezers. The airmen I took to be my cohort shrunk from everybody who lived in the same barracks to a much smaller group that made up my class—a couple of dozen. I began to know the people fate and the Air Force had thrown together, and knowing them changed my self-image big time.

Most of my immediate classmates had some college. I went from not knowing anybody who had been to college to being surrounded by "college men" (as I thought of them) overnight. Their experience ranged from one semester up to three years. I expect if they had graduated, they would have been able to come in as officers rather than enlisted men.

I remember people who had attended the University of Pittsburgh, the University of Colorado, Michigan State, and one guy who had been going to Universidad de las Américas in Mexico. He was the first white guy I knew who was fluent in Spanish.

We all had cleared a battery of aptitude tests to get assigned to the tech school we were in, and, sure enough, everybody seemed to catch on pretty quickly. I amazed myself when I learned to do things in binary I had never been that great doing in decimal.

We quickly moved along to binary-coded octal and I did not get smoked. The "college men" considered me one of them before I considered myself one of them. I talked to them about college, about which I had years of pent up curiosity.

No one admitted to having flunked out. Most claimed to have been bored. A couple had only attended for the student deferment, thought better of it, and joined the Air Force because it was the safest branch of the military.

When I worked up the nerve to broach the subject, none of them could see any reason why I should not look forward to using my GI Bill entitlement when my hitch was over. That was the best news I got since learning that any enlisted man could buy beer in the Airman's Club, a policy probably directed to keeping as many of us as possible out of Wichita Falls, where the local government loved the Air Force but the local boys of a certain age considered fighting with airmen to be great sport. Most of the airmen who went off base tried to promote a ride to Denton to socialize with the women of North Texas State University.

I could never hook up with somebody driving to Denton, so I stayed on base and made my way through tech school with an ease that was a continuing surprise. My anxiety about being tossed in with so many guys with college credits melted away.

After a tech school that was heavy on punched card accounting machines and light on computers, I drew assignments that were mostly about computers. After my experience in tech school, I was confident that I could master a new computer as quickly as anybody else and that turned out to be true.

My first assignment was Randolph Air Force Base, located just north of San Antonio, where I had done boot camp at Lackland AFB. Randolph was headquarters to the Air Training Command. In addition to a huge computerized personnel center that tracked all the students, there were two main flight lines, one for jets and one for propeller driven aircraft. Enlisted men lived in barracks without air conditioning situated near the jet flight line, while officers on the other side of the base had both air conditioning and the reduced noise level of the prop aircraft.

The primary teaching aircraft for the numerous foreign students at Randolph was the T-28, which had not been manufactured since 1957 but was sturdy enough that, in a combat version, it became the primary aircraft provided to the Vietnamese Air Force. Fewer than 2,000 of them were built, a factoid that got my attention when I almost had to buy one.

In 1965, my duty as an auxiliary air policeman took me away from Randolph. Normally, the most exciting Air Police duty was guarding Air Force One when LBJ was in town. On this occasion, a Vietnamese student pilot had become alarmed when he began to get smoke from the engine in his cockpit, and so he put it down at an auxiliary airfield near Seguin.

I was told this story to explain why I was being sent to Seguin to guard a T-28. I had never seen a T-28 that didn't smoke at all, but I supposed there might have been a fire. I was issued an M-14 rifle with only one magazine containing eight rounds, which meant that anybody who came to steal the airplane had better be unarmed or I had better be as good shooting at people as I was shooting at paper targets. Neither seemed likely, but there was a hot phone line directly to Randolph, a distance of about 20 miles.

After a couple of hours of twiddling thumbs, a civilian car pulled up to the gate and dropped off a man wearing a USAF flight suit with captain's bars. I shouldered arms and snapped him a salute, to which he responded with one of those half waves that says, "OK, if we must, but let's get to work."

The captain rummaged around until he found a big fire extinguisher on wheels, which he manhandled out next to the errant T-28 without asking for help. Then he called me over and showed me how to work the thing. He said he would crank the plane up with the canopy open and he would give me the high sign if I should use the machine. Then he thought for a minute and added that if there was so much smoke I could not see him I should just let 'er rip.

He turned it over and the elderly aircraft belched smoke like every other T-28 I had seen. I could see no flames. The pilot goosed the throttle a couple of times and then let it idle while he poked around in the cockpit a good long time. It continued to smoke but not an amount that would alarm me if I saw it on the Randolph flight line.

Apparently satisfied, the pilot closed the canopy and shot me some hand signals I did not understand followed by a salute much crisper that the one he returned when I greeted him. Then I lost eye contact as he taxied to the end of the runway, took off smoothly, and flew away in the direction of Randolph.

I pulled the fire extinguisher back where he got it and picked up the hot line. A voice answered immediately and asked what I needed.

"I need you to send somebody to Seguin to get me. The airplane is gone."

"Gone? Where did it go?"

"A captain showed up and flew it off toward you."

"What was his name?"

"Er...I didn't ask his name. I was busy with the fire extinguisher."

"Airman, do you know what a statement of charges is?"

Yes, I knew. Everybody is told that if you break or lose something that belongs to Sam, they dock your paycheck to pay for it. And if the sum is too great to get it paid during your hitch, they can extend your hitch until Sam is paid.

Sheesh, I was thinking. *Couldn't I go back to just guarding Air Force One?*

The T-28 turned up, so I did not have to pay for it, but that was the most exciting thing that happened during my tour at Randolph, although there was an incident that might have turned out to be more important.

Later in 1965, the squadron commander summoned a roomful of airmen, all of us assigned to highly technical Air Force specialties. We were gathered to hear an Army major offer us the opportunity to become helicopter pilots. It was a friendly audience because most of us did not join the Air Force to be chairborne.

If we signed on the dotted line, the Air Force would release us from the rest of our hitch, and we would fly to Ft. Rucker, Alabama to learn how to fly rotary wing aircraft. Upon graduation, we would become Army warrant officers.

The mention of Ft. Rucker got my attention because my most serious girlfriend (although not my only girlfriend, because I had been dating a WAF I met at Randolph) was stationed there. Flying. Warrant officer. Girlfriend. What's not to like? I raised my hand, and the major pointed at me.

"What happens if we don't graduate flying school?"

"You spend the time you had left on your Air Force hitch as an Army enlisted man."

"What specialty?"

"Infantry."

It had been fun while it lasted. Nobody signed. We all knew why the Army was beating the brush for helo pilots, but that was OK because we were all bulletproof. What was not OK was the living conditions Army grunts faced while waiting to get shot at. We all opted to stay in a situation where the major issue was lack of air conditioning or soundproofing in the barracks next to the jet flight line.

Our next encounter with Sam's needs involved a smaller group of data processing people. We were called to our squadron commander's office and informed that we had been "selected to volunteer" for USAF Security Service, and that was a big deal because we would be getting a top secret security clearance.

This was how I came to be assigned to headquarters, USAFSS, situated on a hill between Lackland and Kelly air force bases, on the other side of San Antonio. USAFSS was the flyboy branch of a then-obscure outfit that has become less obscure, the National Security Agency. My duty would involve compiling top secret communications intercept intel reports—SIGINT, as they say.

When my clearance came through, I worked rotating shifts in a big, windowless box of a building with layers of cipher locks on the inside.

I really, *really* wanted out of there—working without windows, cooped up with lots of electronic gear and perpetually rotating shifts that left me permanently sleep-deprived—but had no chance of leaving USAFSS because of the expense involved in my top secret clearance. The form that started the clearance process required a list of everywhere an applicant had ever lived or worked and references to be named in each place. An agent of the Office of Special Investigations made a personal visit to most of the references, or so the people I listed told me. The older non-commissioned officers told me I could perhaps get out of USAFSS if I re-upped, but maybe not even then.

So, I went over to personnel and asked where I could volunteer for that would offer the best chance of getting me out in the field. Answers: Alaska remote, a listening station aimed at the Soviet Union that could not be reached except by snowmobile or dogsled. Or Vietnam. I put in volunteer statements for both. At that time (late 1965), I was still gung-ho to rout the Commies.

By and by, I got reassigned as I wished, to a listening post on a hill just south of the DMZ, north of Da Nang. I was pleased at the prospect of getting out of that windowless box and I lacked the sense of my own mortality that might otherwise have kept me from cheering over being assigned to a combat zone.

It's customary to take a thirty-day leave before deploying in a combat zone to say your goodbyes and put your affairs in order. It was so customary that if you did not have thirty days accumulated, the Air Force would let your leave balance go negative. I had the days, but I still had to raise the money. After draining my dinky credit union account, I looked around my barracks room for items that could be pawned. There was nothing but my music: an old banged up Kay guitar and my clarinet.

The pawnbroker offered nothing for the guitar and fifteen bucks for the horn. I was desperate and I knew I would get paid before I had to leave San Antonio and that meant I could get the clarinet out of hock. So I accepted a fraction of what my grandparents has borrowed to make me a musician.

My customary pre-deployment leave in 1966 offered up more adventure than I expected, and when I returned to duty from a one-month leave seven months later, I no longer thought I was bulletproof.

STEVE RUSSELL

~14~

NO LONGER BULLETPROOF

In 1966, I was over half finished with what I still called my first Air Force hitch, still on track for a retirement pension at the ripe age of 37. I was looking forward to deploying to a Security Service listening post so close to the DMZ, my colleagues claimed, that our Big Ears picked it up if Ho Chi Minh farted in his sleep.

I was not thinking my assigned slice of the Vietnam War was particularly dangerous. That far from Saigon, I expected to be issued an M-16, but I did not expect to use it. The work promised to be as boring as the location was exotic. I would convert the electronic intercepts to something our computers could read and ship out the raw product for the rest of the conversion from Vietnamese to computer to English.

While I did not think I was heading into mortal peril, I could see advantages in letting others think so. I had taken to carrying a pistol whenever I visited Bristow because I was done being anybody's victim. Going to Bristow aroused more anxiety about having to defend myself with a firearm than going to Vietnam.

I made a copy of my orders to prove I would soon be a war hero and headed first to Bristow, where I found my grandmother had also acquired a pistol. She explained that, in my absence, boys about my age—running in groups—had done home invasion robberies at her home that she was helpless to stop. She called the police and they sent somebody out after the robbers were long gone to write a report. The only thing that really slowed them down was that she had so little worth stealing. At first she was just scared, but then she got angry.

Her report filled me with guilt. I had always lived in fear of being beaten for amusement, or, after I began earning money, robbed. But I had never given a thought to how vulnerable my grandmother would be after I was gone and my mother was able to move out.

The pistol was still in the box from Oklahoma Tire & Supply. I asked her if she had ever fired it. She had not. I asked her if she had ever discharged any kind of firearm. She had not.

I loaded Granma and her pistol in my Volkswagen and drove out to the dirt landing strip the Civil Air Patrol had used. It was deserted that day and I did not see the airplane, leading me to wonder if the CAP still existed in Bristow, but I was not curious enough to deviate from the reason I was there. I drove out to the end of the landing strip, where I had to stop to avoid my exhaust heat setting the grass on fire.

I was lucky to find a spot close enough for Granma to walk to it that offered a view with no houses or livestock fences. There were too many trees for my liking, but there was a hill to catch the bullets. I had bought a box each of .22 shorts, longs, and long rifles—any of which her pistol would fire.

My plan was to set up some bottles and have her fire the different kinds of ammunition to see what she was most comfortable using, but I was already having the thought that the pistol might be more dangerous to her than to intruders. She kept forgetting my admonition to pay attention to the direction the barrel was pointed at all times and to keep her finger outside the trigger guard.

At one point, she had just fired a couple of rounds and she turned around to talk to me. When she turned, so did the pistol, and there I was with an elderly woman's shaky hands holding a loaded pistol and pointing it at me. I don't know if she understood my alarm, but she did understand that her hands were not up to the task of loading the shorts. She did better with the longs and long rifles.

I was thinking the only solution was to leave the pistol loaded—scary as that prospect was—because she had so much trouble loading it. Her solution was to leave it unloaded and just wave it at them. I could see danger in that as well. We agreed that I would take her pistol with me when I went to visit my mother in Arkansas and we would make a decision on my way back.

When I told Granma of my impending deployment, I learned that she was stoutly opposed to the Vietnam War, because the fight was "none of our business," and she was dismayed at my participation. Somewhat deflated by that and by the contretemps over the pistol, I steered my Volkswagen in the direction of rural Arkansas, where my mother lived while commuting to work in the metropolis of Russellville.

When I arrived in Arkansas the same day, I was nonplussed to find that Arkansas existed in an alcohol prohibition time warp. The state was divided between wet and dry counties. There were a few the locals called "moist," because alcohol was legal but surrounded by so many regulations it was hardly worth the trouble.

The nearest place to my mother's home to buy a legal six-pack was Conway, where I learned that the drinking age was 21. I was 19, and after a day of futile attempts to wet my whistle, I went back to my mother's place and described my day. After she was able to quit laughing, she introduced me to her bootlegger, who lived conveniently close.

Scotty was a gangly blond dude about my age with a haircut that looked more military than mine. We became fast friends, and the next day we went hunting for small game. I had three pistols in my car, and I chose the most accurate, a Ruger .22 semi-automatic that I kept in my car for self-defense when visiting Bristow. Scotty chose my grandmother's Hi-Standard .22 revolver—a good choice because the third pistol was an Astra semi-automatic with a barrel just a tad over two inches that only fired .22 shorts in seemingly random patterns.

We shot a few squirrels and Scotty was neither grossed out by eating rodents nor surprised at my insistence that I don't kill things I don't intend to eat. We began to think of taking our hunting a little more upscale, and Scotty suggested there might be ducks hanging out in the small ponds formed by deserted strip mines.

Hunting ducks with pistols would be asking too much of marksmanship, but the furnished cabin where my mother lived had an old .12-gauge shotgun on a rack above the fireplace. It was a side-by-side double barrel with two triggers. I cracked the breech and it looked cruddy in there but not rusty. My mother called her landlord and he agreed that we could use it and said it ought to work, although it had not been fired for a couple of years. Scotty volunteered that he had an old partial box of shells somewhere and when he returned with it we were in business.

It was late in the day when we loaded all the guns into the trunk of Scotty's big blue Edsel and went out to reconnoiter the strip pits. Two things stood out about Scotty's car in addition to the make. I had never ridden in an Edsel before and the interior seemed to have been pretty ritzy before the car got old, but he had removed the rear seat, making what was already a cavernous trunk a payload area that looked suitable to carry my Volkswagen. The other oddity was when he cranked up the V-8 engine, it idled with a deep rumble that caused the whole front end of what I immediately dubbed the blue whale to vibrate— upscale rides can be powerful, but normally without such ostentatious noise.

Given Scotty's profession, I had to ask him why he would drive something like the blue whale. I had never seen anything like it and it had to be easy to spot on the two-lane roads of rural Arkansas. He smiled with pride and allowed that all the cops knew him and knew the blue whale, but they had never been able to catch him driving a load.

The blue whale was an odd beast on the inside as well as the outside. An automatic transmission was no surprise but push-button controls on the steering wheel were. The only radio Scotty had would become a fad in about ten years—a CB radio.

He claimed that his radio was one reason he had never been caught.

As we rolled in the blue whale, the two-lane blacktop became gravel, and after a turn over a cattle guard it became two dirt trails through high grass. Scotty pulled up to one of the strip pits and stopped at a little clearing where somebody had built a fire in the past. In the fading daylight, I could still see the water was clear and there were plenty of big rocks for sitting and climbing in and out without slogging through the mud in the shallows.

It looked to be an outstanding swimming hole, but there were no ducks. Thinking I'd like to fire the old shotgun anyway as long as we were out in the boonies, I picked up the dirty cardboard box and discovered it was just as well there were no ducks. The shells were not birdshot. They were number 2, which is near the small end of buckshot.

Scotty was not sympathetic to my complaint: "Whatta ya expect with luck of the draw? They're .12 gauge, aren't they? They fit the gun, don't they?"

With nothing to fire birdshot at, having an argument seemed like a waste of time, so I shut up and plopped a couple of old shells into the old gun, only to discover the last of the sunlight disappearing over the horizon. Then we heard some familiar sounds.

The first croak sounded like there was a granddad bullfrog right at my feet. It was answered from the other side of the pond.

Scotty asked, "How about some frog legs?"

I like frog legs just fine, but I had to point out that we had no gigs and shooting in the dark seemed both futile and dangerous.

Scotty motioned for me to wait. After some rummaging in the whale, he came up with a flashlight, a little one of the kind that takes two D batteries and has a magnet on the side of it. He flicked it on and the brightness said the batteries were new. It gave me an idea.

I took the flashlight and fastened it to the barrel of the shotgun with the magnet. Wherever the light went, I thought, that's where the gun was pointed. I stood right on the dirt edge of the bank and looked down to where I thought that basso croak had come from.

I played the light along the water's edge, but I saw nothing and I heard nothing. I was about ready to give it up when I thought I heard the same frog taunting me from a distance. I raised the light and there he was on a log twenty-five or thirty feet away. I had the light right on him when he ripped loose another croak.

About that time, Scotty hollered at me to "aim for the head." I was annoyed that he thought I could aim a shotgun when I had never seen its pattern but I had not taken my eyes off the frog and I'd seen chickens with smaller drumsticks than that, so I looked down the top of the barrel at the frog's head and squeezed the trigger.

I've been trained now for being struck by lightning. A flame from the end of the barrel lit the area to the other side of the pond and the report was louder than any weapon I had ever fired. I heard someone scream, "Ooohhh shit!" and I didn't realize it was me until I heard the splash and felt the cold water on my crotch.

When I could see and hear again, I was sitting in the mud with my shiny black GI shoes under water. It was dark and I could not see the flashlight. I cracked the breech to unload the gun and discovered I had managed to fire the other barrel as I slid down the mud bank on my butt.

As I wondered how I was going to get out of there in the dark, all of a sudden Scotty was shining the flashlight on me. He claimed it flew up ten or twelve feet and fell to the ground behind me. The light had stayed on.

Certain the gun was unloaded, I was able to hold it by the end of the barrel and hand it up to Scotty. Then he used the light to find me a place to climb out.

"All of that," I griped, "and I missed the damn frog."

"No, you didn't." Scotty was shining the light on a large spot of froggy bodily fluids and parts on the branch I had shredded with shot. He wanted to switch to pistols and start stalking frogs, but I was ready to go back to my mother's house. I didn't care for walking around in wet pants and I was especially interested in removing the mud from my GI shoes.

Scotty picked up the floor mat from the passenger side of the blue whale and put it on the seat so I would not get the upholstery wet, stashed the pistols in the empty ice chest, and we were off. We had no more passed the cattle guard and turned onto the gravel road and there were red lights behind us.

Scotty glanced briefly in the rearview mirror and stomped on the throttle. The whale bucked and roared and my shoulders were pinned back to the seat as I yelled, "What are you doing? Are you out of your gourd?"

"Did you say something about a policeman?" Scotty snickered. "What policeman?"

Sure enough, the flashing red lights were pinpricks in the distance, and as we rounded a gradual curve, the pinpricks winked out.

The gravel road exited the forest and intersected with the two-lane blacktop. As we neared the intersection, a police car blocked the road and turned on reds. Scotty cocked the steering wheel all the way left as he slid on the gravel, but his perfect 180 just brought him hood to hood with his pursuer.

They soon had us both out of the Edsel and handcuffed while they ransacked the car. I overheard some back and forth about traffic offenses that could be nailed on Scotty. Speeding was out because nobody measured his speed and there was no marked speed limit where he was driving fastest. Failure to stop didn't work unless there was a reason to stop him. There was nothing illegal about the 180.

Then the officer who had opened the ice chest asked over his shoulder, "Where you boys goin' with all the artillery?"

"Down to the strip pits to spotlight frogs," I piped up.

"Don't you boys know it's illegal to spotlight frogs? Sounds like a conspiracy to me."

Scotty was glaring at me. My mouth had gotten the blue whale impounded, at least.

When we got to the police station, they dug into the statute books and claimed to have found a law about spotlighting game. It did not mention frogs, but there was no exception for frogs, either.

While they were discussing the merits of a criminal conspiracy charge, the jailer looking through my belongings found a copy of my Vietnam orders folded up in my wallet. He handed the document to one of the arresting officers, who read it over.

"According to this, Airman Teehee, you are supposed to be in California in about two weeks."

"Yes, sir. If I'm out of jail, that is. I don't know what happens if I miss my connection."

He made some remark about not wanting to interfere with my vacation in Vietnam. He read my mother's phone number off the booking sheet, called her, and told her to come and get me.

I asked if I could have my guns back and they said no.

Before my mother drove away, she asked me where the guns were, probably thinking of the old shotgun she had borrowed from her landlord. I told her the story and she marched back inside. She returned shortly with the shotgun and all three pistols. I asked what was going to happen to Scotty.

"Not much," she replied, "unless they can find a law he broke. I don't think conspiracy to spotlight frogs is going to hold up."

I was on the road the next day back to Bristow, where I found, to my relief, that Granma had decided she did not want her pistol back.

It was a couple of months before I wrote my mother a note asking what happened to Scotty. She said he had to pay to get the blue whale back but he was getting over being pissed at me. If I cared to return to Arkansas for a visit, he had a six-pack with my name on it. We could go down to the strip pits and spotlight frogs.

~15~

THE EMPTY SPOT ON MY DRESS BLUES

The gas gauge in my 1966 VW Bug—the first new car I had ever owned—told me I was not going to make it back to San Antonio. I had spent most of my leave with my grandmother in Bristow and my mother in rural Arkansas. In Bristow, I had found that most of the friends I tried to look up were serving in the military, and one enlistment made me laugh out loud.

Terry's dad was a construction contractor who specialized in public projects in a state where corruption was rampant. He pulled every string he could reach, cashed in all his political chips, to get his son a coveted slot in the Oklahoma National Guard. The weekend warriors represented safety, shelter from the draft, from being jailed for refusing induction, and from getting shot at in Vietnam. The limited number of positions was divided among families with political clout.

Getting Terry into the National Guard was an act of love that burned political capital normally spent on getting government work without being the low bidder. I could only imagine the family complications when Terry tired of being dry-docked in Bristow while all of his friends were having far-flung if not exactly safe adventures. When he could stand it no longer, Terry exchanged his scant Guard duties for an active duty enlistment in the Navy.

This story of giving up a coveted weekend warrior slot that cost his father a small fortune was the talk of Bristow, and I listened to it several times as I hunted for people who would remember me and discovered that most were in the military. I didn't know any of the girls well enough to be looking for them.

Goodbyes said to everybody I could find, I was headed back to Headquarters USAF Security Service in San Antonio to pick up my stuff and head out to California for something called "counterinsurgency training." I heard there would be cushy transportation in a civilian airplane under contract to the military from California to Saigon. I had visions of headphones with several music channels, tiny whiskey bottles, stewardesses—a last exposure to the comforts absent on military aircraft.

I pulled off Interstate 35 near 51st street in Austin to fill up at a Texaco station.

The last decision I remember making was whether to pay with a twenty or with a ten, and I've often wondered, if I had chosen differently, would my timing have changed enough to avoid the drunk coming up the interstate the wrong way in a 1965 Ford station wagon? As it was, we met on the Colorado River bridge, my speed 60 mph or so and his accelerating to highway speed with police already in pursuit.

The police report said I left some short skid marks and the Ford left none. My medical records claim I was unconscious for about forty-eight hours, but I have memories of the crash that are like snapshots rather than a movie, with sketchy bits of sound going with the still photos.

I was somehow one with my car, a melding of flesh and metal. I had arrived at a dead stop from highway speed without noticing. Sounds sputtered on and off like a radio losing reception, sirens wailing and men shouting.

Somebody grabbed my shoulders and pulled me back from my seamless union with the dashboard. I had clutched the steering wheel with both hands as I vainly stood up on the brake pedal, holding on as the collision accomplished the sudden stop my brakes could not.

The steering column had ripped up though the unpadded metal dashboard. The windshield had popped out in one piece and the steering column ended up vertical, the top of my head resting against it, in the space where the windshield had been. The lower part of my face had smashed into the jagged metal where the steering column had been. A tiny difference in the travel of my head would have taken both my eyes into that sharp metal instead of my mouth.

When a rescuer pulled me back, I felt my jaw collapse. My mouth was blocked by blood and what I later found were teeth and bone fragments, and there was an overpowering smell of gasoline from the ruptured front-mounted gas tank I had just filled up. The movement caused such pain that I passed out, according to my memory. According to my medical records, I was already out. I remember consciousness coming and going randomly.

The first responders cut my seat belt and extracted me from the driver's seat. The process was bumpy and every movement caused the pain to blaze. It must've been about this time the police resolved to get my blood tested to see if I was driving under the influence, like the man who had hit me had been.

I don't blame them. I had purchased several cases of Coors to take back for my friends in the barracks. In those days, Coors had a big fan base but was available only in limited areas—it was for sale in Oklahoma but not in Texas. The Coors was in glass bottles stacked on the back seat. No bottle survived, and when they pulled me out of my car I was wearing most of the beer.

Suddenly I was on my back looking at the ceiling of the ambulance and there was motion. Every now and then my airway would become blocked with blood. Several times during that ride I sent a blast of breath out of my mouth and caused a spray of blood and bone fragments.

I wanted to apologize for the mess and explain that I was trying to breathe, but I could not talk and the men tending me in the ambulance did not seem upset.

I learned later that Brackenridge Hospital, which hosted the only trauma center in Austin then, was a straight shot north on Interstate 35 from 1st to 15th. If there is a fortunate place for a life-threatening medical emergency, that would be where I crashed. A quick U-turn on the south end of the bridge and there was just time to enter the interstate but not to reach highway speed before exiting practically at the emergency room doors, having avoided half a dozen traffic lights.

At Brackenridge, they wheeled me directly into an operating room and began to cut my clothes off. I watched what I took to be a scalpel slice down the seam in the leg of my brand-new white Levis. Somebody else was cutting through my blood-soaked shirt.

When those Levis left my body in two pieces, my memory tells me I managed to snag my wallet, flip it open, and hand my military ID to somebody. My medical records say that could not have happened because I was unconscious. I want to believe my memory, but the story in the medical records seems more likely.

Unable to speak to anyone, I interrogated myself. Was I alive or was I making a slow and painful exit from this life? I was not sure which and not sure it mattered. If this was the final exit, I would as soon get it over with.

That is all I can remember of the emergency room. I next came to, off and on, in a room where I would be molested periodically for the hospital ritual called "taking vitals." It hurt. Everything hurt.

I was no longer a participant in my life. My throat was parched, but liquid only came into my body intravenously. Liquid left my body through a catheter. I wondered why they needed me to move fluid from one plastic bag to another.

A couple of days later, when I was conscious and supposedly stable, an Air Force ambulance showed up to transport me to Wilford Hall USAF Hospital at Lackland AFB in San Antonio. Lackland was directly adjacent to my destination at Headquarters Security Service, a windowless box surrounded by razor wire and motion detectors that contained the nerve center of the USAF branch of the National Security Agency.

We are all born unable to speak, having to be fed, and having to have our backsides wiped. But we mercifully forget those times of total helplessness. By the time the Air Force sent an ambulance to retrieve me, I was beginning to understand my situation of total dependence on others without a means to communicate with them. I was not liking it one bit, and I was having a hard time understanding why I should want to live in this condition. Nobody had told me if or when my condition might improve.

Arriving at the hospital that would be my home for the next seven months brought another trauma but ended in redemption. Wilford Hall was only my second hospital admission in my young life. The first had been the emergency room at Brackenridge in Austin I had just come from.

As they unloaded my gurney from the ambulance, they extended the wheels so I would be a little over waist high as they rolled me into Wilford Hall. Somebody neglected to lock the wheels in position. It was not possible to fall on the ground unless the thing tipped over, but when the wheels returned to their folded position, I fell straight down, maybe four feet.

The pain when the gurney made its sudden stop inches from the pavement set off fireworks behind my eyeballs. Because the entire lower part of my face had been smashed in the crash, I still could not talk, but I'm sure I groaned loudly before the pain took away my consciousness again. I learned later that most of that pain had been produced by my least serious injury—a broken collarbone.

When I rejoined shared reality, the gurney was back up high and I was being pushed though some swinging doors to a clean and well-lighted room, where I would get inspected by a team of Air Force doctors.

I had never experienced pain of the magnitude that had been coming at me periodically for the two days since the accident. Stacked on top of the physical pain was not being able to communicate with the people around me. I was not sure I wanted to survive this unless it was going to get better soon.

That's when I saw her.

She was wearing a surgical mask, so all I could see were her eyes, beautiful eyes, and a few wisps of shiny black hair hanging down from her forehead and around her ears where they were not quite covered by her cap. My eyes, wet with tears from the fall, met hers. Oh, how I wanted to speak to her!

125

Without breaking eye contact, she peeled off one of her latex gloves, reached down and took my hand in her bare hand and squeezed it just hard enough so I would know it was purposeful. She did not say a word and I could not say a word.

The doctors were discussing me as a case, deciding what part of me to attempt repair on first. They were talking about me but not talking to me. Their conversation became background noise while my eyes remained locked with the nurse and my brain was shouting what my mangled lips could not: *I love you!...I love you!* And as if the effort to send that signal had been too much for my damaged body, my eyelids got heavy and I could no longer see her, but I could still feel her warm hand in mine as I floated into a sleep state, still chanting silently, *I love you.*

I never saw her again, but when I awakened in an ordinary hospital bed in an ordinary hospital room, the memory of her touch was crystalline and I was no longer ambivalent about wanting to live.

Wanting to live was a good thing, because I was in a plastic surgery ward with what seemed like an endless cycle of surgery, recovery, day duty/open ward, and then back for more surgery. Every month, somebody called about when I would be released for duty. I presume the call came from my squadron or from the personnel office, but they never talked to me.

Some time around my third trip to the operating room, I finally started digging through the blood-soaked wallet that had followed me to Wilford Hall in a plastic bag. I found the pawn ticket for my clarinet, only recently expired.

I thought about who I could ask to make a run to the pawnshop—Louis Fejszes, Duncan MacNaughton, Leonard Zacher—any of them would give it a try. I loved playing clarinet and the horn had sentimental value because of the sacrifices my grandparents had made to buy it.

On the other hand, the accident left me with noises in my ears that would not stop—not for a minute or even a second. The docs taught me it was called "tinnitus" and gave me hope it might go away. That was important because my inability to experience silence had me suicidal and because the tinnitus rendered me tone-deaf. If you gave me a nice loud G chord on the piano, I could not get it to stand out enough to match it with a guitar string.

I could not tune a guitar. I could no longer sing on key. And even if I could tune the clarinet, I could no longer hold the mouthpiece for any reed instrument or control my lips enough for a brass instrument.

Later, I was able to acquire an electronic gadget to tune a guitar, but my days of horn playing were over. While I was in the hospital, I had no time to be interested in music because Vietnam was still in my face.

I can remember everybody on that ward who had not just come from Vietnam.

There was a guy with lung cancer. He died.

There was a guy who had that Alaska remote assignment I hadn't gotten. He fell down in the snow and was set upon by his sled dogs. They ate his ear, and he was getting it slowly reconstructed as I was getting my face reconstructed.

There was a guy who had been rendered quadriplegic by a stock car racing accident.

Everybody else had combat injuries from Vietnam and was getting reconstruction. They were mostly Americans, but also Vietnamese, some of whom did not speak a lot of English. They looked forward to visits from Vietnamese assigned to the Air Training Command bases around San Antonio.

Service people like to tell "war stories," regardless of whether they got to a war zone, and the people on that plastic surgery ward had real war stories. Some didn't remember much about the incident that caused their injuries, but I didn't remember much about my head-on collision, so I'm guessing the blank spots in traumatic memories are common.

I was as interested in stories about life in Vietnam as in the stories about combat. In the stories I could elicit, the government the U.S. was supporting in South Vietnam did not sound likely to command much loyalty. I tried to fact check what I was hearing with some of the Vietnamese patients. While they were cordial enough, my inquiries were stymied by both a language barrier and a political barrier that told me something about the value of free speech in South Vietnam.

I picked up and read *The Prison Diary of Ho Chi Minh*, written in classical Chinese quatrains while he was in a Chinese prison. Some of the reputed beauty of the form must have been lost in translation, but it was hard to find much to hate or even with which to disagree. It also occurred to me that the alliance between China and Vietnam was probably a matter of necessity rather than choice on Vietnam's part.

The final break came when I watched a debate on public TV with a panel of college students against the war and the newly elected California Governor Ronald Reagan for it. The other politician on the stage was New York Senator Robert F. Kennedy, who had been in the senate as long as I had been in the Air Force and whose position sounded like a straddle. He was extremely critical of the way the war was being conducted but did not call for an immediate end to it.

A lot of history came up that I had not known. I also came away impressed with RFK, because when the students nailed him, he acknowledged being nailed, while Reagan covered his ignorance with bluster.

In April of 1967, I overheard my plastic surgeon speaking to whoever was making the monthly call to inquire when I would be available for duty in Vietnam.

Captain William Cocke let his irritation show to a degree that surprised me: "Maybe not in this enlistment. I can't tell, and I'm not releasing him until I'm done."

While the Governor and the Senator and the students were debating the war, my deployment orders were being withdrawn. Dr. Cocke did not have to take "the Teehee call" in May or June, and after leaving Wilford Hall in July, I served out the rest of my hitch in that windowless box I had been trying to escape with the realization that I was on the wrong side of the war I had enlisted to fight. I started writing letters to the editor of the San Antonio newspapers and hanging out with Quakers. It's amazing my clearance was not yanked. I did get "counseled" about "inappropriate behavior."

The listening post to which I'd been assigned was overrun during the Tet Offensive. I would have been KIA or POW had I been there, which would have required reenlistment, but I might easily have reenlisted had I not collided with reality. I don't know how well insulated from that reality I would have been in my Security Service assignment. It may sound funny, considering my changed attitude about the war, but I felt guilty about what happened at Tet.

Dr. Cocke said my scars had not hardened up enough to safely be "revised." However, he said he would give it a try if I were considering reenlistment to get the plastic surgery. The VA will not do plastic surgery on the cosmetic level.

I thanked him, took my honorable discharge, and grew a beard to cover the scars...which is why I've not shaved since 1968.

When my hitch was up, I had a top secret clearance and I was good at operating a computer system like the one that controlled space flights at NASA. But what would give me the confidence not to reenlist did not exactly come from the Air Force but rather from the people I worked with who taught me a little bit about the promised land of college and a lot about myself.

I may be one of the last generation of Indian boys who considered pulling a hitch necessary to becoming an adult. I hear the young ones now asking questions about Iraqis I failed to ask about Vietnamese, and even asking why we should serve at all in light of our treatment by the United States. The only answer I can offer is that I can't imagine an existential threat to the U.S. that would not also be a threat to the Cherokee Nation. It's good that we are finally having these conversations— good for the U.S. and the Indian nations and the young people who always carry the burdens of wars.

Because I did not question the wisdom of my generation's war, it was not so much my choices as my luck that led me to have war stories only once removed, and the survivor's guilt but without the battle ribbon.

STEVE RUSSELL

THE RIDE OF MY DREAMS

The same fates that decreed I would lose the first new car I owned and almost lose my life—while at once robbing me of the opportunity to lose my life in armed combat—had also decided that the man who died almost killing me would not be carrying liability insurance. Because I still owed the credit union for my destroyed car, I notified my insurance carrier.

Within days, I was visited in the hospital by a nice young man named Pat Priest, who identified himself as an insurance adjuster. We were able to agree on the value of my car with relative ease. I got my hands on the classified ads from a Sunday edition of the *San Antonio Express-News* and found plenty of 1966 VW Bugs for sale. I asked for a sum in the middle of what those people were asking.

Mr. Priest chuckled and acquainted me with a reference called the *Blue Book*, which listed a fair market value for my car within a few bucks of what I was asking. I told him it was the first car I had ever owned and so I had kept it in tip-top shape and the records to prove it were in the glove box. Friends from my squadron had visited the boneyard where my white Bug was taken and brought me a picture of the mangled front end. They tried to bring me any belongings that were not destroyed but there wasn't much left. The trunk was in the front and the whole front end was mashed all the way to the passenger compartment.

I did not have to send them back to look for the remains of the glove box because Mr. Priest took my word for the condition of the car prior to the accident and paid the full value. It was enough for me to pay what I still owed the credit union and enough money would remain to buy myself some cheap transportation once I got out of the hospital.

When he paid me for my car, I thought we were done. That's when Mr. Priest informed me that I had uninsured motorist coverage in the amount of $10,000. He watched the dollar signs light up my eyes for a moment before delivering the bad news: the Air Force had a claim against my insurance for my medical care and for the loss of my services while I was in the hospital. While a look at my medical records convinced him I had a "policy limits case," I was going to have to split that $10,000 with the Air Force.

I argued with Mr. Priest, who was an innocent party. He had already agreed that his employer would have to pay the full amount. The only question was to whom, and in that he was on my side. I felt guilty for complaining to him that the Air Force had not paid my premiums or required me to buy the coverage so it did not deserve any of the money. Luckily, I was only writing this on a pad. I could not yell at him because I could not talk. I carried a note pad and a pen everywhere.

Mr. Priest predicted that the Air Force would want an even split, but he intended to write up my injuries and suggest I should get $7,500. I was still outraged, but I understood the law was not on my side and I was fortunate the insurance adjuster was. He sent in the paperwork to the Air Force and we waited.

When I was released from the hospital in July, stripped of my Vietnam orders and therefore in need of transportation, we were still waiting. I bought a 100cc Suzuki motorcycle to get around and after waiting a few more weeks, I decided to employ the GI's atomic weapon: Henry B.

Most of San Antonio had been represented forever by a man who became legendary for his defense of the men and women who served at the five major military installations—so legendary he was known by his first name and middle initial. Congressman Henry B. Gonzalez.

I experienced the legend firsthand when, in the uniform that plainly showed me to be a low ranking enlisted man, I walked into Henry B.'s office in downtown San Antonio. I asked if the congressman was in because I needed to see him. I did not at that time understand how absurd it was for me to come to his door without an appointment and expect more than some happy talk from a staffer.

Henry B.'s receptionist showed me right in. I was almost tongue-tied by a combination of being in the great man's presence so quickly and having looked at the map hanging in his outer office with his district outlined by a colored magic marker. I had just found out I did not live in his district.

He never asked me where I lived. I told him my problem and he summoned one of his staff and told him to draft a letter to General so-and-so with a copy to the JAG office and ask them what is holding up Airman Teehee's money.

Then he turned to me. "I'll have somebody call you when we get a response. Is there anything else?"

"No, sir. Thank you, sir. I'm amazed at how hard you jumped on my problem."

"It's what I get paid for, Airman, what I get paid for."

In a little over a week, I got a call from Pat Priest. "The Air Force just settled your case. If you can come and sign the papers, I'll get you a check."

"How much?"

"$7,500. They paid what I asked for. I expected a counteroffer."

As I got directions to his office, I was thinking, "Thank God for Henry B."

As soon as the check cleared, I was ready to go shopping. At that magic moment, I could afford any mass-produced American car and most foreign cars. Naturally, I moved toward a Corvette.

I didn't just press my nose to the glass at the dealership in San Antonio. I went inside and fondled a red Corvette. After all those years of foreplay, I was ready to consummate the relationship that had existed only in my dreams.

That was when I discovered that auto insurance could be even more expensive than it already was for an unmarried male of 20 years. Add to my age, sex, and marital status the fact that the insured vehicle would be a red roadster with a V-8 and the premium for insuring the Corvette sent the prospect of owning one right back to what Walt Disney called Fantasyland.

Because of the accident from which I was still recovering, going without insurance was out of the question even though it was still legal in many places. I had always bought liability insurance because the Air Force required proof of insurance as a condition of driving on base, but my accident made me an insurance believer.

Whether driving on base would continue to be an issue was unclear. At the time I was shopping for a car in the manner of my dreams with all showrooms open for serious consideration, it was late 1967 and my hitch was coming to an end. I was still trying to sort out how I should respond to the news that the Air Force considered me eligible for "selective reenlistment."

It was ego gratifying to be "selected" and there was talk of a signing bonus, but what did I want to do with the remainder of my life? Beside that question, picking a new ride was almost trivial, but it was a useful diversion, a place for my mental energy to recharge from trying to sort the positives and the negatives of a career I thought I had picked four years earlier.

I was as certain that the conflict in Vietnam was wrong as I had been that it was right when I volunteered to fight.

Another datum that differed since my first enlistment was I understood I could be killed and/or I could experience physical pain on a level I had never imagined. I was fairly certain that I had reached some sort of limit to pain when it triggered the neural circuit breaker that renders humans unconscious.

The reenlistment decision continued to lurk while I continued to stalk new cars. It was late enough in 1967 that 1968 models were for sale, and the pony car phenomenon was still galloping. It was fun looking at Mustangs and Camaros knowing I could afford one.

When I made a deal, it was for a glittery metallic green 1968 Plymouth Barracuda convertible. I could afford the insurance and the price was just north of $3,000. I went from the insurance agent to my credit union and withdrew the purchase price in cash. At the drive-through. That was not a transaction they were used to, so it took some time. I pulled out of the line to let people pass with more normal business, and I realize now that my Suzuki might have weirded out the tellers as much as the transaction.

When I showed up back at the Plymouth dealer with the cash, I learned something about the customs of selling cars. The salesman who had spent over an hour helping me was gone for the day.

No problem, right? The green convertible was right there on the showroom floor and I had the cash to buy it in my pocket. Nobody would take my money. It would be a violation of car sales etiquette, which was a serious consideration where everybody was working on commission.

Could they not split the commission if one person made the deal and another shuffled the papers? If they made a deal in advance, they could, but "my" salesman had made no bargain with anyone to cover for him and nobody was willing to do the paperwork on speculation that they would get paid.

Having failed at a General Motors transaction and now a MoPar transaction, I did not give Ford a shot because the Ford dealer had pegged me for a young GI and so only a looker and, besides, they were still too proud of those Mustangs. I went back to the dealership where I had bought my first new car.

I found the man who had helped me two years earlier still selling Volkswagens. He chuckled at my experience trying to buy a Plymouth and said I would not have that problem at the VW dealer because the salespeople were on salary. There was a small commission on each sale but you had to string together so many sales for that to be significant, the salespeople just treated the commissions as free money, little bonuses.

My Bug had held together well in a high speed head-on. The full-size Ford that hit me did not absorb the impact as evenly. My front-mounted gas tank had been just filled at the time of the accident and gasoline spilled but did not ignite. The other driver did not survive, but most probably because he was sitting on his seat belt and I was wearing mine. This was speculation, but the bottom line for me was that I loved my Volkswagen and the accident had not changed my attitude. I had been shopping a bit more upscale because I could.

I bought a 1968 Bug with all the available options except whitewall tires for under $2,000. I paid in cash and put the rest back in the credit union.

At 500 miles, you bring your new VW back and they will fix anything that was not perfect and give it a first oil change. Something about the "running in period" was thought to dirty up the oil quickly.

When I brought in my dark brown Bug 500 miles later to tell them all I needed was the oil because it was delivered in perfect condition, I waited in a room with a long window overlooking the service bays. From up there, watching them change my oil, I saw the car meant for me coming out of make-ready. It was a bright red Karmann Ghia convertible with a black cloth top. I was in love.

I found the salesman and made a horrible deal when I absorbed the depreciation on the Bug. I gave them my new car and less than $1,000 and I had the ride that would take me though great adventures.

It turned out I had one task to complete before ending my Air Force adventure. I had just turned 21 and the magic age was 18 to register for the draft. When I had turned 18, I had been in military service for a year. Registering for the draft did not occur to me.

Hoping there would be no penalty for tardiness, I looked up the address of my draft board in San Antonio. I did not have to speak to anybody to procure the form I needed, so I picked it up and went on my way.

When I filled it out, I was pleased to see there was a section that allowed me to apply for conscientious objector status. I had considered myself in that status since I got out of the hospital, and it was only the benevolence of my supervisors that kept me from having my top secret clearance yanked.

I had been a good worker and I still was—in terms of getting my reports done—but I was no longer dedicated to the mission, no longer the guy who volunteered for service in a combat zone.

When my draft card arrived in the mail, I saw that I didn't get any of the three or four kinds of conscientious objector status. If memory serves, I was given a 4-A, which meant that I had done a hitch and would not be expected back in uniform unless there was some kind of flaming emergency.

I've never had a problem serving my country, but after the Vietnam craziness, I would want to know the nature of the emergency and I wanted to make a record that, while I was willing to die for my country, I was no longer willing to kill for it.

I sent the draft card back with a polite explanation that there was no room in my wallet for a draft card that did not state my conscientious objection.

I got the card back with a polite reply that the law required them to classify me in the group least likely to be called. The COs would have to go before 4-As.

I returned the card again stating my willingness to perform whatever service CO draftees had to perform but I would not be carrying around evidence of my willingness to kill because that willingness was long gone.

They sent the card back again with a less polite letter stating they had to follow the law and so did I. The law made me 4-A and the law required me to carry the card that said so.

I returned a less polite letter saying my conscience did not consult the law, but if theirs did, then they should do as it told them. My draft card was enclosed again.

The next and final letter from the draft board warned that if I sent the card back one more time, they would forward my file to the United States Attorney for prosecution. I didn't write another letter. I just sent their letter back. With the draft card.

I was never apprehended, but I didn't stay around San Antonio long enough to get picked up on a warrant describing a heavy set guy who was obviously having trouble growing a beard driving a red Karmann Ghia convertible. It seemed to take forever for the hair on my face to cover that scar, but it was not just the scar that made me feel as conspicuous as I have felt in my life.

~17~

VA ROULETTE

The first of many adventures in my little red convertible was striking out for a part of the country I had never visited: the Midwest. My girlfriend from Oregon, Tori Motte, had just gotten out of the Army and intended to use her GI Bill to train for radio broadcasting at a trade school in Milwaukee. My plan for my own GI Bill involved getting into a good university, major to be determined. Milwaukee was not my first choice.

Life decisions had been coming at me heavy and fast.

First, I declined "selective reenlistment." Having qualified for an Air Force career, I wanted loose from the promises I had made in light of what I had learned about the Vietnam War. My conclusion about the war also informed my second decision.

The most common job taken up by people with whom I worked was operating the nearest copy of the monster computer I had been operating for the Air Force. According to the UNIVAC customer engineer, there were only two not used by the military. One controlled all the reservations for Eastern Airlines and the other was controlling space flights at NASA Headquarters just outside of Houston. Working for NASA seemed to me unbearably cool. When I went to apply, I discovered that I would only be working on the space program as a contractor. My employer would be Lockheed, a corporation I perceived—rightly or wrongly—as dependent on the war, and that perception caused me to pass up a sure thing.

The stupidity of the Vietnam War made me feel stupid, like I should have known better. By that time, I knew the U.S. had backed out of free elections because the people would vote for Ho Chi Minh. From the Vietnamese point of view, we had stepped into the boots of their colonial masters, helping Francophile Catholics hold power over Vietnamese Buddhists.

Around this time—early 1968—I learned that Australia would pick up the costs of emigration for U.S. citizens with certain kinds of skills, and it appeared that my computer skills qualified. I sent for the paperwork to apply for a subsidized move only to find that the offer was for white people only. American Indians were too similar to Australian Aboriginals, so I could only apply for the money by abandoning my Cherokee identity. I was not yet tribally enrolled but I had always been Cherokee and did not wish to pretend otherwise.

I threw away the forms half-finished.

"College" was a fine abstraction to me, visualized in almost geographical terms, a place to go. It was time to figure out how to get there. The only people who had the treasure map in my childhood were school teachers, and they apparently saved copies of the map for kids who probably needed no map, since most of them appeared to have family guides.

The best advice I got from my friends was to try for admission to only the best schools because they were more likely to take a chance on me. One friend mentioned Harvard, which he claimed had no requirements at all for the rural poor who could demonstrate ability.

I did not have the nerve to strike out for Massachusetts, and, besides, I was in love with the University of Texas at Austin. Starting when I was stationed at Randolph AFB, located between San Antonio and Austin, I would visit the campus just to sit and watch the students go by.

Yes, Texas women are legendary, and they got my attention, but I would also notice male students striding purposefully across the campus with slide rules hanging from leather scabbards. I would make up elaborate stories about what they would accomplish. It seemed like everybody was carrying a book or a notebook. Pocket protectors, later to be stereotypical nerd gear, seemed cool to me—but so did nerds.

I drove to Austin and cruised Guadalupe Street—pronounced "Guadaloop" even by many Spanish speakers on campus—until I found a rare parking space. Guadalupe is known to students as "The Drag," and it borders one side of the original UT campus, known as the Forty Acres, surveyed for higher education at the same time the tract just south was surveyed for the Texas Capitol.

I made my way to the admissions office, then located in the building with the clock tower that had become infamous in 1966 when Charles Whitman used it as a sniper perch. I waited at the counter until one of the women behind it noticed me, and then told her I'd like to go to school on the Forty Acres.

She started collecting blank forms and telling me where to get my high school transcript sent. I interrupted her to say I had none.

She stopped gathering up papers and really looked at me for the first time. "How old are you?"

"Twenty-one."

"Do you have a GED?"

"No."

She didn't give me a chance to tell her that I took the test and passed but the Air Force would not give me a high school equivalency certificate because, they said, I enlisted in Oklahoma, which required that I be 21. I had been 17 when I passed the test.

"What have you been doing since high school?"

"I was in the service."

She loosened up a little. "You're an adult and a veteran. I think they'll take a look at your application. Just have the high school send what credits you have."

"I have no credits."

"None?"

"I dropped out of the ninth grade."

She put the papers back. "I don't think they will even look at your application."

I was crushed. I had no Plan B. Big mistake. Always have a Plan B, C, and D.

I learned in getting ready to write this story that I was probably mistaken when I said I had *no* credits. I had technically been in the 10th grade, although I would swear that I failed required courses, so it had to be a social promotion. I passed typing and I think I passed speech, so maybe I did have some well-hidden credits at either Permian or Bristow. I was at Beaverton High less than a semester.

Before I could come up with another idea to deal with UT's rejection, I decided to chase Tori Motte off to Milwaukee. I carried along another task on my post-USAF agenda. An old veteran from one of the veteran service organizations had badgered me about getting evaluated for a disability rating. "Do it," he growled, "soonest."

I thought it was absurd. I got out of the hospital in July of 1967 and from that time I went to work every day I didn't have a medical appointment and I pulled the same duty as everybody else. I did not feel disabled.

For reasons going back to my childhood in Bristow, I was put off by going to a Veterans Administration hospital. The veteran who talked me into getting evaluated got my agreement before he dropped it on me that the VA does the disability evaluation. My feelings about approaching a VA hospital were a long story.

My childhood collision with VA care was visiting my grandfather, a Spanish-American War veteran, in his final illness. In those pre-Medicare days, my grandmother was served by the University of Oklahoma charity/teaching hospital in Oklahoma City and my grandfather by the VA hospital in Muskogee.

The VA Hospital in Muskogee is today the Jack C. Montgomery VA Medical Center and it looks as new as the University of Oklahoma Health Sciences Center in Oklahoma City. As a child, I could have identified each hospital blindfolded. I had an early introduction to the "hospital smell," a combination of bodily fluids and chemical cleaners. In

Oklahoma City, the chemicals predominated. In Muskogee, it was the bodily fluids

Grampa was always sick, but he always said that if he got sick enough to check into the VA hospital, he would not be coming back. He had been there many times for outpatient services and I had been allowed to tag along.

Maybe the differing results I experienced shape my memory, but the University Hospital seemed to have bright lights everywhere and the VA Hospital I remember as dark, sometimes with outside light leaking in from window coverings.

My Aunt Eleanor, the registered nurse, had come to watch over Grampa in his final illness and it appeared to be a good thing, since the hospital staff paid little attention. I had learned what a catheter was and that the bag had to be emptied. What modesty Grampa might have had disappeared and his awareness of time and place and persons, perhaps mercifully, came and went.

His awareness was mostly gone when I caught a ride with my mother back to Bristow, where I was alone the night Aunt Eleanor called to tell me Grampa had been right, that he would not be returning from the hospital. I don't remember how the call ended, just how it started, and that I had never heard Aunt Eleanor cry before.

I would have thought it unlikely somebody as mean as she had always been could feel much sorrow. But there it was. Her father had died, as everyone said, "of old age," and she was hurting. Her pain attached a thread of kinship that had never felt real before.

It was probably good that I heard her pain when I was a teenager immersed in my own because it normalized feelings I did not recognize. I went in the kitchen and took out the biggest butcher knife in the drawer. I pointed the tip at my flabby middle and tried to gather the courage to plunge it in.

I'm not the first would-be suicide who failed to account for the possibility of failing a serious attempt, but I was saved from the consequences of my lack of foresight by a failure of courage. That failure opened some hidden floodgate of emotion and I threw the knife into the kitchen wall so hard I had trouble pulling it out the next day, a day that showed up too quickly after I cried myself to sleep while fully dressed and woke up with broken pieces of memory overlaid by a determination never to darken the door of a VA hospital.

Less than ten years later, in 1968, I was being released from active duty and had to get examined at a VA Hospital to determine my disability rating from the injuries that had kept me hospitalized for seven months. Because of the choice I had made to head for Milwaukee, the examination took place there.

It seems like most services offered by the VA involve groups of vets rather than individuals. The disability screening was no exception, and the group I was in had a wide range of ages, from one-hitch wonders like myself to "lifers" who had been in some branch of the military for at least twenty years.

If you make a disability claim, you get another going over like the physical you took at induction. The process differs in that the VA treats veterans more respectfully than the military services treat their recruits. Nobody yelled at us and we were not paraded around naked.

There were two results from a day of being poked and prodded and cross-examined. First, somebody decided I needed my "wisdom teeth" removed. They were buried under my gums behind what I had left of my unwise teeth.

Since I had never known they were there, I didn't expect to miss them, so I consented to some dental destruction that involved being reclined all the way back in a dental chair while two guys worked in my propped open mouth with tools that appeared to me the same size as the tire tools that came in the trunk of my Karmann Ghia.

I left with a mouthful of bloody gauze and a bottle of pain pills. Some weeks later, after my mouth had healed up, I got a notice of the second result from my day at the Milwaukee VA Hospital: I had been found to have a service-connected disability of 10%.

That finding seemed to me preposterous. After my seven months in the USAF hospital, I did the same work as the people around me—not 10% less.

Since my discharge, I had driven across the country to a big city I had never set foot in and got myself a job that paid more than any expectations I had. In my off hours, I was knocking on the doors of the local colleges and I was about to volunteer for Eugene McCarthy's antiwar presidential campaign.

I was engaged in politics, working full time, and trying to get into school. Therefore, it seemed to me at age 21, I could not possibly be "disabled." What the 10% disability meant in my life was that I had a higher priority than a non-disabled veteran when seeking care at a VA facility and I got a monthly cash payment of about $21. I was offended at being called "disabled," but not offended enough to send back the money.

STEVE RUSSELL

~17~

MOTHER, I TRIED

My grandparents always told me I was smart, that college was the promised land, and I needed to go there to make something of myself. They had worked all their lives and poverty was a bitter draught they tasted every day. They wanted better for me and they knew hard work alone would not be sufficient.

"College" was a fine abstraction of which they knew nothing. Neither did anyone else in my family.

I had just gotten out of the Air Force, having served four years where the college kids went to dodge the draft. From my college-educated colleagues, I had some clues my grandparents could not give me and my teachers did not give me. I had come to visualize the GI Bill as money and it was burning a hole in my pocket because the promised land was more real to me than it had ever been before.

To say that college was my *only* focus would be an exaggeration. There was the relationship with Tori Motte, the playwright at Beaverton High School whose address I was careful to acquire before I escaped, the only opposite sex relationship that survived my disfigurement.

Before moving to be near her, I had seen her only twice since my escape from Oregon, but we had been corresponding for the six years since I played the lead in one of her plays at Beaverton High School. The two of us had, independently and for different reasons, joined the military one year apart. My Air

Force hitch was four years and her Army hitch was three, which meant we got out at the same time. I had taken a short leave after I finished tech school at Sheppard AFB, borrowed my mother's car, and visited Tori at Ft. Rucker, Alabama.

I have two potent memories of my first trip to the Deep South in the summer of 1964. There was a bit of unpleasantness in rural Alabama when I interjected myself verbally into an argument by a black guy who was denied service in a little restaurant in the back of a service station. He looked to me like a GI, because of his shiny shoes and short hair...like me. I did not know that denying service because of race became illegal in July of 1964—the very month of this encounter—nor (I suspect) did the old boys who followed us into the gravel parking lot to school us on the southern way of life.

The young fellow was a GI and we were both on short leaves and had no time to fool with what we were fooling with. I had to pull out some gravel embedded in my cheek and we both bled enough on our shirts that they were goners, but we had no lasting physical injuries, so we shook hands and drove off to our respective military assignments.

The other memory is taking Tori to a drive-in movie in Dothan, Alabama, and engaging in such steamy necking that I don't remember much about the movie except a Pink Panther with a cool theme song. Those deep kisses led me to claim the term "girlfriend" for the first time in my life and following her off to Milwaukee would seem like a natural thing to do after we finished our hitches in 1968.

In early 1968, Tori visited me briefly in San Antonio and then started off toward her tech school in Milwaukee while I was still working up the nerve to make my futile effort to enter the University of Texas. We kept in touch by telephone, so when I was ready to head north, I knew she was visiting her mother in Dayton, Ohio. I had not met her mother, and if my feelings were strong enough to move me to a strange city, I thought getting to know her mother was a good idea. So my path to Milwaukee was less than direct.

We cruised around Dayton in my Karmann Ghia with the top down and the heater going full blast, as was the radio. It was early March and it was snowing—not enough to remain on the ground but enough to make cruising with the top down a memorable bit of fun at our age.

That night, her mother fixed dinner and all seemed to be going well. Tori had a contract to stay at a dormitory near her tech school for the duration of her classes. The classes would be about two months, as I recall. We were not intimate enough to share living space at the time even in the unlikely event her mother would approve, so I headed out for Milwaukee first.

In Milwaukee, I saw my first Great Lake. It reminded me of the gulf coast in Texas, but I knew the water was fresh. I was not tempted to verify that by tasting the water because it was still so cold. There were fishing piers with lockable barriers close to the shore and the ice on the Lake Michigan side of those gates was taller than I was—at three inches over six feet, I would still be looking up at the ice. I blew my first day in Milwaukee just driving around the Lake Michigan shoreline.

The next day, I quit playing tourist and found an apartment as close as I could get to the University of Wisconsin-Milwaukee. It turned out to be near Tori's school as well. After hanging around on the UWM campus for time enough to connect with the academic vibe, I went looking for the admissions office.

I could cut and paste the dialog from the University of Texas admissions office. Texas took a little longer to turn me away than Wisconsin, but the result was the same.

I made a quick run to nearby Marquette University. I got my hands on a catalog, took one look at the tuition, and decided that getting admitted would do me no good at all. I could not afford Marquette. At that time, the GI Bill paid $130 a month. Unlike the Gulf War GI Bill, there was no provision for covering actual expenses. That rendered private schools out of the question without additional financial aid. I drove to Madison with applying to that UW flagship campus in mind, but I chickened out.

That left M.I.T.

That would be the *Milwaukee* Institute of Technology, no relation to the school of a similar name in Massachusetts. The name has now changed to Milwaukee Area Technical College to avoid confusion with the other school. Since it was where rejects from UWM and Marquette often landed, it was also known locally as "Mother, I Tried." The tests for admission were whether you could cloud a mirror and whether your tuition check bounced, so I knew I could take some classes and hoped they would transfer to a real university because MIT was accredited.

The academic sticker shock at Marquette reminded me that I had only paid rent for a month and I needed to find a job. My time delivering Tulsa and Oklahoma City and Odessa newspapers informed my next move. I went to the public library and looked at *The Milwaukee Journal* from the previous Sunday. The employment ads, I knew, usually started running on Sunday.

Sure enough, there was lots of help wanted in Milwaukee, and I filled over two pages of a spiral notebook with hand-copied ads for "computer operator" or "data processing." I knew I would not find the UNIVAC behemoth I had been operating, but it had slave systems from both UNIVAC and IBM for input and output off the mainframe and I also had hands on experience with machines from RCA and Honeywell and Burroughs.

I started making phone calls, which quickly turned into interviews. Before I got to the bottom of my first page of help wanted notes, I was hired by a data processing service bureau attached to Midland National Bank, located smack dab in downtown Milwaukee on Wisconsin Avenue. I was not a city boy, and I felt like I had jumped right into the deep end.

Parking was scarce and expensive at both ends of my commute. On the plus side, there was no appreciable learning curve at my new job. The only machine I had to learn was the "micker," as we called the Magnetic Ink Character Reader (MICR). It was like the sorter we used for punched cards, something I had used in various forms ever since tech school, but instead of holes it read the numbers across the bottom of checks and deposit slips. The major difference was that punched cards are a uniform size and weight while checks and deposit slips make uneven stacks that are much harder to handle. I got accustomed to the micker quickly.

To get from my job to my apartment, I would drive down Wisconsin Avenue—the main drag—and turn left at Lake Michigan. I never got tired of seeing so much fresh water in one place. It lacked waves the size of the oceans, but there was enough wave action that it had real beaches.

By the time Tori showed up, I had a routine down and I had finessed the parking problem somewhat by purchasing another motorcycle. I had left a Suzuki at my mother's house in San Antonio, having traded my little one on an X-6 Scrambler.

When I got my money moved from the credit union in San Antonio to the bank account into which Midland put my paycheck, I bought a BSA Thunderbolt. It was a tamer version of the BSA Lightning, with one carburetor instead of two. The Thunderbolt was a brawny touring machine that would thump down the highway all day at 70 mph.

The longest ride I ever made on that beast was from Milwaukee to Elkhart Lake, Wisconsin, to attend the 1968 June Sprints at Road America. With Tori on the back, we twisted and turned through the Kettle Moraine with spring flowers and greenery on all sides. It was breathtaking natural beauty and, on the motorcycle, we were actually in it—not just seeing the flowers through a window, but smelling them.

The race itself was a bit less exciting. We sat on bales of hay at a curve tight enough that the racers had to slow a bit. On each lap, there was the racket made by the downshift into the turn and the higher pitch of the engines as they accelerated out of the turn. Unlike on television, knowing who was ahead and on what lap was not likely. As we sat there with tall plastic cups of beer and corn on the cob served on the end of a stick and dipped in butter, I quickly found I was more into Tori than I was into the race.

Later, we swam in a nearby lake with other young couples. Standing in cool water chest deep on me, Tori had her legs around my waist for support and we both could feel my erection pressing urgently on her inner thigh. The electricity in her deep kisses would keep my mind on her during the week when she had classes and I was still chasing college when not working.

I considered broadcasting to be a wise choice, an excellent pursuit because of what I knew about Tori's acting chops. We never spoke about what she was learning and I never had much to say about my data processing work. We would just meet every weekend and go out to hear some music. We heard Cream and Little Richard and I had tickets for The Doors, but Jim Morrison got himself arrested and The Doors cancelled.

I never learned to dance but what passed for dance in those days required nothing but a minimal sense of rhythm. On the few slow tunes, I would hold her close and kind of shuffle around the floor in the same general direction as other couples.

My attitude towards women had gone through the first of two major changes, the social one, after my seven months in the hospital. The handful of girlfriends I had in San Antonio came to visit me. They would take one look at my ruined face and there would not be another visit.

Tori was able to handle my disfigurement, and my gratitude for that knew no bounds. I was never handsome in the first place, but I could make my way in a world where men are not judged by their looks to the degree women are. Having my face destroyed cured me of ever treating women that way again. I had gotten a taste of being judged by my external appearance and the taste was bitter.

The second major change was political, and it came much later, when I finally made it to the promised land at a major university. I did visit a lesser promised land with Tori.

One August night at the end of Tori's studies, we finally consummated the relationship that taught me the meaning of "heavy petting." I had moved out of the apartment and into a fine old house across the street in which each room was rented to a student and we shared a bathroom down the hall. There was a garage where I rented a space that cost more than my room but was big enough for both the Karmann Ghia and the BSA.

We were returning from one of our nights on the town listening to local music. We had been drinking what made Milwaukee famous but neither of us was drunk. We got off the BSA and before we could get in the car in which I would take her home, she attacked me in the dark garage. I was nuzzling her neck, dropping a kiss here and there, when all of a sudden she grabbed my belt and started opening my pants.

I was amused at first and I reached inside her bra and started massaging her nipples. To my surprise, she didn't stop taking my pants off, and we were soon down on the cold concrete. When the location of her hand convinced me she was serious, I managed to talk her into retiring up to my room to do the deed.

Within the week, I understood why she was in such a hurry to lose her virginity. She was about to dump me after we had been whatever we were for about six years.

Where was it writ that Tori had any more social skills than I had? She had talent coming out of her ears, but I am sure that I was for her what she was for me—an opportunity to be paired up.

After she accepted me as a person appropriate to play the lead in one of her plays, after she became my first serious girlfriend and the only girlfriend who could still look me in the face after my face was destroyed, who am I to hold it against her that she knew no graceful way to break up with me upon deciding I was not her One True Love?

I was 21 years old when I first got my heart broken. While I regretted her decision, it never occurred to me that I had a right to stop her from moving on. I had picked her up at her dormitory so many times the management knew me, but they had to tell me she left no message. I wrote to her care of her mother in Dayton and got no reply.

I had followed her from San Antonio to Milwaukee but only because I was rejected in Austin. Now I had the best job I'd ever had and was enrolled in a community college, taking classes I hoped would transfer to a real university. If I gave up the job and the classes to chase Tori, I had nothing to say if I caught her beyond, "Are you sure?"

It's been fifty years now and what I feel is warmth and gratitude for her friendship. I looked for her periodically over the years, but I was looking for a disc jockey or a newsreader. When I got in touch with her ten years ago, I learned that she did not find a job in broadcasting and so, using her veteran preference, she tested into a position with the postal service. She was retired in a small Oregon town; I was attending an academic conference in Portland. I had a rent car, but I settled for a long phone call. We were both paired, and both of us were satisfied with our lives.

~19~

LIFE LESSONS

My affair with Tori Motte went on from 1962 to 1968 and left memory trails in Oregon, Alabama, Texas, Ohio, and Wisconsin. This was a big deal for a 21-year-old kid who never had a girlfriend in his hometown. As a life experience, it became a bigger deal because of the times in my first career as a judge—particularly the years as a police magistrate—I watched kids and even some adults destroy their lives over heartbreaks that were as real as mine but would have been temporary.

There was nothing temporary about my feelings for Tori, but the crushing weight of her rejection was as temporary as being chased away by a clerk in the admissions office at the University of Texas. It does not cheapen my love to understand it does not confer ownership of another human being and thinking it does is uncomfortably close to the lines I've read in too many homicide confessions or offense reports from standoffs with the police: "If I can't have her, then nobody will have her."

I don't claim precocious wisdom or moral superiority. Nor do I claim the strength of character to fight off those feelings. I never had those feelings. The best explanation I can offer is to remember all that heavy petting that never made it to the logical outcome. What was turning me on was not so much what I was doing as what she was doing. Her enthusiastic participation made me feel in those moments like the most important man in the world. The times I tested the edge of her comfort zone were buzzkills. There was no excitement in feeling like a rapist.

How that sense could come to a young man with so little experience with women is just another blessed mystery, but if a young man reads these words who is also mystified but is having more normal contact with women in his teenage years, it would be worthwhile to treat those normal contacts as the learning opportunities they are. At least, trust me on this: if you require words to communicate with a woman, you do not yet know her well enough to consider merging your fortunes with hers, and if she's not a potential partner you need to put the "s" in "safe sex."

When Tori disappeared, I was not seeing anyone else, but not because of any understanding with Tori. I was working to make money and working to end the Vietnam War (my view of why electing Eugene McCarthy was important). When my classes at M.I.T. cranked up, all of my time was taken. I did two semesters at the community college, trying to take classes that would transfer up the academic food chain while understanding the curriculum was weighted heavily in the direction of introductory material that might not transfer.

In the summer, I started with English Composition, Introduction to Mathematics, and Introduction to Computer Programming. That last one was my attempt to sneak a "gimme" into my schedule and it backfired when my sure thing A did not transfer.

The mathematics class did not transfer at first, but I got it reconsidered when the class I landed in at the university level used the same textbook. The English class was a required course everywhere, so I knew I had to take it in spite of never having passed an English course in high school. Those three classes were my part-time load in the summer and I was pleased to have As in all of them.

I had been in the military since I was 17, and that made me a bit of a hothouse plant. All my decisions had been made for me and now life lessons were coming heavy and fast.

When I moved out of my Milwaukee apartment on my way to the old house split up into rooms for students, the landlord told me without having looked at the place that I did not get my cleaning deposit back. He said the condition didn't matter, since he always kept the deposit and if I didn't like it, I could sue him. The last evening I spent in the perfectly clean apartment, I bought a big box of fried chicken with lots of side dishes. I knew it was more than I could eat.

When I had enough food, I emptied the balance of the fried chicken on the carpet, along with mashed potatoes, lots of gravy, and even some coleslaw. I stomped on the chicken so there were bone slivers in the carpet, and then I took the two-liter bottle of Coke I had not bothered to refrigerate, shook it well, and sprayed the all-American sugar water everywhere I could not reach. In the bathroom, I plugged the toilet and flushed until there was plenty of water on the floor but not enough to seep through to the lower floors. The water was clean, but the landlord would not know that.

I considered leaving a note to tell him that if he did not like the condition of the apartment, he could sue me. But in the end, as I tossed the contents of all the trash cans hither and yon, I decided to let the mess speak for itself. I understand now that if he had sued me, he would have gotten nothing, because he had already stolen enough to pay for the cleanup.

Another collision with the real world happened when the data processing service bureau where I worked tasked me to carry some of our work product to Bell & Howell in Chicago, a short drive in the company car. When I went to return the car keys, I also handed over a $10 bill I had found clipped to the visor on the driver's side.

The fellow in charge of the car rolled his eyes and then shook his head like I was such a damn fool he should make me ride a mule next time. He seemed to think about it for a couple of beats and then he asked if I had been stopped by a cop.

"No. Why should I get stopped by a cop?"

"Wisconsin plates. The sawbuck stays on the visor in case you get stopped by a cop who's on the take. He'll reach in and take it and let you go and you never had to run the risk of offering it."

"Oh."

Some twenty years later, I was in a class at the National Judicial College with some judges from Cook County, Illinois. I repeated this story.

"What year was this?" one of the Chicago judges wanted to know.

"1968."

"I call bullshit," he said. "Ten bucks wouldn't get it in 1968." He went on to tell a story of a courtroom where, if you had a case on the uncontested docket, you needed to clip a $20 bill to your file before handing it to the bailiff. Failure to do so would cause your file to stay on the bottom of the stack until the end, when the cheapskates would finally get their routine matters heard.

I was lucky to be working in Milwaukee rather than Chicago, but both cities were intimidating. I never lost the awareness of being from the boonies, but I needed a job processing data. Data had to get collected in the boonies but was processed in the cities. Some of our data traveled on phone lines. A machine would read paper tape or magnetic tape at one end and produce a copy anywhere there was a telephone.

Using this machine, I became acquainted with a woman a little over 100 miles away. Sort of acquainted. I did not know her last name, what she looked like, her family situation. She had a pleasant voice and a sense of humor.

One evening, as we were signing off, she said, "If you were to come up here, I'd treat you right." Could she possibly have meant what it sounded like she meant? I decided there was only one way to find out, and I was on the road as soon as the swing shift was over.

I had no trouble finding her house. As she let me in, she cautioned me to keep it quiet so as to "not wake the kids." Shortly afterwards, I saw my first naked woman with stretch marks. There was little foreplay, but she did orgasm, trembling all over...and then she was ready to go again.

158

Afterward, I learned that I had just had sex with a married woman. Her husband was working out of state.

"I'm on the pill," she assured me.

Oh. My. God.

Sex with Tori had been unprotected. STDs were not deadly then, but this was not about STDs. I had no STD and Tori could not have one. Pregnancy was the thought hammering in my stupid skull. Getting somebody pregnant would shake the trajectory of my life. There was no woman I would rather face an existential crisis with than Tori, but I hardly knew this woman who had topped off a couple of hours of wild sex with an offhand remark that proved she was smarter than me.

Seldom has a life lesson hammered me so instantaneously.

In my first semester at the Milwaukee Institute of Technology, I experienced love at first sight for the second time, if it's fair to count the nurse at Wilford Hall USAF Hospital whose face I never saw.

Kitty Lyons sat in the row to my left and a little bit behind me in the math class. The first time I turned and saw her I lost most of what happened in class that day. I had not yet heard the phrase that had to have been coined for her, "drop dead gorgeous." Her hair was long and shiny and (I learned later) natural blonde, and she wore a dress, a custom already dead among college women. When I was able to breathe again, my first rational thought was: *out of my league.*

I had to will myself back to planet Earth when I realized she was speaking to me. She had missed the last class. Would I mind sharing my notes? The class was about number theory rather than arithmetic and I was enjoying it more than I anticipated even before I noticed Kitty, so I was taking good notes.

I showed her my "notes"—three or four sentences—and I was quick enough to understand her look of dismay. I told her that I never write down everything the teacher says, but rather just what it would take to cue my memory. I assured her that I could reconstruct the lecture from those few sentences.

I normally hung out in the snack bar between classes and studied, since there was not enough time to go anywhere off

159

campus. I persuaded Kitty to come along, purchased my usual hot tea and one for her, and proceeded to unravel for her the story the teacher had offered in the previous class.

A college lecture is a story. I knew this long before I started constructing my own lectures. If I tried to write as quickly as the teacher spoke, there was no way I would be able to grasp the story. I was already a writer and I understood that a story hangs from a series of conceptual hooks and if I could jot down the hooks then reading them would enable me to reconstruct the narrative that came in between because I had listened to it carefully the first time I heard it.

Kitty was impressed and wanted to know where I learned that. I could not tell her beyond that it seemed to me common sense. Because I missed most of high school and nobody in my family had done college, nobody was going to advise me, so I had to put together my own repertoire of survival skills. How to take notes was an easy one, but it did make sharing my notes with others difficult.

The next semester—the fall session in 1968—I took four classes: Spanish, zoology, psychology, and Kitty Lyons. I followed her into the zoology class and contrived to become her lab partner. We began dating. I learned that she came from a rigid Irish Catholic family and she was at M.I.T. to keep her close to home and away from pernicious influences.

Most of the time we spent together was in the school snack bar. She spent some weeks of that time knitting me a bright blue sweater. I remembered how cold it had been when I first arrived in Milwaukee and I would have been grateful for the sweater even if it had not come from her hands.

The clubs I used to frequent with Tori Motte were off limits according to Kitty's mother, so our dates were normally movies. When I took Kitty to see *2001: A Space Odyssey*, her mother made some vague complaint about drugs, but she went ballistic over *The Graduate*. Her complaint was specific but misguided. She said it was about an older married woman who has an affair with a young guy, that it was unfit for her daughter, and we needed to stop seeing each other. That is not what it is *about*, I told Kitty. That's just something that happens in the movie.

But I quickly gave up arguing about *The Graduate* and resigned myself to being *persona non grata*. I could not interfere in Kitty's relationship with her mother and if this movie were not the breaking point there certainly would be another one coming. Still, Kitty expressed intent to ignore her mother's hostility to me and it did not take long for me to become a willing accomplice, picking her up and dropping her off at places other than her home.

As I spent more time with Kitty, I had become less gaga, more rational, no less attracted. It was my rational side that told me I was no less interested in live music venues than I was when I was dating Tori and somebody was going to come to town I didn't want to miss but didn't want to see by myself. A concert may sound trivial, but my choice of lifestyle was not.

I had not been drunk since my getting out of the USAF party, but I still drank. Usually tequila, which was not at that time a respectable beverage that far north. Dope smoking, sure, but I had never smoked enough to "go psychedelic." I did not know what that meant. I expect I would have been keen to learn with or without Kitty.

Given my political commitments, I knew that I would likely spend time in jail, and I needed a significant other who would back me up.

The major research paper Kitty wrote while we were together was an examination of the graduation rate of scholarship basketball players. She concluded long before it became common knowledge that universities were exploiting the NBA dreams of kids often picked out of dire circumstances and given an opportunity to go to college.

The kids got enough help to maintain their eligibility. When they could no longer play either because no longer eligible or because of injuries, the universities would cut bait and troll for another tall kid with good hands and starry eyes.

We talked about racism and about the war in Vietnam and I did not expect to have any deep political disagreements with

Kitty. Still, I was sure I would get locked up at some point, and that when I did, her mother would have kittens. I had no doubt that the two of us would have a good life and do good left to our own devices, but I could not act on my feelings without being the cause of a war within her family. I could see little good for Kitty in that scenario.

All of this came to a head at the end of the fall semester in 1968 when my exile from Kitty's home had left me able to see her only at school. I had quit my job at Midland National Bank for a better one at the *Milwaukee Journal*—not as a writer, but in their computer room.

I told Kitty I would start trouble in her family if we proceeded toward marriage and I just could not balance a certain harm against a speculative benefit. I had nothing to offer her, it seemed to me, that was as certain as the damage to her life.

I hoped I was wrong. I hoped she would show me I was wrong. She did not.

After that contretemps, my heart had been broken twice and there was another Wisconsin winter on the way. When I quit crying, I called the personnel office at the *Journal* and told them something had come up and I could not accept their kind offer. If my relationship with Kitty would not be on a marriage track, I had no reason to stay on the Midwest side of a vast cultural distance from the Southwest.

I collected some official transcripts—my grade point average had come down to 3.7 when I got a B in the five-semester hour zoology class because of my inability to draw what I was seeing in the microscope. Then I bought a trailer to carry the BSA back to where it was warm. I wasn't sure if I was headed for Austin or for Norman, Oklahoma.

I went to Bristow and had a visit with Frank Sanders, the principal of Bristow High School. He helped me decide, although not exactly in the manner he intended. I told him I had a GI Bill entitlement and I looked at it as if it were money to spend. I was in a position to claim resident tuition in either

Oklahoma or Texas. Which is the better school, I asked, the University of Oklahoma or the University of Texas?

I did not tell him about my two semesters at M.I.T., figuring I could bring it up if the conversation turned to scheming about how I would get admitted.

He laughed loud and long. My cheeks were burning when he was done laughing and he informed me that it was not a close question. Texas was the better school, but OU was the best Oklahoma had to offer and he knew of no reason to think I could handle the work at either school. He told me I needed to get my high school diploma, take the SAT or the ACT, and then ponder the options dictated by my grades and test scores.

I don't remember what I said but I hope it was insulting.

I was halfway to the Red River before I cooled off enough to think about what I would do when I got to Austin. I never understood what "Boomer Sooner" was supposed to mean, anyway.

As I drove south, my mind wandered back and forth between education and the other problem that I remained in love with Kitty Lyons. Either she was going to have to cut the apron strings without my fingerprints on the scissors or I was going to have to accomplish something that would render me an appropriate match in her mother's eyes.

I resolved to keep in touch with Kitty and try to conquer the University of Texas. I was doing my best to resist another possible outcome. My resolve not to make trouble between Kitty and her family might evaporate in a blast furnace of lust.

As it turned out, my sexual fantasies of Kitty did not ripen into obsession. I had already been the first sex partner for one lady and I was not keen to repeat the experience. It's a hard job (no pun intended), but somebody has to do it—just not me.

I found I could drive with a twice-broken heart and think at the same time. It was a bit harder than walking and chewing gum, but it was necessary because at my destination in Austin, there was a door I would have to kick down.

STEVE RUSSELL

~20~

KICKING DOWN THE DOOR

In Milwaukee, I had hugged the fringes of the counterculture, but there were limits. How countercultural can you be when you work in a computer room in a downtown bank tower while collecting college credits at a community college? I wore a clip-on necktie at work, a bit of fakery that has been necessary all my life because I was never motivated to learn how to tie a real one. I had to have the first bank account of my life because my paycheck was deposited into the bank where I worked.

Between the insurance settlement from my accident in 1966 and having a good job, I had joined the middle class. That meant, by the standards of my childhood, I was rich. I accumulated stuff—at one time, I almost bought a sitar. Because there was a tiny crack in the *kadu ka tumba*, the lower of the gourds, it was dirt cheap and I would say it sounded just fine if I knew how it was supposed to sound.

I looked in every men's clothing shop I could find for a Nehru shirt or jacket. They were stylish at the time and could never be sullied with a necktie, but I could never find one big enough. It was not these matters of fashion that would make me an Indophile, but I had yet to discover Gandhi's writings.

When I returned to Austin, discovery was on my mind, although I could not say exactly what I hoped to discover. The counterculture was attractive background noise. The conversation with Frank Sanders focused me on the University of Texas at Austin—my preference in the first place. My application had not been denied because I had not been allowed to submit it. Little had changed. I was a year older and I had a transcript showing two semesters at a community college.

I went all the way to San Antonio to add my Suzuki to the trailer moving my BSA. Coming back up the highway to Austin, I had the top down and my data processing credentials— certificates from three years of varied courses—in a file on the back seat. Just south of Austin, I heard a ruffle of paper and looked in the rearview mirror. My credentials, as well as some resumes I had printed, were sailing in a cloud behind my Karmann Ghia.

I stabbed the brakes once and then quickly decided to hell with it. I'm not going to be a computer nerd. I'm going to be a student at the University of Texas and this time I will not take no for an answer.

Finding a place to live in Austin topped my agenda. There was no way I would be able to park my car with the trailer behind it anywhere near the campus. I was looking after the spring, 1969 semester had started, so I expected finding a place to live—let alone park—would not be easy. I was wrong. Just north of UT, I noticed a "room for rent" sign on the front of a big old white bungalow. Against an additional set of odds, there was an empty lot next to the house that was being used for parking.

I pulled into the vacant lot, set the brake, and walked up to knock on the front door, where I met an elderly gentleman who seemed skeptical of would-be renters. He cross-examined me for most of an hour, and I had to wing it a bit when he wanted to know my immediate plans. It did not seem politic to say I intended to kick the door down at UT.

He liked that I was older than most people wanting to rent that close to campus and it sealed the deal when I agreed to stay the semester and paid him four months of rent up front. He was dividing up the house to rent and I got an enclosed back porch on the second floor with a new bathroom. It was vacant because he had not gotten it ready in time for the beginning of the semester.

I spent the rest of the day hauling my stuff up to the second floor. It took a while because between the Karmann Ghia and the trailer, I was carrying all my worldly possessions. The trunk, the jump seat, the passenger side, and my Air Force duffel locked between the two motorcycles were all full.

I found a hardware store nearby and bought a heavy chain and a lock, with which I attached my trailer to a telephone pole in the lot next door, leaving both motorcycles locked to the trailer. Late the next morning, I circled the Drag until a parking place opened up. As I walked up the West Mall to the UT tower, it seemed like my previous attempt was days ago rather than months.

I am not sure if the woman behind the counter in the admissions office was the same one who sent me away the previous year. If so, she did not remember me, because we had the same conversation. In light of my veteran status, she was willing to take my application if I would send for whatever high school credits I had, a willingness that evaporated when I told her I had none. A year later, I had convinced myself that I had passed typing and probably speech, but I was not sure where the evidence was, and it was just too much trouble to chase down less than a year of credits.

This time, when she tried to shoo me away, I didn't leave. I asked to speak with her supervisor.

"She's gone to lunch."

"I'll wait."

When the supervisor came back, she was friendlier and more sympathetic. Unlike the person at the front desk, she was willing to put in my application, but her opinion was that it would be futile, and she did not want to blow smoke.

I believed her, so I asked to see *her* supervisor.

The wait was not as long, but the guy seemed to be busy. He had stacks of paper on his desk. Still, he gave me the first chance to tell the whole story about passing the GED but being deemed too young to get a high school equivalency certificate. He was not impressed by two part-time semesters at Milwaukee Institute of Technology. Cutting to the chase, he asked me why I thought I could do the work at UT.

"Why do you think I can't? Look, I'm just asking for a chance. If I can't do the work, I'll go away and never bother you again."

"Bother me again?"

"You don't think I'm going to give up if you turn me down, do you? You can have the police remove me and when I get out, I'll be back here asking again."

That appeared to amuse him. He spelled out an offer slowly.

He would order me admitted to the summer sessions. There were two of them, and I had to take a full load the whole summer—twelve semester hours. I would be admitted on academic probation.

I had to ask what that meant.

In the summer of 1969, I needed to take twelve hours, fail nothing, and finish with at least a C average, meaning that a D would have to be offset with a B. This did not sound like a big deal, since the GI Bill demanded that I be a full-time student. I thanked him profusely and left the Main Building and the next thing I knew I was at the Drag, having walked on air down the West Mall. I had four months before classes would start, but I felt like I became a University of Texas student right then.

On my transcript, it would say:

"Admission Record: Individual Approval.

"Deficiencies: All."

Even a completely deficient UT student was still a UT student. I read over the catalog again and again, drooling over the choices I had to make. In addition to making choices, I had to get ready to be a full-time student for the first time.

Within the first week in Austin, I got myself a data processing job in the evenings, but this "scholastic probation" stuff made me wonder if working full time was feasible. On one hand, I considered the university my one shot at the promised land and therefore my top priority; on the other hand, I had gotten accustomed to the middle-class life. That dilemma resolved itself when the supervisor of data processing where my boss rented computer time made some obnoxious comment about dope smokers. I took up for the dope smokers and won the argument on points, but, for the only time in my life, before or since, I got fired.

I cannot recommend getting fired even when it's a firing like mine—for a silly reason and not at a time when I was desperate for income. I don't hold with the notion that adversity builds character. Adversity is just adversity, and that's how it felt in spite of the objective facts.

As much as I sustained a real ego blow getting fired, the idea of keeping my mouth shut the next time somebody said something asinine never penetrated the fog of depression. I lack the STFU gene that makes things easier for those who have one. My inability to STFU would cause trouble for me that first summer at UT, but the unpleasant firing sprung me loose from a full-time job and forced me to think hard about looking for a less expensive place to stay and a job I could handle with my serious academic load.

My plan had been to take required courses to get them out of the way. That plan got sidetracked when I became entranced by a woman who took me seriously as UT student material but not as boyfriend material because she was paired up with a Chicano from South Texas named Candelario Saenz. Both were studying anthropology. I met Candy first and he introduced me to his girlfriend, Barbara Worley. They were as old as me but with much more academic credit, and the fact that the two of them both took me seriously was a delight beyond anything I expected.

I met them when my job search was dry and I got the idea of giving up possessions to fund my schooling. I knew the GI Bill only paid $130 a month and that would be insufficient. What I did not find out until I was attending classes was that the piddly payment never showed up in time to help me buy books. I paid for the summer sessions on my own, but I was counting on the GI Bill in the fall. I had never used it in Milwaukee because I was only a part-time student and I was making plenty of money. The fall semester would start in late August and I would not see a dime from the GI Bill until late October. It turned out my situation was so common that the University of Texas had an established protocol for veterans. Every semester, I got a short-term loan at close to zero interest, and when I got that first big GI Bill check (containing two or three months of payments), I would pay back the short-term loan.

Before my savings were entirely depleted, I put index cards describing both motorcycles on a bulletin board at a hippie dive called Alice's Restaurant run by a fellow I came to know as Silent Jack, who ran a karate dojo in the back of the eatery.

Candy, the male half of the anthropology couple, bought the Suzuki, and the more I came to know him the more impressed I was with how intelligence met inquisitiveness in this small-town boy from South Texas. He and Barbara personified the virtues I expected to find at a university. We did a lot of student-type stuff that was normal to them and thrilling to me.

One day after the fall session started, we were in my Karmann Ghia with the top down, Candy riding shotgun and Barbara in the jump seat. We rolled up on the guard post in front of the UT campus, known to students as "St. Peter's Gate" because it was so hard to pass. I started to turn away to hunt for a parking space, but Candy told me to head into the campus "and watch her work."

The guard signaled me to stop. I stopped, but before I could say a word Barbara stole away his eye contact and spun a tale as complicated as it was nonsensical. We had forgotten something in a particular building and needed it right then and couldn't we just dash in and get it and we would be right back? It was my first observation of a Jedi mind trick practiced by an attractive young woman. The guard had no chance and this brand-new student got the rare privilege of cruising the inner campus drive during school hours.

Back before I ever attended a class, Candy and Barbara had allowed me to tag along to a professor's house. The professor had a large collection of student guests and he folded me right

170

in. He grilled steaks while the students—me included—smoked dope from the professor's stash to tune up our appetites. I would think of that evening years later, when I watched an Austin police officer explain to high school students why marijuana needed to be illegal. It would destroy their motivation, he warned, and they would be unable to handle serious academic work or decent jobs. Most of the conversations I heard that night at the professor's house were about academic subjects, and everybody seemed as fired up as their blunts. I was no exception. The professor was serving some very good weed, but my high from his party favors was nothing compared to my high from being accepted in that company as just another UT student and also from being able to follow most of the conversations.

I was not shocked about the marijuana. In those days, you could practically get a contact high walking up the West Mall. Among serious students, there was more dope smoking than drinking. I had seen more hard drinking in the Air Force than I would see at UT.

Being thrown into a backyard full of stoned anthropology students was so pleasant and I was so excited that I altered my summer plans slightly even though I did not know exactly what anthropology was. I remember a conversation with Barbara that veered off into primatology, but she reeled herself back in and explained that the major division in freshman course offerings was between cultural and physical anthropology. It was much later when I heard the wisecrack that physical anthropology is the study of human beings for people who cannot stand live human beings.

Becoming friends with Saenz and Worley was a random event that resulted in my first two classes at the University of Texas being introductions to anthropology, cultural and physical. Those two courses had profound influences on my conduct when I became a university professor.

The freshman required courses at a research university are normally taught by graduate students, and I was better off getting my introduction to university education from professors so I could see the clear distinctions from both high school and the community college.

Professors at a research university profess, and what they profess is tilted toward their research agenda. Since I was under the gun to pass my first twelve hours, I was motivated to search for what my professors had published. I expected to need every advantage I could get.

The cultural anthropology course was a lot of fun until we started talking about Indians. I was under the impression that I knew something about Indians because I am one, but I would not mention that because I was there to watch rather than to be watched.

The professor was an active volcano of what are called in these times microaggressions against Indians. Combining that with my lack of the STFU gene was a recipe for disaster. The friction between my secret identity and the professor's view of his own cultural competence was played out in his grading, and he gave me the only C I would ever get as an undergraduate.

The physical anthropology course contained some material about racial differences I found hard to stomach but lacked the knowledge base to challenge. Like the cultural course, the format was readings followed by lectures that went far beyond anything in the readings and essay examinations written in "blue books," sold for the purpose at the University Co-Op. I experienced the physical course as a harder slog than the cultural course, but quitting was not an option. Going into the final exam, I was on track to earn a B.

My research on the professor pointed me to an article he had recently published in a professional journal that dealt with something he mentioned in his lectures but which was touched only lightly in the textbook. I became convinced that a question based on his article was highly likely. Based on other material I had absorbed in and out of the course, I became persuaded that the central point of his article was incorrect. At this time, I had not yet been hammered by the cultural anthropology professor.

I had never taken a blue book examination before that summer and I quickly decided that the challenge was not so much answering the question as composing a clear and concise essay with a topic sentence, discussion, and sum up at the end. Even for a born writer, that's hard to accomplish on the fly.

So, I wrote out a succinct critique of the professor's last article. I rewrote it a couple of times until it had polish beyond anything I had written in a blue book, which at that point was not saying much. The essay was short, and I committed it to memory.

I went into the final exam loaded for bear...and the bear did not appear. The professor did not ask the question I had anticipated and for which I had prepared. After calming down as much as I could, I did quick answers to the questions he did ask. At the end of the last answer, I printed in big letters: OVER. Then I turned the blue book around and wrote the essay I had prepared about the professor's errors on the back of what I had written to his questions.

Since I had a B going into the final, I must have gotten an A on that exam, because I got an A for the course. I had been argumentative with both professors. One punished me, and one rewarded me.

In my own teaching, I have always been partial to students who care enough about the material to have original thoughts even if those thoughts run contrary to my own. I learned how I wanted to teach in my first semester at the University of Texas, a semester guided by two unlikely friends, both of whom went on to do dissertation research for their Columbia University PhDs in Africa and to become professors of anthropology.

For the remainder of the summer of 1969, I reverted to my original plan and took a required English course and the first half of the required government course. Both of those classes were taught by graduate students and I got two more A grades, making my scorecard for the summer three As and a C. I had taken a full load, failed nothing, and had no grade below a C. I thought I was done with scholastic probation, a mistake that would give me a fright when it came time to graduate.

STEVE RUSSELL

ALONE IN THE PROMISED LAND

I was born and raised in a town of about 5,000 souls and found myself on a university campus of some 50,000, not counting the city of Austin or the growth in population every two years when the Texas Legislature came to town and ran up the price of cocaine.

Austin, the birthplace of outlaw country music, and Austin, the Silicon Valley of the Southwest, were far in the future when I arrived, and the University of Texas was the center of everything.

I had paid rent to the end of the spring 1969 semester. I was to start classes full time in the summer and I was unemployed. Just before I panicked, another piece of insane luck came my way. I had taken to hanging around the University Y, because at that time the office of Austin's underground paper, *The Rag*, was in the basement and the fine old building across the Drag from UT was a center of left politics and hippie culture.

There was no air conditioning—always a major drawback in Texas—but there was a public area with a radio the size of a steamer trunk that must have been as old as the building. The antique had great sound quality and it was usually tuned to KUT-FM, public broadcasting from the University of Texas. I had no radio except the one in my car, and the car was doomed to be sold after the funds were spent I acquired from selling my Suzuki scrambler, my BSA road bike, and my motorcycle trailer.

I was shedding possessions more quickly than I had acquired them but still clinging to the Karmann Ghia. I knew I would have to find part-time work, but I was determined to be a full-time student for that first summer when my chance to continue at UT was on the line.

In the interest of finding employment by the fall semester of 1969, I made sure every friendly acquaintance knew about my situation. That bit of self-promotion combined with my age and veteran status brought me an offer to manage the dorm in the top floor of the Y when the previous manager graduated.

My problems were solved. I got a free room right across from the campus with a parking space in back, and the Y even paid me a token sum, less than $100 a month. Small sums of money got to be important when I learned I had to wait for the GI Bill.

The "job" at the Y amounted to just being the person who knew where to call for help. Keeping order was part of the job description, but the residents were serious students and therefore were not rowdy.

There was an Egyptian student who was studying engineering on a scholarship from his government. Because his scholarship did not include living expenses and his visa did not allow him to work, he had to be creative.

When his family sent him a little money, he would buy a big sack of turkey necks and tails. I opened the kitchen on the first floor and he boiled the meat off the bones over several hours. By stretching it out with some rice, he made that broth last for a couple of weeks.

I am sure he got as tired of tasting turkey broth as I was tired of smelling turkey broth, and some of the other residents got enough olfactory overload to complain to the management (me). I responded to the complaints with enough doubletalk to qualify myself for White House Press Secretary.

The University of Texas was the same promised land to him that it was to me, and I learned a little about his life because we often hit the books together. I would share the tea that I made by boiling Lipton teabags in a saucepan. His creativity with the turkey parts made me wish he was a U.S. citizen so he could qualify for the commodities that provided much of my calorie intake when I was a child.

Across the cultural divide, my good intentions were broader than my knowledge base. I was not completely innocent of the facts, but I lacked the insight to put together that an Egyptian was probably a Muslim and Muslims do not eat pork. The meats we most commonly acquired from the commodities program were bacon and Spam, the latter in cans that opened with an attached key and were adorned with a white label that claimed in black type that they contained "pork shoulder"—generic parlance for Spam.

There was a Native Hawaiian guy living on top of the Y as well, and he would have been a problem if the Y had any interest in the sexual activities of the residents, but it did not, and, if it had, I would probably have turned down an otherwise perfect gig. I did wonder if things would get loud should two of his lady friends show up at the same time, but it never happened.

In addition to the perpetual turkey broth, I began to unlock the kitchen downstairs in the mornings to feed breakfast to as many kids as we could ferry over from East Austin, the African-American side of town. Housing segregation had been enforced for generations by bank redlining. At this time, the lawsuit to desegregate Austin schools was still pending in federal court.

An organization called the Community United Front had sprung up in East Austin in imitation of the Black Panther Party, and feeding breakfast to schoolchildren who would not otherwise get it was equal parts good deed and shaming the school district for expecting hungry kids to compete with kids who didn't have to worry about food.

The kids probably preferred to ride with me even though I would stack them in my Karmann Ghia in a grossly unsafe manner, because they liked rolling with the top down and the radio blasting. We stretched the money contributed by UT students in lots of ways. I acquainted them with SOS ("shit on a shingle," GI-speak for creamed beef on toast) and I would fill a huge coffee percolator that the Y kept for public meetings with powdered milk and add chocolate syrup.

Author transporting kids for a free breakfast in the famous Karmann Ghia convertible. Photo © Alan Pogue. Used by permission.

The kids were a lot of fun and those daily duties were over when we got them delivered back to their segregated school and we got the kitchen cleaned up. Having to get up early probably got us to bed early in the evenings and kept us more awake for studying than if we had the money and the time to go honky-tonking.

I was there to study and so was everyone else lucky enough to live on the top floor of the University Y for next to nothing right across the street from the campus. The only downside was the lack of air conditioning, but it would have cost a fortune to cool a building that old.

In daytime, we would hang out in the air-conditioned comfort of the Texas Union across the street. During exam weeks, every room on top of the Y would have a light showing, every window was open, and everybody had at least one fan moving so much hot air you would think the Texas Legislature was in session.

Before the summer of 1969 was over, it was clear to me that I would meet the conditions to seek a degree from the University of Texas. I designated the College of Education as my academic home and began preparing myself to be the high school teacher who had never appeared in my life to tell me I was college material.

It was during this time I met a UT student who was studying Portuguese. I had managed to reach nominal adulthood with little exposure to European languages. The indigenous languages spoken in Oklahoma were not "foreign," and the Oklahoma attitude toward language study was summed up in the observation that English had been good enough for Jesus.

The Spanish I studied at MIT had proved a useful supplement to the Tex Mex I had picked up when I had delivered the *Odessa American* in a Spanish-speaking neighborhood. When I overheard Heather Harris reading her Portuguese textbook out loud, I thought I was hearing Spanish with a funny accent.

When she only laughed a little at my goofy questions about Portuguese, I had plenty more questions. The answer to the last one was "Yes!" and I awoke the next morning naked, in Heather's bed, and noticed for the first time that she had a roommate. I was not exactly embarrassed as much as I was unsure of the etiquette that would be expected of me. It was a one-bedroom apartment and Heather's turf was the living room, where the sofa became the double bed Heather and I were occupying.

A little bit of recon quickly established that my clothes were beyond my immediate reach and the women were conversing as if I were not present. All of my modesty had been left in Wilford Hall USAF Hospital back in 1967, so my comfort was not the issue—theirs was. Or so I thought until Heather decided to come back for seconds while her roommate was present.

This began a relationship of which I am not proud. She gave and I took and I fooled myself by hiding behind a literal idea of "honesty." I never hid my attempt to marry Kitty Lyons or my continuing interest in Kitty. I never told Heather I loved her.

The foolery was convincing myself that I would not feel the way I feel right now as I write about it—like a selfish bum. Heather and I had great fun in and out of bed, but she was looking straight past my protestations that this was not serious in the way we understood serious: forever or until further notice.

The definition of "further notice" is idiosyncratic but enough of my generation are divorce survivors that we consider a split at some point to be normal. The fact of splitting is predictable, but the reasons and the results remain mysterious. And romance remains what it is, so we proceed with our eyes wide shut.

There were several points in my relationship with Heather when I should have known that remaining in it was dishonorable. The only defense I can offer is that I had never ended a relationship. I had been dumped, but never in a straightforward manner from which I could learn anything beyond my own inadequacy.

The only other woman I treated as badly as I treated Heather has accepted my apology. I've been unable to offer an apology to Heather because I don't know where she is. She dropped out of UT and was in and out of Austin even before she decided that I represented over a year of her life she would never get back.

While I did not lack sexual companionship in my first year at UT, I still had unfinished business in Wisconsin. I had no understanding with Kitty Lyons that I would wait for her and I don't think I would have agreed to be celibate on speculation.

Before the year passed, one of my phone calls at the pay phone in the hall of the Y convinced me that Kitty had, on her own, grown up. If there was trouble within her family, I would not be the villain. She had left Milwaukee and begun to study at a four-year university in Oshkosh.

There was still much to work out. She was still Catholic, sort of, and wanted to continue a cultural Catholicism. I knew lots of Jack Catholics and I got along with them, so I could see no problem being married to one.

How did I feel about raising my children Catholic?

"That's not going to happen," I said, because faith comes from within—or not—and can't be passed down like the old family Bible. Even if it were possible, it would be immoral by my lights.

After a long silence, she asked if I would have any objection to my children learning the catechism and attending a Catholic school.

Of course not. Anybody who has had an argument with a Jesuit knows that Catholic education is not inferior, and Christianity is part of the cultural landscape. Lots of literary devices turn on Christian imagery and some modern plots are lifted right out of the Bible. An educated person needs to know that stuff and I want my children educated.

She decided that was good enough. As soon as finals were over in spring of 1970, I headed my Karmann Ghia once more to Wisconsin, this time Oshkosh rather than Milwaukee. I rented a hotel room downtown, where Kitty joined me and I tasted a little marital bliss in advance of the ceremony.

I learned there was a series of "counseling sessions" I was supposed to attend with a priest. I was unhappy at that news until she informed me that she had arranged mine to be done with Fr. James Groppi, the radical priest in Milwaukee who had started the tactic of closing the main arterial roads of the city with sit-ins. I had always admired his civil rights work and studying anything with him sounded worthwhile.

Kitty broke the bad news (counseling) followed by the good news (Fr. Groppi) and I could see that she knew me well at the time she made the arrangements even if she had not known me in the Biblical sense until the Oshkosh hotel.

With these agreements made, the ceremony was a detail, so we headed to Milwaukee to break the news. She arranged for me to spend the night at a relative's house so she could try to soften up her mother, who we would go to see together the next day.

The plan seemed foolproof until the next day, when I drove for the first time in a year to Kitty's home in a middle-class neighborhood of Milwaukee with lawns and flower beds neatly trimmed as if by a cosmic barber. Upon hearing our news,

Kitty's mother looked me in the eye briefly before responding, "I think I'm going to be sick."

I bit my tongue hard enough that I remember the salty taste of blood and I became a silent witness to the screaming and the tears, my worst nightmare acted out in front of me.

If I said anything at all, I don't recall it. I had thought my admission to the University of Texas made me somebody equal to other young men of my age, almost white.

Whatever the reasons, it was plain that Kitty's mother still did not consider me an appropriate match and that Kitty was not prepared to withstand the emotional tsunami. I was shocked at my own inability to take up for myself...the scene just made me feel empty inside. My heart did not hurt so much as it shrank to nothing.

The hurt came later, on the drive back to Texas, but right then my six-foot three-inch body would have fit in a shot glass and left room for tequila. When I was sure she would not be coming with me, I left Kitty with a gold ring I was still paying off and I took with me an emptiness that became a sharp pain and then receded to numbness as I drove straight through from Milwaukee to Austin.

Lying on my bed, exhausted from the driving marathon, I was still unable to sleep, or so I thought. I kept hearing a conversation between the woman I had wanted to be my mother in law and the man I had wanted to be my father:

"I think I'm going to be sick."

"Useless as the teats on a boar hog."

Over and over, they repeated. Real words from real people. Was I awake or asleep?

Then I could not decide. They sounded so real.

Now I think I was teetering on the brink of a fugue state. I was tripping someplace acid had never taken me and I didn't want to go.

It was daylight when I awoke for sure but I was uncertain which day. I cursed myself for going off half-cocked in a fog of love and lust, exaggerating my own worth based on a few A grades from the University of Texas.

I briefly tried to convince myself Milwaukee was a nightmare, but that void in my chest returned and I knew I was going to be alone. I had nothing to offer.

STEVE RUSSELL

~22~

DAIRYLAND WISDOM

My disastrous courtship of Kitty Lyons was not everything from Wisconsin that shaped the rest of my life. I had followed politics from an age when most kids would be in kindergarten, as I learned to read from front-page news in the *Tulsa World*. While I had a lively interest in foreign affairs, I could not do much about Korea. If I could get involved, it would have to be in domestic affairs.

Racial segregation was an offense to common decency, but I was a witness rather than a victim. Still, it seemed to me to be the most pressing domestic political issue, and it's the only domestic political issue I can remember from my childhood, other than the controversy over where exits would be located on the Turner Turnpike, which was actually a bigger deal in Bristow than the segregation issue that dominated national news. Bristow got an exit but the Main Street businesses quickly learned that having an exit does not mean people paying for a 70-mph speed limit in a world of 55-mph limits will tarry in small town Oklahoma.

The segregation issue was slower to surface on the local level and it was resolved without the nastiness and violence that was all over national news. It was just a fact of life that made no sense to me.

My home was on the dividing line where the pavement ended and the street turned to sticky red mud when it rained.

After a serious gully washer, the city would send a road grader and a gravel truck to make 12th Street look like a street again.

I understood the dividing line but I thought it was between people who had money and people who didn't. It was perhaps that misunderstanding when I was of preschool age that caused me to look for playmates on either side of the street. My grandparents didn't police the color of my playmates, so I only found the practicalities of segregation after I was predisposed to find it absurd.

There were not a lot of signs explaining the customs—everybody just knew their place. There were no black people in the downtown barbershops or restaurants, except to shine shoes in the former and wash dishes in the latter. In the two movie theaters, the blacks sat in the balconies, but I don't remember any signs saying so. The train depot had signs designating two of the four restrooms "colored."

I thought somebody should do something about it, but I was just a kid and there was no leadership. I had still never heard of Gandhi. The Student Nonviolent Coordinating Committee would not arise until the 1960 sit-ins in Greensboro, North Carolina.

Nonviolent action in the form of sit-ins began, as far as I know, two years earlier than Greensboro. The venue was Oklahoma City at Katz Drug Store. If Katz was not the first, it was one of the first. I felt like I knew Oklahoma City because I had been there with my grandmother when she got cancer treatment at the University of Oklahoma Hospital. Still, at 11, I had been too young to go alone. Was I too young for a sit-in? Of the people who did it at Katz, the youngest was 6 and the oldest was 17. I would have fit right in. When I gained some perspective on my times from my studies at UT, I considered civil rights to be the defining issue of my generation and my failure to attend the Katz demonstrations tragic.

On other issues, there was room for good faith disagreement, but you were OK with racial segregation or you were not and my tribal identity made the white supremacy side of it problematic even before I knew that many of the discriminatory laws being contested in other states originally applied to Indians as well as African-Americans.

Indians in Oklahoma experienced little of the segregation *de jure* that was common in the Confederate States of America because Indians used to run things. The state was cobbled together starting with Indian Territory, comprised of the lands belonging to the Five Tribes. Most of the rest was Oklahoma Territory, where the survivors of many small tribes and some large ones that fielded strong armies were involuntarily settled on reservations. All of the state but the panhandle was legally recognized at one time as sovereign Indian land. The three counties of the panhandle were "no man's land" on the maps and havens for vice on the ground because they lacked a functioning government.

All of the Five Tribes—called then the Five "Civilized" Tribes—had taken up chattel slavery to some degree, and many slaves had walked the Trail of Tears with their owners. The practice of slavery was tied to plantation economies found in the Southeastern United States. The Plains Indians and the remnants of woodland tribes from the Midwest had no use for slavery.

Tolerance for slavery that had existed in Indian Territory meant that when the Jim Crow laws arose in the former Confederate states to delay the results of emancipation, they would find their way into tribal law for the same reason. The goal was to protect the former owners from social interactions with the formerly owned.

The peculiar history of Oklahoma as the ending point of federal Indian policy—One Big Reservation—meant that Indians still served in legislative bodies after white settlers were admitted to the state. The Five Tribes had met in constitutional convention beginning on August 21, 1905 and drafted a document that was similar to what became Oklahoma's Constitution, but the state of Sequoyah was a nonstarter when it was submitted to Congress for ratification.

Two years after the state of Sequoyah was rejected, Congress approved a virtually identical constitution for the new state of

Oklahoma. Plainly, the issue was not the document. The reason for rejecting Sequoyah might have been a direct influence of racism—not wanting an Indian republic surrounded by more conventional states.

My opinion is that the influence of racism was more indirect. The Civil War was supposed to have settled the slavery issue, but it did not settle the tension between slave and free states, a tension that lives on now—in the 21st century. Sequoyah, a creature of the Five Tribes, would have been culturally attuned to slavery and therefore its bastard child, Jim Crow.

Establishing Sequoyah would have left Oklahoma Territory, the Osage Nation, and No Man's Land as distinct geographical areas that were not contiguous and therefore might have been three more states to work into the complex task of absorbing the former Confederate States of America. The solution that prevailed made one state. The Osage Nation filled the hole in the proposed state of Sequoyah, and so all of what is now Eastern Oklahoma came from Indian Territory, which was joined with Oklahoma Territory to become the state in our 21st century map when No Man's Land became the panhandle. Oklahoma was admitted as the 46th state on November 16, 1907.

There was a great deal of overlap between the membership of the Sequoyah and the Oklahoma constitutional conventions, the former having been dominated by the Five Tribes. Indians would not make laws to disadvantage Indians, and so segregation by law in Oklahoma only applied to black people. This history made my experience of segregation inconsistent.

There were no Hispanics in Bristow when I was growing up there. In Odessa, where I got sent to finish the sixth and eighth grades and where I briefly attended high school, the high schools were imperfectly segregated—African-Americans went to Blackshear, Hispanics to Ector. White students were split between Odessa High and Permian High.

I went to school with one brown kid in Odessa during my enrollment in Permian High School to finish the fall semester of

1962. The customers on my *Odessa American* paper route would teach me how to pronounce Spanish names, but not quickly enough to suit me. All the teachers called the one brown kid in my Permian class "RAY-mos" but he called himself "RAHM-os." Even when I did not know how to pronounce enough Spanish to order Mexican food, I still understood that it was rightfully up to Ramos how we should say his name.

It was in 1964 when—having finally given up on high school in fall of 1963—I enlisted in the Air Force. All of my four-year hitch was spent in Texas, and all of it in San Antonio except for a couple of months in tech school at Wichita Falls. In San Antonio, it's possible to get along exclusively in Spanish, although few people do.

One of my bosses at Randolph AFB, Dave Treviño, was happy to help me out with Spanish when I asked him, but he would not speak Spanish in front of his own kids. I argued with him about the advantages of being bilingual, but he wanted his offspring as distanced as possible from the discrimination that was still playing out in fights over voting rights and education funding.

From living in Odessa and San Antonio, I came to understand racial discrimination as something white people practiced to hold themselves up as superior to black and brown people. Indians were by appearance brown people but did not fit because the brown people in those days were sorted by country of origin—most often Mexican-American. "Latino(a)" and "Chicano(a)" came along later and "Hispanic" came along after that.

Indians were not in those days known as "Native" Americans, but it did occur to me that if the naming convention for brown people were followed, we would be "American-Americans." I never worried much about my own label, because I always knew which side I was on in the discrimination derby.

When I got out of the Air Force and chased a girlfriend off to Wisconsin, I was spoiling for a fight on the civil rights front because I had missed the Oklahoma City sit-ins on account of my age. During Freedom Summer, 1964, I had just finished boot camp and was working on tech school.

Hanging around the Eugene McCarthy campaign in 1968, I quickly noticed that the people who were anti-war seemed to be pro-civil rights. That observation would have kept my limited time to do politics focused on the coming election even if the war had ended. I was as ignorant as the rest of the nation that Richard Nixon had treasonously sabotaged the Paris peace negotiations, but I did not need that knowledge to scoff at Nixon's claim of a "secret plan" to end the war.

The Wisconsin Primary was held the first Tuesday in April 1968. My chance to vote for McCarthy would have to wait for November, because I was registered to vote in Texas. We won handily. I had expected it to be a lot closer. That put a spring in my step until Thursday, April 4, when a radio news report made me feel as though Milwaukee were suddenly in the path of a raging forest fire.

Dr. Martin Luther King, Jr. had been shot in Memphis. In the matter of minutes it took to formulate the question, the radio announcer was back with the result: MLK was dead. Inner city Milwaukee was known as "the core." White Milwaukee—which is to say most of Milwaukee—expected riotous mobs of black people fanning out from the core to destroy property and endanger lives.

At work the next day, it appeared that every window on Wisconsin Avenue contained a poster with MLK's likeness. Some print shop must have worked all night to produce that many posters, and whoever guessed that having a big photo of MLK as a talisman would prevent bricks flying through a window had a lucrative payday for that idea.

The NAACP and allied organizations got a permit to have a memorial march across the Milwaukee business district. Midland National Bank, where I worked, was displaying the magic posters. In addition, the biggest males on the staff were sent downstairs to "guard" the premises during the march.

I was one of the big guys. We were wearing normal work attire. For me, that was a white shirt with a clip-on tie. We had no uniforms or weapons. We were instructed not to start anything and not to get in a fight no matter who started it. I didn't know anything about game theory, but the instructions sounded like a recipe for lose-lose.

The parade announced itself with an incredible racket. I had never seen that many black people riding Harley-Davidsons, most of them tricked out with touring gear. The blocks-long line of black people of all ages was plainly there in memory of MLK, because they were anything but rowdy. Some men were carrying handheld bullhorns, but I didn't see much use for them.

As I watched those people file by, I felt a sense of personal loss from the death of a man I had never met or even seen from a distance. I had been confident that I would hear him speak—maybe another March on Washington, or maybe a rally in some city within a day's drive. I had been waiting for the opportunity to hear MLK, but it hit me all at once that I had been waiting too patiently.

Not only would I never hear him, it seemed to me that a movement was without a leader. I understand now what I was not seeing then from my days at a community college and my evenings at the bank. My idea of a problem had become that the transactions from that day had to balance before we could go home. If the totals were off, I prayed that they would be off by a nice odd number rather than 10¢ or $10 or $100.

While I had my nose in books and balance sheets, the black power movement was rising. I did not know that the Student Nonviolent Coordinating Committee was less than a year from calling itself the Student National Coordinating Committee and giving up on nonviolence. I did not know that leaders like Stokely Carmichael and H. Rap Brown were taking black power to places MLK did not support.

I also did not know of an FBI program called COINTELPRO that undertook infiltrating civil rights organizations and sowing enough discord to keep the movement from speaking with one voice. With all of these things I didn't know, it's amazing that the things I did know about what MLK represented had me standing on Wisconsin Avenue in a wet shirt from a cascade of tears that would not stop.

The sidewalks were as full of humanity as the streets and so I was able to slip away without my colleagues taking notice and join the march. I walked off my emotional outburst if not my sadness and returned to work, making my way upstream against a human current that was still moving.

My idea of politics still centered on elections, but that mooring was shaken by the murder of MLK and shaken again almost exactly two months later, when Bobby Kennedy fell in a spray of bullets from a Saturday night special. It was like I had been stunned by one blow and then hit again before I could fall down. I was Gene McCarthy's man, but RFK was our backup plan and everybody knew it.

McCarthy had won the Wisconsin Democratic Primary. I was far from the youngest person willing to push paper for McCarthy but I was a newbie at age 21. We did no electioneering in the Air Force and I had been there since my 17th birthday. As far as I knew, we anti-war people had done what we were supposed to do when McCarthy won the Wisconsin delegates in a free and fair election.

Those delegates set off for a Democratic Convention just down the highway in Chicago and encountered a nomination process rigged for a man who had not found time to campaign in the primaries. The rigging was flagrant and the process was anything but free and fair. Many of our McCarthy delegates got shut out of the convention.

Those who got past security into the convention venue found the anti-war movement leaderless without RFK, hopelessly splintered. The intention of every McCarthy delegate I spoke to had been to hang in there while our man had a chance and then get behind Bobby Come Lately (as we called him) to defeat the war hawks. Most of the Kennedy delegates had no reciprocal plan. A WWII bomber pilot from South Dakota, George McGovern, tried to put together a last-minute surge but the fix was in and resistance was futile.

While the McCarthy delegates who made it inside struggled vainly to produce an anti-war candidate, those who did not get admitted found that their floor credentials did nothing to ward off the Chicago Police Department billy clubs.

My illusions were crushed on the streets of Chicago along with my interests. *Kaleidoscope*, the local affiliate of the Underground Press Syndicate, ran photos of the bloodshed and dubbed the contretemps "Czechoslocago," a reference to how Soviet tanks were snuffing out the Prague Spring at about the same time.

We had no Alexander Dubček, but if we had, it felt like he would at best be beaten bloody and at worst assassinated. My feelings about the government did not improve when I learned that *Kaleidoscope* had been busted for obscenity. It was not over the first time they printed pictures of people having sex, but rather over printing pictures of sex between a black man and a white woman.

I had become an instant fan of *Kaleidoscope* when I came to Milwaukee, both the cultural and the political aspects of it, which often overlapped. One such overlap was in a continuing feature called, "Jesus, Christ!" The column followed the antics of one Christ T. Seraphim, a local judge who harbored enough establishment biases and prejudices to offer unintentional comedy to those court watchers fortunate enough to be only watching.

Editor John Kois wrote in the May 24, 1968 issue of *Kaleidoscope* about the obscenity bust:

"No one is bitter. When we decided to publish an underground paper last summer, we accepted the inevitability of a bust as part of the price we'd have to pay in attempting to establish a free press in Milwaukee."

Kaleidoscope endured boycotts of its advertisers and its printer, arrested vendors, and all the other petty harassments that followed the underground press.

In 1972, John Kois had his conviction for obscenity reversed in the United States Supreme Court, with Justice William O. Douglas writing in a concurring opinion that "the vague umbrella of obscenity laws was used in an attempt to run a radical newspaper out of business." *Kaleidoscope* had ceased publication in November of 1971, leaving *Kois v. Wisconsin* as a fitting memorial.

One more bit of politics stuck to me from Milwaukee, which was a union town to the degree that when the brewery workers threw up a picket line, the locals would not cross it to drink free beer in the hospitality houses at the breweries.

Not very long after John Kois wrote his fatalistic comment on the *Kaleidoscope* obscenity bust, I was on my way into a grocery store in the university area where I lived. I was stopped by a middle-aged man in jeans and a flannel shirt who looked Indian and barely spoke English. He carried a sign with a black thunderbird on a red background and the message, "Boycott Grapes!" In smaller type across the bottom were the letters UFWOC.

I took a leaflet from the picketer and paused to read what was a shocking fact sheet about the working conditions of the people who picked the grapes. I did not cross the picket line and I resolved to quit eating grapes until I was satisfied things were better in California, the home of UFWOC–the United Farm Workers Organizing Committee.

My commitments to the farm workers and to the underground press followed me back from Wisconsin to join civil rights and opposition to the Vietnam War on my personal political agenda.

FOLLOWING THE FUNNEL TO THE
UNDERGROUND TUNNEL

The political commitments I brought back from Wisconsin turned out to have a practical use in how I was able to fit in at the University of Texas when I began classes in the summer of 1969. There's no denying that it's hard to stand out in a crowd the size of the UT student body, but making friends is easy. You will see the same people repeatedly in courses that focus on their interests, there are student organizations devoted to all sorts of interests, and if you don't see an organization that suits you then all it takes is three students and a faculty advisor to start your own.

The people who put out *The Rag* were my posse before I ever attended a class, but that particular method of fitting in would not have been pleasing to the UT administration. When I arrived in Austin, there was already a lawsuit pending between the New Left Education Project (the official name for the miracle of functioning anarchy) and the UT Board of Regents over our right to distribute *The Rag* on campus.

The case was won in the Supreme Court by David Richards, working as a volunteer for the ACLU. David started out as Mr. Ann Richards to the general public but the legal profession knew him as a major force in civil liberties law and an expert on voting rights litigation, in which the Texas Legislature offered a target rich environment. The Austin power couple had split amicably by the time Ann was elected governor of Texas.

Had David Richards not made the lawsuit end well, I doubt we would have gone away. *The Rag* was the center of my extracurricular universe. Upon arriving in Austin, I looked up the office of *The Rag*, and I quickly became a hanger-on just as I had moved toward the *Kaleidoscope* circles in Milwaukee. Working and going to school, I had no time to elbow my way to the *Kaleidoscope* staff. I was better fixed to pursue a place on *The Rag* and I soon learned it did not require much pursuit. If you hung around, you would be put to work.

The Rag had started in 1966 in reaction to the election of John Economidy to edit *The Daily Texan*, the student newspaper of the University of Texas. He went on to right-wing establishment politics and he certainly foreshadowed that as *Texan* editor.

One of the original founders of *The Rag*, Thorne Dreyer, worked up an article for *The Texas Observer* in 2006 about government surveillance of political activities in Texas and he discovered that Economidy had become a bit less hard core and was a criminal defense lawyer of some repute. Dreyer was able to confront Economidy with documents showing that, during his time as editor of *The Daily Texan* in 1966, he was an informant for police agencies seeking to suppress peaceful dissent. Economidy commented: "No doubt about it. As a journalist, it definitely was not appropriate."

Perhaps Economidy's memories of his one year term as *Texan* editor doing his best to sabotage the counterculture by conducting surveillance of Janis Joplin, Jerry Jeff Walker, and Kinky Friedman, among many others, became less fond as countercultural values became mainstream. The campus surveillance for which he informed went on to track intimate details of people who are now professors, editors, and serving at every level of government. I am part of that rogue's gallery, and not the only judge to have that distinction.

Thorne Dreyer was also a surveillance target as the original "funnel," responsible for dealing with letters to the editor in the column of that name because, at first, he *was* the editor—funnel was considered a less authoritarian term, pending the growth of what came to be called "the miracle of functioning anarchy."

Like most people in the underground press, Dreyer made some of the news he covered—but that was no secret. Dreyer is still practicing journalism after all these years as editor of The Rag Blog, host of Rag Radio on the Austin community station, KOOP, and freelancing when he can.

I had first read *The Rag* in 1968, the year I made my first, futile effort to become a UT student. When I came back a year later, my reading of *Kaleidoscope* had made me aware of the national phenomenon called the Underground Press Syndicate.

I didn't know much about the UT campus or Austin or even recent statewide politics, so my feeling about *The Texan* was that it was free and worth about what I paid for it. (In fact, it was funded from student fees, so I *did* pay for it.) The writing did not meet my SOTA standards. Depending on context, SOTA might mean "Student Occupational Therapy Association" or "Student Older Than Average." SOTA standards in the latter sense mean the humor is no longer juvenile and the content is no longer anodyne.

I was a serious student but having survived a military hitch that left me keenly aware of my own mortality, I was for lots of sex, drugs, and rock 'n' roll. I was more into folk music at the time, but you take my meaning. *The Rag* existed in my culture; *The Texan* did not.

Most of the cultural disconnect I experienced was not so much that I was evolving—although I was—but that I had found people whose cultural lives played in minor chords with a strong backbeat, the inner music that left me out of step where I was born.

Back in the buckle of the Bible Belt where I came from it might have been shocking to learn what happens when sex becomes, as Dustin Hoffman's character in *The Graduate* said in trying to explain his dalliance with Mrs. Robinson, "like shaking hands."

In the four months between my arrival in Austin and my first class, I had sex with more different women than in my entire life before 1969. As best I can remember, the total was seven, and most of the women took the initiative. I developed the common sense I lacked before and started asking the birth control question before doing the deed with anybody, although I must admit it was sometimes just barely before.

I like the world where sex is normal and expected between men and women of a certain age better than the one where sex is commodified. That is a tricky word to describe it, and I suppose it suggests sex workers, but comparing my new environs to those of my childhood showed me a much longer continuum than different kinds of sex work, and it is all permeated with commodification. Prostitutes and dominatrices, topless dancers, and some masseuses are probably sex workers, but what about waitresses who know they get better tips when they maximize femininity, or waitresses at Hooters or Twin Peaks?

Can you argue with a sex worker who claims that a perfect Bible Belt wife, virgin at marriage and faithful to one man, sells her body, but only sells it once and therefore has to take care to get a maximum price connected to a secure retirement? We are, at least, a generation removed from legal coverture, under which marriage renders two people one, and he is the one.

Same sex relationships appeared to take a bit longer to get started among my cohort in Austin, but since I assume the hormonal surge hits gay and straight around the same age, I would guess that getting started late is the influence of heteronormativity or overt discrimination or even direct threats to life and limb in circles where "beating up queers" is recreational activity.

When sex was no longer the defining quality of a relationship, I found myself paying more attention to women in non-sexual ways. That was good, because it was in Austin that my political attitudes toward women took the turn my social attitudes had already made back in the USAF hospital almost three years before I arrived at UT—when I had gotten a taste of being judged by my physical appearance, found it not to my liking, and, therefore, had quit judging women that way.

I had not heard the slogan, "The personal is political," but I was about to live it when I arrived at UT. I was still carrying around ideas like jobs being identified to men and women. After all, that's the way the jobs were advertised. If you were hiring for the electric company, you would not advertise a lineman job under "Help Wanted—Women."

That attitude fell to being challenged by women, who pointed out that if they could not do the work, they would be wasting their time and asking for embarrassment. If God did not intend women to climb light poles, then why would God need a law or a custom to make sure they did not?

One of the women I worked with on *The Rag* rebuilt the engine in her Volkswagen, and she did it so quickly and correctly that people started hiring her to do the same for them. Most of her customers were men.

It's a good thing I came to Jesus on that issue, because now I have a daughter and a daughter-in-law who are better with hand tools than the men they married and also better than I am.

The next domino to fall was equal pay for equal work. I was never on the wrong side of that issue because the common-sense appeal of the right side is overwhelming, but I had to be convinced that it is a problem. The justification for paying women less, if I understand it, is that men need to make more money to support a family. That never flew for me even back in Oklahoma, because there are just too many single mothers. I suppose if the fathers were paying child support like clockwork, that might shore up the differential pay argument a bit, but that was just not so and still is not so. Even if the facts supported men needing to make more money, what about the idea that the employer is hiring a job done that has a fixed value? That value does not change depending on the sex of the person doing the job. The policy arguments are so obvious that it's almost embarrassing to write them down. I would not parse such a clear issue except that I know equal pay for equal work is still a problem all these years later and long after paying women less was declared unlawful.

For women demanding equal rights, overt employment discrimination of various kinds is the low hanging fruit. None of the justifications put forward will stand up to good faith questioning. It gets harder when the issues are feminine stereotypes and the related issue of why women in most organizations tend to get trapped in the lower parts of the organizational chart. Having a woman supervising a man is an issue, but it's an issue nobody wants to talk about, and bringing it up elicits denials rather than justifications. It's not women generally who can't handle supervisory roles, the excuse goes— it's the particular women who work here.

The Rag joined other underground publications in having to accommodate the women who did most of the work and belatedly discovered they were constructing their own glass ceilings. The women woke up to men running things in "alternative" institutions, and when the women woke up, the men had to walk the walk they had been talking.

We had arguments about whether a fruit stand ad showing a woman eating a banana was symbolic of fellatio and, if so, was it therefore a sexist act to publish it? Locating the edge was a continuing struggle, but when an upscale restaurant that catered to the rich and powerful refused to assign women to the lucrative evening shifts because being served by waiters rather than waitresses is "more elegant," we knew which side we were on.

I am writing from post-truth America, so it seals my status as a geezer to say that I care passionately about objective truth in news reporting. At the time when *The Rag* was taking on what we called scornfully the "straight press," it was avant-garde to utter what is obvious today: to ignore a challenge to the status quo is journalistic bias that supports the status quo.

Ragamuffins (as the staff came to be called) would make the news and then cover the news, often writing in the first person. This was said to demonstrate bias.

We ran a report from the picket line over refusal to let women work the evening shift at Headliners by one of the women doing the picketing. Her bias was plain, but so was the felicity of equal opportunity. I always wondered what the average UT student would think of how *The Daily Texan* treated the boycott of the University Co-Op.

I wrote most of the boycott coverage when the boycott itself was undertaken by the Committee to Oppose Racism and Apartheid (CORA). It took three students to register a student organization like CORA, and the three were myself, Betty White (who would become my first wife), and Richard Moore, an African-American prelaw student.

Our beef with the Co-Op was the advertising and sale of Polaroid products at a time when Polaroid was exporting its ID-2 machine to the Republic of South Africa for the purpose of making "passes"—internal passports—convenient to create but hard to counterfeit. The passes made enforcement of apartheid much easier. The pass could be inscribed with some special dispensation for work, but the big deal was that if the police saw a nonwhite person who appeared out of place, they could arrest for mere failure to produce a pass.

CORA was not a well-known organization. Our only major action prior to the Polaroid boycott was to reserve the display cases outside the Chuck Wagon snack bar in the Texas Union. Alan Pogue, principal photographer for *The Rag*, did blow-ups of the famous and gory pictures of the Sharpeville Massacre on March 21, 1960. South African police had opened fire on a mass demonstration over the pass laws, killing or wounding approximately 250 people. Bleeding people, even in black and white and rendered fuzzy when blown up, are not the kind of images to get customers in the mood for a hearty lunch, and I expect the Union might have regretted that particular exercise of the First Amendment at a public university.

The Sharpeville display had the desired effect of opening up a conversation on campus about apartheid. In the U.S., the violence would come from the KKK rather than the government directly (although some law enforcement officers did moonlight in sheets). Our generation knew Jim Crow firsthand and so was not disposed to support apartheid. Our problem became showing links between the U.S. and the Republic of South Africa.

When national anti-apartheid organizations began to focus on Polaroid's ID-2 as a piece of modern technology critical to enforcing South Africa's pass laws, we noticed that the University Co-Op was running ads for a sale on Polaroid cameras. We followed the Gandhian paradigm, talking with Co-Op management and giving them a chance to do the right thing. When they didn't, we threw up a picket line covering the busiest times of the day, every day, from 10:00 a.m. until 2:00 p.m. We put out press releases explaining ourselves, and we expected the one to the *Austin American-Statesman* would line a birdcage, but we got the same silence from *The Daily Texan*. We got an audience with the elected editor, who informed us that, in his opinion, covering our picket line and boycott as if it were news would amount to endorsing it, something he was not prepared to do because he didn't know a lot about the issue, did not trust us to get it right, and didn't care enough about it to inform himself.

The picket line was up for a couple of weeks, and it was difficult to keep it up. We would not put anyone on the picket line who did not know a great deal more about apartheid than what was in our leaflet, and that meant a few people were on endless recycle, two at a time to cover both doors, four hours a day.

As we attempted to begin a third week, Co-Op management invited us in to have another talk. We readily agreed but made them wait until after the rush hours were over. At the meeting, the Co-Op complained that our boycott of Polaroid was taking down sales in the entire camera department. That moment, when a manager owned a bit of vulnerability, kicked off something that might be unfamiliar to persons only involved in politics during the last ten years.

It was common back in the brown shoe days, and it was called a "negotiation." The method has been in disuse for a long time, but the result is commonly that nobody gets everything they want but everybody gets something.

We would have preferred that the Co-Op quit selling Polaroid products entirely. What we got was the Co-Op agreed to no longer advertise Polaroid products even when offered a subsidy by Polaroid and to take down the Polaroid posters immediately. We retained the right to do informational picketing about apartheid, the pass system, and the ID-2, but we agreed not to ask people to quit patronizing the Co-Op.

After the negotiation, we, CORA, felt that we had won and struck another blow against apartheid. The editor of *The Daily Texan* decided that our agreement with the University Co-Op was news. While that was better than nothing, I had harbored thoughts that we might see an article from which an innocent UT student could learn what apartheid was, what the pass laws were, what Polaroid had to do with it, and why at least some UT students cared.

Those thoughts were entirely too optimistic for the student newspaper at a research university in the early '70s, at least in Austin. Negligent decisions by *Texan* editors made the underground press seem as necessary from the campus as in the community. What was newsworthy off campus turned on race or class or sex or political point of view and that's the way most newspapers had been in our lifetimes. We expected better at what the Texas Constitution called "a university of the first class."

I had read of my journalistic hero, Will Rogers, sending hotel bellmen out to acquire the local newspapers in every city Rogers visited on tour. From those readings, I knew that major newspapers had not always spoken with one voice and squelched all others, but I was clueless about how things changed or how they could change back.

The Daily Texan had an elected editor. When enough students awoke to that, those elections involved students generally rather than just the J school and the Greek organizations. Reawakened democracy brought a stunning run of elected *Texan* editors who showed the possibilities that had always existed but had atrophied from lack of exercise: Lori Rodriguez (1971-72), Michael Eakin (1972-73), Buck Harvey (1973-74).

When *The Texan* joined the real world, I joined *The Texan*, pissing off some journalism students by scoring one of the paying gigs they took to be theirs by choice of major. Instead of the occasional op-ed for which I had to beg and wheedle, I got a regular column with my mug shot at the top. I contrived to be wearing a United Farm Workers button when the mug shot was taken, and so I appeared with a tiny black thunderbird that only the sharp-eyed would notice.

The thunderbird was a signal to any sharp enough to notice that I was throwing in with Mr. Dooley, who famously called upon newspapers (in an Irish brogue I will not attempt to duplicate in writing) to "comfort the afflicted and afflict the comfortable."

~24~

SCHOOLING MEETS EDUCATION

In my first long session, fall of 1969, I took my first philosophy class with Richard Zaner, one of the most memorable professors I had at UT. I was not the only one who thought so. Students lined up to get his signature on permissions to add his courses. We often wound up sitting on the floor, which I'm sure gave the fire marshal indigestion, but Zaner was worth it.

After each of Zaner's lectures, small groups of students would repair to the Texas Union to continue the conversation begun in class. That was how I met Mike Mott, a prodigiously talented guitar player. We became good friends over philosophy, folk music, and LSD. Such were the times.

It was around the time Mike and I became guitar picking pals that the board of the University Y had the epiphany that the real estate at 2200 Guadalupe had more value than could be unlocked by offices for public service organizations, an auditorium for rent, and a low dollar dorm on the top floor. They ordered the historic building demolished and I was homeless again.

Along with Mike's brother Fay (AKA Butch), an MD doing an internship in Austin, and his sister Frances (AKA Chickie, an undergraduate heading for veterinary school), we tried renting a house on Wonsley Street, which was then at the north edge of

Austin, as a semi-organized crash pad. The theory was that splitting the rent enough ways would make it doable.

In practice, too many people wanted to be free riders, and Butch got stuck with more than his share of the expenses. I paid late when the GI Bill was late, but I paid. Before hippie irresponsibility doomed the Wonsley house, we did have some good times.

One of the best ones was the night Leonard Cohen played at the municipal auditorium. His guitar work was rudimentary, but he was a poet's poet and the audience ate him up. After the fourth or fifth encore, management turned on the lights and told us to leave.

There was a rumble of protest in the audience and a rhythmic stomping and clapping that shook the building. Before it could get ugly, Cohen came back out and invited us all to get our music making equipment and meet him "over there," pointing to the park called Auditorium Shores.

We walked across the street and waited a half hour or so and Cohen did not appear. After some discussion, we determined to make the long drive out to the Wonsley house to fetch our guitars and a selection of rhythm instruments. Because of the distance, it did not seem promising.

When we returned, there were just a few people left, less than fifty, but just about everybody had some kind of instrument. So, we sat down and joined the picking. We hadn't been back long when Leonard Cohen showed up.

We finished the song in progress and asked Cohen for one. He smiled and said he did not bring a guitar. I handed him my Goya. He strummed it once and said, "Very nice." He launched into "That's No Way to Say Goodbye" in the people's key of C, which everybody seemed to know.

Leonard Cohen stayed there swapping songs with the remnants of his audience until the sun came up. Chickie had insisted on coming in a separate car, stating her intent to make it back to Cohen's hotel room. When we left, she was locked in an embrace with Cohen trading deep kisses. She was not back by the time I had to go to classes.

So, did Chickie Mott do the deed with Leonard Cohen? Beats me. When I razzed her about it, she just grinned like a cat that had swallowed a bird and was trying to ignore the feathers.

While I don't know if she got into Leonard Cohen's bed, I do know that she got into vet school. That is no small accomplishment. Pre-vet students have to take the same highly competitive courses that pre-med students take. There are a lot fewer vet schools than med schools. I call attention to her academic accomplishments to reiterate that few people who partake of sex, drugs, and good music come to a research university for that purpose alone. You don't see a lot of this conduct at exam time, but after the last exam is turned in, it's Katy bar the door.

I had my first and only bum trip at the Wonsley house, but I had already become convinced that acid held no magic for my creativity over three or four years of using it irregularly. It seemed to amplify whatever mood I was already in. I was trying to learn to finger pick my six nylon string Goya and LSD convinced me I should try the same on a twelve steel string Fender. It makes my fingers hurt just to remember the bloody result.

What followed the demise of the Wonsley house was a year of the student version of couch surfing. I shared an apartment near the campus briefly with Heather, who had taught me the difference between Spanish and Portuguese when I first arrived at UT. I usually had a bed, but sometimes I was on the floor. The student anti-war movement was cranking up and I was in the middle of it.

At *The Rag*, I progressed from scut work to writing regularly by the simple expedient of turning in more copy. I don't mean to suggest that writers escaped the scut work. The paper really was a functioning anarchy in that nobody gave orders and, if they did, why pay any attention? You can't fire volunteers.

A 1970 semester brought the worst grades I got as an undergraduate: nothing but Bs. I attribute that to three or four trips to jail as well as some close calls. I do not think it was heartbreak, because I found diving into the books to be a welcome respite from thinking about what was and what might have been with Kitty Lyons in Wisconsin.

Heather had re-caught me on the rebound but it would be more correct to say we caught each other. At that particular time, I think I wanted her more than she wanted me.

After that awful semester without an A grade, I resolved to pay more attention to why I was at the University of Texas. The next semester, I got only one B, and that was from a professor who sucked me right into his orbit with his fascinating backstory.

Eduard Taborsky had been Czech ambassador to Sweden at the time of the Communist coup in 1948. He chose exile and got put on trial *in absentia* by the government that would serve the Soviet Union faithfully until the Velvet Revolution in 1989, when there were no longer Soviet tanks to quash dissent.

Taborsky had been a junior diplomat at Munich, where the Czech delegation tried to sleep on tables outside the suite where their country was being fed to Nazi Germany in return for an illusory promise of peace. The Czechs were not allowed inside the meeting. He later became personal secretary to Eduard Beneš, President of the Czech government-in-exile. In that role, Taborsky discovered evidence that led him to believe that the number three Nazi, Rudolf Hess, had parachuted into Scotland snapping at bait dangled by British Intelligence.

So what if Taborsky gave me the only B in a semester full of As? The man had lived the history that shaped the Cold War conflict into which I was born. I took a second of his courses in 1971 and a third that summer, earning the A grades I found he gave so rarely, and the next year I became his grading assistant.

My time as Taborsky's grader let to a difficulty for some of his students that repeated several times. Having been sentenced to death by a Communist government, Taborsky was a high profile anti-Communist on campus. As such, he attracted students from the political far right. I was by that time, thanks to my work in *The Daily Texan* and my arrest record, a high profile leftist. It was amusing to see the looks on their faces when I showed up to proctor the first exam.

As I found out when I got that lone B from Taborsky, he was a tough grader. He gave me a list of points relating to each essay question and suggested that I add up the number they hit. I had permission to call the close ones to the next higher half point in favor of excellent writing. Too many of the far right students did not study and relied on Taborsky's anti-Communist views to boost them to a passing grade. Instead of answering the exam questions, they would unload industrial strength anti-Communist diatribes that hit none of the points Taborsky had in his model answers.

Because I did not enjoy failing anybody, I would give them a D- if they managed to write their names on their bluebooks and spell them correctly. Most recipients of my mercy grades would leap to the conclusion that the leftist grading assistant had pencil whipped them. They would appeal my grade to Taborsky, who never once raised one of my grades but often lowered them. He did not believe in mercy grades.

Taborsky was one of several professors who hired me for the sorts of academic tasks that made me feel at home in the mythical "college" that played such an odd role in my childhood, as a goal without a reason beyond the assertion that I was smart enough to do it and so I should. In my heart, the promised land was keeping its undefined promise and the possessions I sold off in the pursuit were utterly insignificant.

The relinquished possessions included, at last, the red Karmann Ghia convertible that had been number three in my esteem among relics of my middle-class life, behind my typewriter and my guitar. Butch Mott borrowed it to drive to San Antonio in 1971 and managed to roll it on a sharp interstate turnaround lane. I caught a ride to San Antonio with denizens of the Wonsley house and we were able to manhandle it right side up. The windshield was smashed and the body dinged pretty badly, but I was able to drive it back to Austin after replacing the oil that leaked out while it was upside down.

Butch determined to pay for the repairs and, since I knew I could not hold out much longer, I just sold him the car. He admired it as much as I did, but the car apparently did not reciprocate his feelings. It died within the year by spontaneous combustion. I made a pilgrimage to the boneyard where it was taken to say goodbye and was unable to see any evidence of where the fire started or why.

I did not mourn over material possessions. I was finding my niche at the big university. My favorite place was not open to undergraduates, so naturally I had to find a way in. The Main Library was a closed stack collection housed in the university tower. The ceilings were low, the windows small, and every bit of space not occupied by books was devoted to study carrels for graduate students. There was a table with a bookshelf above the work space and a light that made the desktop useable.

In years of working in the stacks, I never once got evicted by the graduate student whose carrel I was using. I would get to the stacks after my last class and by the time I left it would be dark outside. It smelled like books in there, like learning, and in those carrels I felt special, like my immediate research or study topic would save the world and achieving that result was all on me.

I was never fond of taking exams, so I would often generate a paper topic off the syllabus and offer to write it in lieu of however many exams I could escape. No professor ever turned me down, and I could often get a note from the professor about my research needs that would get a stack pass. In my last two undergraduate years, 1971 and 1972, my significant other worked in the library and she would just let me in a fire exit.

While I was in love with the books in the research library, I could not say the same for textbooks because paying for them was a constant struggle. I thought textbooks were expensive, but everything looks expensive when you rely on the GI Bill and it never starts when the semester does and you start needing textbooks. When I first began developing university survival skills myself, as I had done of necessity at the community college in Milwaukee, I thought to get a jump on reading assignments by diving into the textbooks early. Instead, I had to find ways to do without them at UT. The issue had not arisen in Milwaukee because I had a great job and was going to school part-time. That meant more money chasing fewer books, and I hardly noticed the expense.

Borrowing from a classmate is only a stopgap, because when exam time rolls around—whether interim exams or finals—you will both need the book at the same time.

The undergraduate library usually had previous editions of textbooks. Most syllabi are detailed enough that you can find the subject in the textbook if you have an earlier edition, and even if you can't borrow a new one to account for the differences, reading the older book is better than reading nothing at all.

Usually, I could acquire the books before the semester was over, but my ongoing hassles with money and books pushed me into a discovery in the summer session of 1971 that probably improved my grades. Before the semester started, I would go over to the University Co-Op and eyeball the textbooks. The purpose was to see if I could adjust my schedule to make one book do double duty. When I could, the emphasis and the reading assignments varied enough that I was getting a deeper dive into the materials than either professor expected.

The apogee of this accidental discovery was when I signed up for a political science (government) class and a literature class and a philosophy class in the fall of 1971 that all used Plato's *Dialogues*. There was a great deal of overlap between the philosophy and the literature classes, but the government class only used *The Republic*. Still, dropping a relevant mention of a piece of Plato not assigned had to be an attention-getter.

Not everything went my way in the promised land, of which I knew nothing and so had to draw my own maps as I went. Early in the summer session of 1970, when I was taking half of the required history course, I was sipping hot tea in the Chuck Wagon and complaining about the reading materials. An acquaintance overheard my bitching and dropped a syllabus in front of me.

There were more readings and more interesting readings. It was like I was chowing down on a Big Mac and he was showing me a round, juicy patty of Kobe beef on a fresh baked Kaiser roll. I noticed that the course number differed from the one I didn't like by only one digit, so I had to ask if that was an alternative required history course.

It was, but it was for Plan II students. All I knew about Plan II was that it was an undergraduate honors program that offered more flexibility than normal majors. It was early in the semester, so I rushed over to the Plan II office to see if I could have what I thought was a more interesting required history course. The only way for that to happen was if the big kahuna head of Plan II signed off on the add card.

I needed the add card right away—summer sessions move right along—so I went into a situation that would require buttering up with an inadequate supply of butter. The way to get what you want from a professor—and I would be no exception—is to engage the professor in an intelligent conversation about his research interests. I had to go see the big kahuna knowing only that he had a PhD in history and it was about five years old. In the half a day between asking to see him and getting in, I did not have time to find his dissertation topic, let alone an abstract of his dissertation.

He, however, found time to pull out my academic record—what there was of it. He started the conversation asking who I thought I was and it went downhill from there. Having just recently arrived at UT, I was living the dream, and I was not willing to risk that, so I swallowed my pride and took the history class I had been assigned.

I tried to talk my way past a required English course with similar results. I do think I was a better writer than the graduate teaching assistant I was trying to avoid, but I lacked the ability to articulate what I knew how to do. Before the course was over, I had the teaching assistant convinced of the truth of it and I think he would rather that I had succeeded in jumping past his class. I took my effortless A and then had a good time in a sophomore level English literature course in the spring semester of 1970, taught by a professor who required more effort for the A.

During the first week, Professor Ruth P.M. Lehmann spent about fifteen minutes per class reading out loud to us—*Beowulf* in Old English. In 1988, she would publish her own translation of Beowulf, but in 1970 her ability to verbalize both Old English and Old Irish left me awestruck by what happens in the place my grandparents called "college."

I filled the rest of the English requirement with cross-listed anthropology courses, finishing up required English in the spring of 1970. The cross-listed anthropology courses were a surer thing for being interesting. I got hired in 1970 for more academic work by tall blond Professor Bernth Lindfors, whose specialty was African literature by black writers working in English. There were lots of parallels between black African writers pushing against white colonists and American Indian writers doing the same.

Following those parallels, I joined the African Literature Association as a student member in the summer of 1970 with the idea of racking up some scholarly publications while still an undergraduate, starting with a paper I had written for Lindfors comparing imagery used by South African poet Dennis Brutus with similar work by Jon Donne. I was using work I had done for Lehmann's class in writing a paper for Lindfors, an easy decision for me because I took both classes the same semester—spring of 1970.

Turning in the same paper in more than one class is an ethical problem unless both professors know and approve. However, once you have done some original research, it belongs to you and it informs all your subsequent work. I was beginning to save my work for future use, but in the case of Lehmann and Lindfors, I got permission.

My involvement in the African Literature Association was short lived. The ALA had its national convention in Austin in the summer of 1970, which I attended. I enjoyed meeting some of the people whose books I had been reading, but the meeting produced a major uproar around the question whether it was politically correct to produce Athol Fugard's plays. Fugard is a South African playwright who was at the time correctly opposed to apartheid but who was incorrectly white. I wanted no part of an organization that considered the color of a playwright a serious political question, so I quit the first professional association I joined.

I hoarded my own research materials and did my best to take courses that would relate to courses I had already taken. I was always writing papers for academic credit whether or not a paper was required according to the syllabus. Outside of classes, I continued with *The Rag* and associated political endeavors. The rest of my time was taken up finding endless part-time jobs, dealing with textbooks, and trying to promote a stack pass to the Main Library every semester. Except, of course, when I was in jail.

25

MY LIFE OF CRIME

By the time I was settling in at the University of Texas, it was plain that candidate Richard M. Nixon's "secret plan" to end the Vietnam War was still secret. Almost two years of the Nixon administration had passed and the war was still doing what wars do.

When I finished my four-year USAF hitch, I made a bargain with myself to do whatever I could to end that war I had been supporting, but I hoped to limit any prison time to four years, balancing my contribution to prosecuting the war with a contribution to ending it. I was not looking for illegal anti-war activities, but I had not been in Austin for a year when illegal anti-war activities came looking for me.

The Student Mobilization Committee (SMC) was founded in 1969, one of several offspring of The Mobe, as the National Mobilization Committee to End the War in Vietnam had become known. The Mobe attracted a lot of star power and showed great creativity.

Norman Mailer wrote *The Armies of the Night* about The Mobe's 1967 March on the Pentagon. Phil Ochs gave a concert at the Lincoln Memorial and Mailer got himself arrested on the steps of the Pentagon along with over 600 others as poet Allen Ginsberg, future founders of the Youth International Party (Yippies) Abbie Hoffman and Jerry Rubin, and The Fugs attempted to levitate and exorcize the headquarters of the U.S.

military. The Fugs were a band formed by poets Ed Sanders and Tuli Kupferberg in the year I enlisted, 1964, and named after a euphemism coined by Mailer in his acclaimed novel, *The Naked and the Dead*.

The University of Texas branch of SMC regularly applied to the Austin City Council for parade permits to march against the war from the campus to various locations downtown, and at first the permits were granted as a matter of course—just as if students opposed to the war were citizens cloaked in the First Amendment.

Representatives of veterans' groups took to speaking against the permits, claiming that to oppose U.S. policy in Vietnam was to favor Communism and therefore granting the parade permits would do the same. Debating the merits of that proposition might have been fruitful, but the City Council was more inclined to raw political calculus and, at the time, students were not allowed to vote where they went to school. Parade permits became complicated and expensive and rare. To the SMC, the regular denials were organizing tools.

I did not attend SMC meetings for the same reason I stayed away from meetings of Students for a Democratic Society (SDS). There was too much esoteric factional backbiting to retain my interest. When the National Council of SDS meeting was evicted from the UT campus in 1969, I took the side of SDS and the First Amendment. That involved nothing more than fetching the keys to open up the University Y for a band in the auditorium and some small groups meeting elsewhere. The bulk of the business was at the Catholic Student Center but small caucuses were in other student religious centers and the Y.

The Austin meeting saw the earliest presentation of a paper titled "You Don't Need a Weatherman to Know Which Way the Wind Blows," from which the violent faction that framed the organization from the establishment perspective derived its name. At the time, it was just a clever title carved from a lyric by the future Nobel Laureate, Bob Dylan, in "Subterranean Homesick Blues."

A friend's FBI file referred to me as a "leader" of SDS—which was nonsense, since I was never even a member—but if asked about my presence on the fringes, I would point to the Port Huron Statement (the SDS founding document) and ask my critics to specify which parts they thought incorrect.

As long as I did not have to attend the meetings, I also took the side of the SMC and the First Amendment. A major march was planned for "Vietnam Week" in April of 1970 and the parade permit was sought months in advance. The denials became almost comical because other permits would be granted in the same meetings and there was no serious question that the SMC applications were being nitpicked and ultimately denied because of disagreement with the purpose of the parade.

The first week in April, 1970, the SMC was denied a permit in the same meeting where permits were granted to the UT Round Up Committee and the Knights of Columbus. The day of the march, April 18, Councilman D.R. Price told the *Austin American Statesman*, "We can't vote to keep them off the sidewalks—but if we could, I would have."

Downtown Austin. April 18, 1970.
"You have no parade permit, so get out of the street."
"The First Amendment is my parade permit."
"You're under arrest."

There was still no parade permit. I was wearing a flight cap that read "Veterans for Peace" and a few remaining bits of my military uniform. The SMC had made the decision to walk on the sidewalks because they had been denied a permit. I was not a member of the SMC and I felt the First Amendment was my parade permit.

In front of the Texas Capitol, at 11th Street and Congress Avenue, there was a line of Austin police officers and a smaller number of Department of Public Safety officers. They all wore full-face visors and carried gas masks. The SMC crowd, waving "U.S. Out Now" signs, completely covered the sidewalks on the west side of Congress Avenue. The downtown newspaper had a record of underestimating antiwar crowds and it estimated the crowd at 5,000.

With a few other hardy souls who thought the Constitution applied in Austin, I was lined up in the driveway of the Capitol. One by one, we stepped into the street. In pictures taken that day, there appears to be about twenty feet between those of us doing civil disobedience. Each of us was warned individually to get out of the street and each of us, as we failed to do so, was taken into custody, handcuffed, and put in a paddy wagon parked around the corner that eventually held twelve arrestees, seven charged with disorderly conduct and five with failure to obey a lawful order. On the way to jail, we serenaded the driver with "We Shall Overcome."

I became acquainted for the first time with the city jail, an environment where every surface was made of metal, resulting in every little sound bouncing from one hard surface to another until it died. I wondered if the jailers were issued ear protection but as they brought us out in turn to be photographed and fingerprinted, I could see their ears were as unadorned as mine had been on the Air Force firing range and jet flight line.

After we were all immortalized for government databases, those who wished got their one phone call. I don't recall that I used mine, because I had stated my intent to have an antiwar parade if I were the only participant and I did not want or expect to be bailed out.

I had a protocol in mind I tried to follow whenever I was arrested for political activity on purpose, starting with this arrest. Do not accept any bond short of a personal bond. Give away all food to other prisoners. Talk about why you are there to anybody who will listen.

It was a sound plan, but the hard part was very hard—waiting for something to happen, for the outside world to take notice. If I had been allowed to bring or have delivered one of the textbooks I had been able to buy, then sitting in jail would have been good for my grades instead of dragging them down. As it was, the only reading materials allowed were the downtown newspaper and the Bible. *The Austin American-Statesman* was so much birdcage liner and I had already read the Bible.

So, I sat in a metal box within another metal box with metal walls and metal ceilings and metal floors and tried to meditate, which required either ignoring the cacophony or working it into a mantra. After a long noisy night, somebody bailed me out.

Not having had any sleep, I was inexcusably rude to the bondsman. He told me I needed to check in at his office once a week or he would go off my bond. I hurled a few expletives and told him I would not check in and he could go off the bond because I didn't want to be bailed out in the first place. But I had signed a promise to appear and that meant I would appear.

There was some dismissing and refiling of charges, and by the time I came to trial in August of 1970, I don't remember whether the charge was disorderly conduct or failure to obey a lawful order. I was represented for free by the civil rights law firm that would later employ me. My defense was simple—that the order to not be part of a parade was unlawful because a permit had been denied based on the content of the parade's message. I testified in my own behalf.

The arresting officer testified that I had said some things to him as rude as what I said to the bail bondsman. I was surprised but I honestly could not remember what I said, if anything, so I turned to the arresting officer and told him that if I said that, I owed him an apology. I did not say it to impress the judge; I said it because it was true. I was found not guilty.

219

While the Austin City Council was denying parade permits to antiwar students, the Ohio National Guard was shooting them dead. On May 4, 1970, four Kent State University students were killed. Two were antiwar protestors; the other two were walking between classes. The national response rocked my immediate environs like the killing of MLK had when I was living in Milwaukee. The violence continued when, four days after the Kent State shootings, eleven people were wounded at the University of New Mexico by bayonets in the hands of the National Guard. Six more days passed and two students were shot dead at Jackson State University in circumstances similar to Kent State.

I was in the military and then I was a college student and there was no great difference between the people who surrounded me in both endeavors. The great majority were kids of similar ages of similar abilities of similar loyalty to the United States and—not least—of similar courage. In response to the killings, some 4 million students from over 450 college campuses and numerous high schools left classes for demonstrations and teach-ins.

In Austin, we lacked time to fiddle with the nitpicking ninnies who had been dredging up one excuse after another to deny a parade permit. The SMC was no longer in control. The entire organization was a tiny caucus within the numbers of students who wanted to take to the streets.

Within days of the Kent State shootings on May 4, a rally in front of the tower made infamous as Charles Whitman's sniper perch in 1966 quickly turned into a march down the West Mall to Guadalupe Street, aka the Drag, which was taken over in its entirety without a parade permit. The police set up a line south of the campus on 19th Street. When orders to disperse were ignored they opened fire with tear gas grenades.

Having learned to tolerate tear gas in basic training, I parked myself by the water hose at a service station on the corner of 19th and Guadalupe and rendered first aid to people under the mistaken impression they were going blind.

Meanwhile, hundreds of demonstrators ran around the police line and continued toward downtown by way of the Capitol Complex. When they figured out their line had been flanked, the police reformed in front of the Capitol on 11th Street, where I had been arrested parading without a permit a couple of weeks before.

Having been delayed by my first aid duties, I was half way between the Capitol and the new police line when I heard the grenade launchers go off again. When I rounded the last building and there were only ancient shade trees and bronze statues in front of me, the canisters began landing at my feet. This was the first time I saw a tactic I've seen many times since: the police order the crowd to move in a direction and then they fire tear gas in that direction so that obeying requires entering a cloud of gas. I did not understand it then or now unless the goal is to give cause to arrest those who disobey and to disable those who obey.

I threw a couple of canisters back where they came from—a harmless act since the police all had gas masks—but quickly decided there were too many canisters and not enough demonstrators unafraid of picking them up. I retreated back to the Capitol with people running past me on both sides.

I entered the Capitol by the south door and walked on toward the rotunda, expecting to sit it out in air-conditioned comfort after I found a water fountain to ease the burning in my eyes. I had no plans to get arrested.

Others had the same idea about the water fountain and there was water all over the tile floor. About the time it was my turn at the cold water a shirtless demonstrator came running into the building with two cops in hot pursuit. He slipped on the wet tile and they were on him with riot sticks. One particularly spectacular blow, a roundhouse swing from above with the long black club, struck the cowering target across his bare back. I would have thought it enough force to break his back but it broke the club. While the cop stared dumbfounded at the remains of his weapon, the fellow who had vandalized city

STEVE RUSSELL

property by allowing the club to be broken on his back got up and ran.

The south doors were still opening and shutting and the pop of the tear gas grenades was sounding awfully close when a white cloud came wafting into the rotunda. I have in the past expressed the opinion that the police actually fired tear gas inside the Capitol, but on reflection I never saw the source of the gas—just the gas.

The plan to sit it out in the Capitol was not working, so I approached the officer at the information desk and asked how he wanted us to get out. He gestured toward the north entrance, which was blocked by a cottony-white fog.

"I can't go through that."

"You will if you don't want to go to jail."

I took a deep breath and plunged in at a trot. Just as I was able to see the light of day though the tear gas, I found myself approaching a gas-masked cop from behind. He evidently thought—not unreasonably—that I was about to attack him. He whirled around in my direction—whether to shoot me or skewer me with his bayonet I couldn't tell.

I raised my hands and performed the unlikely feat of taking a deep snort of tear gas, swallowing, and breaking into a run at the same time. I felt rather than saw the steps and stumbled down them, trying to find a relatively safe place to stop and vomit. The next thing I felt was the metallic snap of handcuffs on my wrists. I still had no visuals, but the audio portion of the program was interesting.

"Get up against that car."

"What did he do?"

Silence.

"Well, what are you going to charge him with?"

Pause.

"Aww, I saw him throwing rocks. Assaulting an officer."

"I didn't throw any rocks!"

"Don't hand me that bullshit, boy."

222

I continued handing him that bullshit all the way to the jail, since it was true. In the police station, a cop recognized me from my last arrest at the Student Mobilization Committee march.

"Well, back again, I see."

"Yeah. Only last time I was guilty of parading without a permit. This time the charge is assault and I'm not guilty."

"You were out there, weren't you?"

"Yes, I was out there and I'll be out there again. Can't you see that we have a duty to be out there? Those four students at Kent State were only the beginning. The only way you are going to stop us is to kill us all."

"We don't wanna do that, Steve. We don't want to do that."

I believed him. If ordered to shoot peaceful protestors, most Austin police officers would regret the order, but they would follow it.

My treatment at the jail was much better this time. There were no insults and I was allowed to make a phone call within an hour. This time I took the chance, because I had no plans to get arrested and I wanted somebody on the outside to know where I was. It took a long time to get bailed out, but part of the reason was confusion over the charges.

It turned out that I was arrested within about a car length of a group of lawyers who were present as ACLU observers. I was unable to see at the time, but the lawyers witnessed the arrest happen while I was leaning against a car puking.

The charges were slowed down while the police looked for somebody to swear that they saw me throw rocks. When nobody was willing to undertake that feat of imagination, they booked me for failure to obey a lawful order and either the ACLU bailed me out or I was released on my own recognizance.

When the case came to trial later in the same month as the civil disobedience on purpose arrest, it turned out that the lawful order I was supposed to have disobeyed was a general order to disperse given at the police line on 11th Street. I had never been anywhere near that line, and even if I had been, I was doing my very best to disperse at the time I was arrested and for some time before I was arrested. The charge was dismissed without trial.

My first political arrest was on purpose. The second, not so much. The third was like being struck by lightning.

I am a creature of habit, and when I was an undergraduate my habit upon rising was to go to the Chuck Wagon and have a hot cup of tea and a donut.

One morning like every other morning toward the end of the fall semester in 1970, I would not be finishing my donut because I was surrounded by Austin police officers, who announced I was under arrest.

Naturally, I asked the charge.

"Indecent exposure."

I was mystified and wondering how I became important enough to send someone to get pictures of me skinny-dipping. Even if they did that, who would testify they were offended?

I got even more suspicious of the arrest when the arresting officers put me in a holding cell and told me to drop my pants, bend over and "spread 'em." And what would I have secreted up my ass while in the police car? I invited them to come in to the holding cell and make me, but they declined the invitation as I expected.

The questions running through my mind were not useful, it turned out. I was thinking of exposure punishable by fine only, the charge you got for taking a leak in the parking lot or skinny-dipping. I was charged with the more serious version: exposure for the purpose of sexual arousal.

During this arrest, I got the look at the Travis County Jail that I had been spared when the assaulting a police officer charge failed to fly. Everything the newspapers said about overcrowding was true. There were not enough mattresses or blankets. What the courts had found to be cruel and unusual punishment was easily observed.

I spent the first night in a holding cell on a concrete floor with my head a few feet from an overflowing toilet. In the crush of sweaty bodies, it occurred to me that getting into a fight could mean death or serious injury before deputies could break it up.

The county lockup as an educational experience was enhanced by friendships made when I gave away my food. I learned that heroin was available in the jail and that it was possible to make a rig for shooting it up by cannibalizing a ballpoint pen. The downside was you had to poke a hole in your own arm because the pen would never be sharp enough. The guys desperate enough for this method had veins like leather.

Late the next day, I got interviewed by the personal bond office and the bond was granted. I went to see Cam Cunningham—one of the lawyers who had witnessed my arrest while puking on the Capitol grounds—and his first reaction was to ask if I had been wearing baggy shorts with no underwear. Even he did not anticipate the degree of lawlessness in this case, but he was beginning to see the light when he returned from a talk with the prosecutor.

The offense involved a report of a guy who had long hair and a beard like me masturbating while seated in a car nothing like mine in the West Campus area. Cam gave me the date and time of the report so I could try to figure out where I had been at a date and a time about four months earlier. Try that sometime.

That was when I did something really stupid. I went back in Cam's office, pulled out the file, and jotted down the name and address of the victim. Then I went and knocked on her door. The charge I was investigating was a gross misdemeanor. Had I scared her, I could have been charged with a felony called retaliation, a possibility that never occurred to me.

God must watch over babies, drunks, and wannabe lawyers, because she recognized me immediately as the guy in the picture the police showed her. The police report claimed she had picked me out of a photo array, so I asked her how many photos she was shown.

Only one, she said. Mine. She told them I was not the perpetrator. They thanked her and left and then swore falsely that she had identified me to get a warrant for my arrest, leading to my tea getting cold and my donut left unfinished. She was outraged and embarrassed. She promised to call the prosecutor and unload on him. After obliviously dodging the retaliation bullet, I soldiered on trying to find an alibi, as Cam had instructed.

A college student—at least one who always attends classes—knows his whereabouts at certain times, but the offense did not match my class schedule. I had procured a calendar page of the month the offense was reported to have happened, and I x-ed through the days I was in class and circled the day for which I was trying to account. There was something familiar about that circle.

It took over a week of racking my brain and talking to everybody close to me, but I finally nailed down the day. Then I looked at that semester's class schedule and got the time. I *had* been in class when some guy was exposing himself in the West Campus area—it was just not my class.

I had been speaking to a government class about the United Farm Workers, in front of approximately a hundred students whom I did not know and who did not know me before that day. I called the professor to ask him to verify the day and time and to ask him if he'd be willing to testify without a subpoena. The day and time were correct and he would be happy to testify.

Alibi in my pocket, I went to visit with my lawyer. Cam told me he had been in the courthouse on another matter when the assistant county attorney stopped him in the hall to tell him my case had been dismissed because the victim had called to complain about the investigation. They made her come to the office in person and she came but she also pitched a fit about the whole deal and said she no longer wished to testify even if they managed to arrest the right guy.

After Cam quit chuckling, he read me the riot act for looking up the victim. What if I had looked enough like the perp to cause her to make a mistake? What if I looked nothing like the perp but I scared her just by knocking on her door? I told him I had to visit her in person so I could show her his picture—Cam was also a big guy with long hair and a beard. He was not amused, so I admitted to kidding and apologized for my horrible judgment.

Collectively, these arrests produced a lawsuit in federal court called *Russell v. Miles*. I was the plaintiff and the Austin Chief of Police, Bob Miles, was the defendant, along with every other officer who touched any of the cases. The youngest lawyer in the Simons, Cunningham law firm, John Howard, was attorney of record, but by then I had experienced difficulty getting placed for student teaching in the spring semester of 1971, so I identified law school as my backup plan. Since I had begun to call myself prelaw, I had to do the work on *Russell v. Miles* myself.

After I filed the lawsuit in 1971, I couldn't get arrested if I tried. In the spring semester of 1972—my last as an undergraduate, after which I was to be a summer freshman in the School of Law—the university had withdrawn permission to use the Texas Union Ballroom for a dance because they found out belatedly it was to be a gay pride event. Some of us vowed to be taken to jail over the issue, but I showed up to the scene late just as they handcuffed Rick Ream, another straight supporter, and put him in a squad car to take him away. Frustrated, I hopped on top of the police car and demanded to be arrested even though I had not made it to the ballroom. Four cops grabbed me—which was no surprise—but instead of handcuffing me, they just pitched me out of the way and the car drove off with Rick inside.

In the fall semester of 1972—my first year of law school—I did get arrested by the University of Texas cops because I would not produce my student ID while dining in the Chuck Wagon. They knew who I was and they knew I was registered. I was not suing any UT officers, so they had no problem arresting me, but the prosecutors were not interested and they chucked me out of jail with no charges filed.

All of the causes of action in *Russell v. Miles*—false arrest, false imprisonment, malicious prosecution, violation of the Civil Rights Act of 1964—survived a motion to dismiss, but the chances of winning money damages were minimal. The Miles in the caption was Bob Miles, the Austin Chief of Police, and the parties included every officer I could identify as having touched

227

any of my cases. The probable outcome was an injunction against any further misconduct for the purpose of locking me up. In light of my workload, since I was in law school at the time, I settled the case for a promise not to do it again and a court order to destroy my arrest records except for the one case that was out-and-out fraud. I could not relate that one to any antiwar activity.

These arrests continued to be brought up every time I ran for election. Five years later, I had not been a judge on the Austin Municipal Court for a month when I was shown my mug shot and compete rap sheet being passed around in the police station. Somebody had disregarded a federal court order, but it did not seem worthwhile to file a contempt motion when the only people paying attention were unlikely to vote for me anyway.

It could have been worse. My political enemies might have learned that I was once arrested for conspiracy to spotlight frogs.

26

READING NEWS; MAKING NEWS;
REPORTING NEWS

My first graduation from the University of Texas—from anywhere, actually—was scheduled to happen at the end of the spring semester of 1972. I had identified myself as prelaw as of one year before my graduation date, when I discovered I could not get placed in any school district in Central Texas to do my mandatory student teaching unless I shaved the beard that had hidden the ugly scars from my accident since 1968.

I could not imagine getting up in front of a bunch of teenagers in a condition that would invite being nicknamed "Scarface." I explained the reason for the beard and how long I had been hiding behind it. To my delight, I was restored to having an opportunity to graduate on time when the UT College of Education set up a student teaching program just for me at the Gary Job Corps Center in San Marcos. Three other students, all men, joined me as the first student teachers assigned to the Job Corps. We took turns driving the 35 miles to San Marcos and exchanged teaching ideas while on the road.

Our orientation was a bit depressing. The teenage students were all black kids from urban areas or white kids from the boondocks. As might be surmised, there was a bit of mistrust between those two factions. We were told not to assign any readings, because the average reading level was third grade. We would be showing lots of films and the biggest challenge would be keeping order. One orientation speaker joked that we should just try to keep broken furniture to a minimum. I was not certain he was joking.

The four of us were split up into separate classrooms. We were training for "social studies," which in the Job Corps meant how to look for a job, how to apply for a job, how to keep a job, and basic civics—voting and jury duty and such.

Reading had changed my life, so I took the caution against reading assignments as a challenge. I quickly confirmed they did not do much reading, but I diagnosed the reason as nobody had ever given them anything they wanted to read. I pulled together paperback readings about the civil rights movement by sacrificing my own collection and begging among friends with similar interests. Those books became my lending library. The biggest problem was getting the books returned, and there was one book that both black and white students would "borrow" and never give back. I could not get enough copies of John Howard Griffin's *Black Like Me*, and Griffin's book sparked some lively class discussions but no fights.

My other effort to push printed material was something I had laughed about with the other three student teachers. I'm not sure which of us made the joke, but when I quit laughing, I decided it was worth a try. There were a couple of pornographic book stores on Sixth Street in Austin, and a bit of investigation showed me places that sell paperback "fuck books" remainder them the same way regular bookstores do. They cut off the covers and send them back to the publishers to have their accounts credited with returns. I convinced the stores to let me have the remaindered books. I figured that if I was going to give away fuck books to teenage boys, I was less likely to get caught if they had no covers.

I did not get caught with the first boxes of remainders from the porno bookstores and they were able to fill the boxes for me one more time before the semester was over. The kids were not only reading them—they were reading them and trading them for other books they had not yet read.

My next attack on the reading problem almost got me kicked out of the program started for me. I was bringing in only slightly out of date copies of *The Black Panther*, the underground newspaper produced by the Black Panther Party in California. One of my supervisors picked up a copy of *The Black Panther* and leafed through it. The next thing I knew, I was at a hearing to decide my fate. If I got kicked out, I could not complete my student teaching and so I would not graduate.

My supervising UT professor, Jo Ann Sweeney, drove down to San Marcos for the hearing. She recommended that I apologize and throw myself on the mercy of the Job Corps management. I did not like that idea—I thought if there were any mercy to be had, we would not be having a hearing about kicking me out.

The teacher who had discovered the paper testified about the circumstances.

When my turn came to cross-examine him, I asked, "What is your objection to *The Black Panther*?"

"These kids are always getting in fights, and that newspaper advocates violence, black on white violence."

I asked the teacher to show the hearing officer the part of the paper that advocated black on white violence.

After a long pause, he pointed out a picture of a Black Panther Party member carrying a rifle.

"That's a serious rifle all right, but could you show me where the fellow holding it advocates using it on white people?"

After another long pause, he could not.

The hearing officer decided I could stay, but the newspaper had to go.

I did not like the result, but Professor Sweeney told me to accept it if I wanted to graduate. I did.

My final stroll off the beaten path was that I had my class produce a literary magazine that I dubbed, *Write On!* It contained a couple of short stories and a lot of poetry, some of it awful and some of it pretty damn good. I duplicated enough spare copies that every kid who published something could send the proof home to his family.

Clearing the student teaching hurdle kept me on track to graduate at the end of the spring semester in 1972. I was admitted to the University of Texas School of Law for the summer session and wait-listed at Yale Law School for the fall session. I guess I was not very good at taking advantage of what resources exist, because I can't imagine that UT did not have a prelaw advisor. Looking back on it, I expect I had no prelaw advice because most prelaw students were in the College of Arts and Sciences and I was in the College of Education, reflecting my original goal to teach social studies at the high school level.

The major mistake my ignorance of the process caused was that I generated a list of law schools to which I intended to apply, only to find out that they all wanted essays on different topics and most of them wanted money, which I did not have. My recollection is that UT did not require money and I just wrote Yale and told them my situation. Yale plainly accepted my application in spite of my inability to pay a fee.

The first time I heard of a prelaw advisor was when I became one for the University of Texas at San Antonio twenty-five years later. My self-taught practice was to recommend three applications: one to the law school most likely to accept my student, one to the law school the student would choose if all things were possible, and one slightly down the academic food chain from the school thought to be realistic...just in case. I referred to these three applications as realistic, dream, and insurance. Had I followed my own advice, I would have considered the University of Houston realistic, Yale my dream, and Texas Southern insurance. My list would be dominated by state-supported law schools in Texas because I was clawing for the free tuition available to veterans after the GI Bill was spent. Yale was a private school but it was intended as a dream. If a private school were just impossible, then my dream school would be the University of Texas.

When I discovered I had intended more applications than I could complete, I did what I could. The only two I finished were Texas and Yale. I know the difference between luck and skill, and my law school admissions were the former. I applied having graduated *magna cum laude* from a first rate undergraduate school and with a Law School Admissions Test score that was high but less than knock your socks off high—by the scoring method of the time, I was in the top third or fourth percentile but I knew a "perfect" LSAT would not walk me into Yale.

When I did the arithmetic, it appeared to me that one C I got in cultural anthropology in that first summer session was the difference between *magna cum laude* and *summa cum laude*. I knew that I would be applying to at least one first tier law school and so I thought it would make a difference. The professor who punished my resistance to his wisdom did not get tenured at UT. I looked him up at the school where he did get tenured and wrote him a plea to change my C to a B on the bases that I didn't deserve the C in the first place and every other professor who evaluated my work at UT found it worth an A or a B. He did not answer.

I made one more error in light of what I know now. I never told UT I was Indian until I requested a graduation notice to my tribal newspaper. I never told Texas Law or Yale I was Indian. I had to tell Yale about coming from rural poverty to explain why I could not send money, but I did not tell them of my tribal connections because I was seeking to avoid the affirmative action stigma. I now consider that an error because the affirmative action stigma is unavoidable. Your enemies will assume you only got a first rate education because of affirmative action whether or not it's true and your friends won't care.

When I addressed my law school applications in 1972, my undergraduate grades were outstanding but not the very best and my test scores were the same. There were plenty of law schools where I could have blown the doors off the admissions office, but because of my poor planning I ended up with completed applications to only two law schools, both first tier.

I still needed to graduate UT, so I was required to visit the Main Building again for a "card check." In those primitive times, there was a file for each senior containing a punched card for every class passed, and a clerical person was assigned to sort the cards and make sure every graduating senior had enough courses and the right courses to fit their degree plan. When the card check took place, my two law school applications were on the way.

I handed in my paperwork and the middle-aged woman in the office started thumbing through my cards. She suddenly stopped, looked over another piece of paper, and started giggling. The giggles quickly turned to laughter and by the time she was able to pause, she was out of breath.

Her amusement gave me a sinking feeling. Since my admission on "individual approval" in 1969, I had never been able to shake the apprehension that somebody was going to tap me on the shoulder and say, "I'm sorry, Mr. Russell, but there was a mistake in your admission. We were hiring for lawn care that day and your application got in the wrong stack." This is common enough the psychologists have a term for it: "imposter syndrome."

I did not get called an imposter, and I understood her amusement when I got over my bureaucratic near-death experience.

"Did you know," she asked, "that for most of your time at UT, you were on scholastic probation *and* on the Dean's List?"

No, I had not known. Three years after my one conversation with the admissions officer who extended the offer under which I was admitted, I could not be sure if he didn't tell me or I didn't remember I was supposed to make an application to get off of scholastic probation. Because I didn't apply to get off, I remained on scholastic probation while earning academic honors. I can see the humor in that now. It took a long time for the *je ne sais quoi* feeling to go away.

When I got the results of my two applications, I lacked the nerve to hold out several more months for Yale because the waitlist is not a sure thing and, even if I got called in, I could not see where the money would come from. At Texas, I would be exempt from tuition.

There were two more issues that seemed less weighty. First, I was back to driving junk—a 1965 Ford Falcon with many mechanical issues that made driving to New Haven problematic.

Second, my wife Betty had several incomplete papers standing between her and graduation. Relocation seemed likely to make her graduation harder and I did not wish to be separated from her.

So it was that my last undergraduate semester, spring of 1972, segued right into my first law school semester in the summer session of the same year.

Almost exactly a year later, the Watergate hearings began, with gavel-to-gavel coverage on commercial TV. The law school snack bar, known informally as "Keeton's Casino," after Law Dean W. Page Keeton, brought in a TV and the hearings played every day and all the time. I was still on *The Daily Texan* staff while a law student, and so I had access to the tickers for all the major wire services. I devoured the copy coming over the wires, only a tiny bit of which made it into the paper.

The head of President Nixon's appellate team was UT Law Professor Charles Alan Wright, who literally wrote the book on federal court practice and who would always answer a couple of questions for the student press when we could catch him. His understanding of his role as a teacher balanced a bit the problem that he was least available to talk when he was most newsworthy—that would be during President Nixon's trips to the Supreme Court.

It was a bit ironic that I had joined the paid staff of *The Daily Texan* not terribly long after a comical issue of *The Rag* ran that intended to troll the campus paper. In addition to some written copy, I contributed a picture of myself taken in our tiny apartment by my wife Betty. I was sitting on a toilet about to put a copy of *The Daily Texan* to a use I had actually experienced with newsprint in those outhouses on the other side of 12th Street in Bristow. My only excuse is that I didn't have a birdcage to line.

Moving to the student newspaper soon after I started law school in the summer of 1972 was about needing the money but also about having a bigger audience. The experience gave me more than I expected. There is nothing like working on a daily newspaper to teach the life skill of nailing deadlines. I also had to learn how to give up chunks of my deathless prose when necessary, because the editorial staff had a hard limit on the amount of newsprint real estate we could tear away from Longhorn Sports, rewritten wire service news, and Muffy Spindletop's election as queen of the Floating Keg Festival.

Working for *The Texan* taught me much more than I expected and getting paid to learn new skills was just gravy. I ended up leaving the student newspaper in the spring of 1974 over a censorship dispute. In one of my many columns supporting the United Farm Workers of America, AFL-CIO, I referred to a particular brand of wine as "scabrous dregs." *The Texan's* censor was convinced that was libelous; I remain convinced it was not. "Scabrous" sounds disgusting in the context of food or drink, but it's a bit of word play referring to the status of the grapes from which the wine was fermented— "scab grapes," picked by non-union hands during a strike.

I was able to replace my newspaper money with research assistant money at the law school. In the summer of 1973, I scored one of the last Law Students Civil Rights Research Council internships working for the United Farm Workers in the Rio Grande Valley. LSCRRC had been a vital part of the civil rights movement, but it was dying of success. Killing of civil rights workers had died down, the KKK had pulled back under whatever rock hides it between eruptions of hate, and the contributions that kept LSCRRC in the fight were drying up.

Most of my close friends knew I was Indian and wondered why I did not throw elbows to be placed with *Dinebeiina Nahiilna be Agaditahe* on the Navajo Rez. I think now that if I had taken that path, I may have gotten to be friends with Peter d'Errico a lot sooner. Peter was a legal studies professor with the University of Massachusetts at Amherst who had cut his teeth at DNA and who remained a force in Indian law for his entire career. Maybe I could have met Peter at DNA, but fate takes curves.

Around those curves, Peter and I, after being colleagues from a distance in academia, would both wind up writing opinions for Indian Country Media Network, as *emeriti* professors.

Author working security for a United Farm Workers rally
in the Rio Grande Valley, 1974. Photo © Alan Pogue.
Used by permission.

The reason I did not hustle for posting to the Navajo
Reservation was—and most non-Indians don't understand this—I
thought at the time that I was not "Indian." I was Cherokee.
DNA might as well have stood for *Det Norske Arbeiderparti*
(Norwegian Labor Party).

By the time I got sucked into the Texas Indian Bar
Association in the early '90s, I had begun to identify with all
indigenous people pushed together by the U.S. government and
to love the Navajo Rez and to have friends there, but going there
in 1973 would not have been a homecoming.

I had started with the UFW when a farm worker in
Milwaukee who barely spoke English convinced me not to cross
a picket line to shop for groceries. Had I not gone with the
UFW internship, I would never have met César Chávez. One of
my great regrets from the Movement days is that I not only did
not know MLK, I never even attended an event where he spoke.
I considered Chávez to be Indian by blood when "Indian"

gained meaning for me, and a man of the stature of MLK. I will always be grateful to have known him and proud to be associated with him.

Because of my size, I was always one of at least two bodyguards stationed near Chávez at all times when he visited Texas. In photos of Chávez speaking to a crowd, all eyes are on Chávez except at least two big guys whose eyes are on the crowd.

In this photo, two persons are candidates for public office and two are not. The candidates wear their name tags on the right side so they are in the face of persons with whom the candidate shakes hands. The candidates are the author, running for re-election to the County Court at Law, and friend of the author Amalia Rodriguez Mendoza, running for District Clerk. Both won. The non-candidates are the author's late second wife, Donna Mobley Russell, and Cesar Chávez, who has just discovered the author's name tag, "Judge Steve Russell." He is saying, "That hippie who walked with me in the Valley is a judge?" © Alan Pogue. Used by Permission.

In Texas, there had been a strike in the melon fields in 1966–67. The litigation from that strike had finally ended in the U.S. Supreme Court in 1972. The Court upheld the wins for the farm workers based on unanimous fact-findings of a three-judge panel. Among the important facts were that the Texas Rangers took on suppressing the strike by violent means.

Among many other incidents, the three-judge trial court addressed the injuries of two farm workers who, according to testimony from the Texas Rangers, had bumped into each other trying to escape arrest:

"The following day two physicians examined Dimas and Rodriguez, and on June 6, 1967, Dimas was examined by a third doctor. Their reports reveal a very different picture...

"Dimas was hospitalized from June 2nd through June 6th. He suffered a brain concussion, multiple bruises on both sides of the neck and other bruises behind his left ear, on his left side, on the right side of his back, on his left forearm and left wrist. Dr. Casso testified that X-ray negatives revealed that Dimas had received a severe blow to the lower right portion of his back causing the spine to curve out of shape away from the impact point. Dimas also sustained a laceration which required four stitches to close.

"Rodriguez had cuts and bruises behind his right ear, bruises on his right elbow, on his right upper arm, on the right upper portion of his back and on his right jaw. His left little finger was broken and the nail was torn off.

"It is difficult indeed for this Court to visualize two grown men colliding with each other so as to cause such injuries."

In the earlier strike, there had also been gunplay by persons the Rangers made no serious attempt to disarm.

Knowing this, we who bodyguarded Chávez were sworn to his vow of nonviolence. If shooting started, our instructions were to throw him down and get on top of him—prepared to take the bullets. I had no problem with the vow of nonviolence, but I always thought that if an assassin didn't kill him, his bodyguards might. His bodyguards were always the two biggest guys known to the union who agreed to the rule of nonviolence. The man being protected came with a great deal of moral stature in a small physical package. As it happened, there was shooting before and after his visits, but no assassination attempts.

The year after my internship, a grower shot some farm workers on a picket line near the edge of his property. The local TV station sent a crew to the grower's home, and before he chased them off, he commented on the question whether he had been shooting at the workers on purpose or a warning shot was misdirected. "I didn't shoot *at* 'em," he asserted, "I *shot* 'em."

The shooting naturally stirred up the Austin UFW supporters, and we collected a bunch of food for the strikers and took it down there. The strikers called for a march to protest the violence and so I called up *The Daily Texan*, where I had worked under a previous editor, to offer a lift south to a *Texan* reporter.

I would have understood if the editor had told me it would be improper for a journalist to ride to the demonstration with people who intended to demonstrate. I did not agree but I would have understood.

The editor was friendly enough, but he told me his travel budget was stretched and he had to save the money for the forthcoming College World Series in Nebraska. He expected the Longhorns to be playing for the national championship. Would I like to publish an opinion piece when I got back?

I accepted his invitation but I was disappointed with his priorities.

The next year, 1976, when I ran for Justice of the Peace before my bar exam scores returned, *The Texan* endorsed my opponent. *The Rag*, put out by a new group of people I barely knew, endorsed me.

Two years later, when I met the minimum law practice requirement in the Austin City Charter, I was appointed a Municipal Court judge. *The Texan* editorialized that I was doing a good job when I engineered a sit down between the cops and students after some extreme celebration of football wins led to arrests. I did not feel I had done anything significant enough to deserve the editorial attaboy.

My view of *The Texan*, like *The Texan*'s view of me, had ups and downs. The differences came with electing the editor. It remains an excellent student newspaper, as student newspapers go, and always has great potential waiting to be tapped.

If I were a student, I would care more about the election for *Texan* editor than for the head of Student Government. This is not to claim that the UT Student Government—which has a budget and a bully pulpit—does not matter.

I cherish my time at *The Texan* but don't ask me to choose it over my time at *The Rag*. I did not exactly start a writing career with the Underground Press Syndicate, because I always felt in my bones that I was a writer no matter what other people said. I started a *publishing* career with the UPS.

I was useless as the teats on a boar hog if all the world was setting terrazzo. But every publication in every venue was more evidence that the world might find some use for me after all.

STEVE RUSSELL

~27~

CHEROKEE NAMES

In the economic circumstances of my childhood, I might have envied many things. I suppose I did, but there was nothing I wanted as much as a family of my own, to whom I would be a provider rather than a burden. After my grandfather died, I had a conversation with my grandmother in which she warned me that she was unlikely to live to see me graduate high school. I could not break the news that I did not expect to graduate high school, but I took her point.

My elderly grandparents did the best they could with their limited resources and the years they had left, but I lived in the shadow of the cold fact that they would be gone before I was educated and I would be alone, my only inheritance their constant reassurance that I was smart and I could make something of myself.

While that reassurance conflicted with virtually all of the feedback I got elsewhere, it turned out to be an inheritance of such value that I wanted to pass it on. Still do. That's why I choose to spend what my cancer diagnosis and sundry complications convinced me would be the last months of my life writing about how I managed my material and emotional needs. Both of those accomplishments seem improbable without the legacy from the elders named Russell.

In their honor, the name I wished to pass on when I got a family became "Russell." By the end of my Air Force hitch, I had decided I was unlikely to disgrace the name, and my Cherokee father was Cherokee only when convenient. He had taught me little besides the meaning of "useless as the teats on a boar hog." I carried nothing from him but the name Teehee and possibly a gene for schizophrenia.

I was aware that the Teehee family has a distinguished history within the Cherokee Nation. Family legend had it that I was a direct descendant of Houston Benge Teehee, who served in Tahlequah city government, Cherokee County government, Oklahoma state government, and most famously as Register of the U.S. Treasury. In that role, he signed the currency and the bonds sold to finance World War I.

My namesake was supposedly Ginatiyun Tihi, Stephen Teehee, who was Houston B's father. Ginatiyun served Cherokee tribal government in a number of capacities. I did not find out the principal role for which he was known until I was a judge poring over old issues of the *Cherokee Phoenix*. Ginatiyun Tihi—who I had known for serving in legislative and executive positions—was primarily remembered as a fair and impartial judge. In a time when much tribal business was done in English, Tihi stayed with Cherokee.

While it's an honor to be thought associated with such a man, he was not my namesake. According to my mother, Stephen Teehee was a living friend of the family when I was born, although *he* certainly might have been named after Ginatiyun Tihi. Houston B. Teehee is a collateral rather than a direct ancestor.

The family story about Houston B. did not hold up, but a look at the Cherokee section of the Dawes Rolls—the master rolls that determine eligibility for Cherokee Nation citizenship—shows more Russells than Teehees. While I am not related to the Cherokee Russells and I am related to the Teehees, being publicly called Russell would not imply I am unlikely to be Cherokee.

I went back to the lawyer who had gotten my disabilities of minority removed after I got my accident case settled in late 1967. As was typical of me, I had cut a deal with Pat Priest (representing my insurance company) when I was too young to enter a binding contract. Priest was an honest man (and he too would later become a Texas judge) but I had to get a court order saying I was qualified to do what I had already done.

After I got a judge's permission to take the insurance settlement from my accident, I hired the same lawyer to change my name. I never told him why and he never asked, because the only reason a judge could deny a name change is if the purpose is fraud.

When the order was signed, I was required to take it and a copy of the pleadings to my squadron commander so my military discharge would have the correct name on it. I peeked at the petition and found that the lawyer had attributed a reason to me: that the name Teehee had subjected me to ridicule. While that was true, it had nothing to do with why I would give up a fine old Cherokee name.

I first learned of that embellishment while I was waiting to see the officer who had taken over my squadron while I was in the hospital. When my turn came, I saluted and then shook hands with my new commander...Major Eugene Tehee. The spelling difference was not significant. He was Cherokee; I was embarrassed. He was very kind and did not discuss my petition.

I wanted my discharge papers to say Russell and the degree I hoped to earn to say Russell and the children I hoped to have to carry the name that had come to mean so much more to me than Teehee ever did.

The name Teehee had come from my biological father, with whom I had only two more interactions after my escape from Oregon. The first came at the beginning of my time at Wilford Hall USAF Hospital in December of 1966. My father in Oregon and my mother in Arkansas had been notified of my accident and that my condition was critical. It remained so for some time after the doctors deemed me stable enough to be moved from Brackenridge Hospital in Austin to Wilford Hall at Lackland AFB. The medical facilities at Bergstrom AFB in Austin were not adequate to care for me in my condition.

Both of my parents showed up. When my father came to my room I was unable to talk and I had tubes going into and out of my body. That I was living was a miracle of modern medicine. I don't remember what he said and I could say nothing. There was a point when I needed my airway cleared, a matter of dangling a tube down though the tracheotomy hole in my neck and turning on suction.

I thought it was pretty disgusting but so were a lot of things that were happening to me. Having an IV, having a catheter, being surrounded by mysterious electronic gear were all new experiences, leaving aside being naked in front of many strange women in circumstances that did not involve swimming or sex.

I pushed the call button to get a nurse to clear my airway and a nurse did not come running lickety-split. They had me on monitors at the nursing station and they knew it was not an emergency.

My father went ballistic. He stormed out of my room and I could hear him down the hall yelling at the nurses. I was mortified. I was dependent on the nurses for everything and I thought their work was first-rate. Even if that were not the case, making enemies on the nursing staff was the last thing I needed.

I asked for a note pad and wrote on it that I wanted him to leave and not come back. For that one time, he honored my wishes.

Two years later, I was managing the dorm on top of the University Y and wondering where I would get the money to enroll in the fall semester. I got a letter addressed to me at "The University of Texas." It had miraculously gotten forwarded. My mother must have told him I was at UT.

I sold enough of my possessions to pay tuition and fees for the summer, but the fall semester was still a problem. My father's letter came at a bad time, just as I was colliding with financial reality.

He did not apologize for terrorizing me seven years earlier. He did not apologize for roaring into the hospital where I was at death's door and starting fights with the medical personnel on whom I was completely dependent for everything from being fed to having my butt wiped.

It would have been touching if he had apologized for not leaving me the broken accordion he promised when I was 4 or 5 years old. Every interaction I had with him in my entire lifetime was stacked up with grievances.

By return mail, I unloaded on him. For the first time in my life, he had some encouraging words for something important to me, getting a university education.

"No thanks to you!"

File that remark under tacky but true. I was in a financial bind. He was not the only member of my family who had not helped but the others had conducted themselves as family in other ways. I put his letter in the round file and forgot about it instantly.

Within two weeks, I was reminded. I got another letter with his return address. I opened it and unfolded the piece of paper it contained. The paper was blank, but folded inside were two $1 bills.

I choose to believe his meaning was literal, because irony was not anything I would ever expect from him. It made me briefly feel sorry for him that he was so broke at his age. He would have been about 42, and I expect he did not volunteer to be broke like I had. He had five kids, Bonnie having been born a year after my escape, to whom he owed a duty of support; I am informed that the two bucks arrived after Barbara overcame her beliefs about divorce and made her dash for freedom.

It was too much trouble to send $2 back, so in honor of my biological father's contribution to my education, I had a "steak dinner." There was a place on the Drag called the G & M Steakhouse where, for a buck and a quarter, you could get a "chopped steak" (a glorified hamburger), a baked potato, a piece of Texas toast, and a "salad" that consisted of nothing but iceberg lettuce with a glop of dressing. It was a measure of my poverty at the time that I considered G & M a treat, only rarely indulged.

While I wanted nothing to do with my father, my suspicions of a genetic cause of his behavior had gotten deeper. If that is correct, then he was ill and the harm he did was a product of his illness. I understand that on an intellectual level, but I can't forget and the sheer volume of evil makes it hard to forgive.

I know now that his violence continued through another marriage after Barbara to a woman who was by all accounts sweet and protective of him. He disappeared in the winter of 1985; his body surfaced in the Willamette River in spring of 1986. There was a report of somebody taking a dive off one of the bridges in Portland about the time he went missing. I've often wondered if it was one I considered doing the same from when I felt trapped in Oregon. That would be a bitter irony.

By the time I learned what became of my father over a year after his body was found, I had extensive experience in mental health commitment cases, first representing persons resisting being committed and then hearing those cases as a judge. Clifford Teehee had been riding what we called the "commitment carousel."

A person mentally ill enough to be a danger to himself or others had to be institutionalized by court order. While he is locked up, the psychiatrists try various medications at various dosages until they find a sweet spot where his destructive impulses are under control but his mind is clear enough to function outside the lockup.

This works for a while, but as the patient feels better over time, he decides that, since he feels normal, he *is* normal, and does not need psychotropic medication. He quits taking his meds and his condition deteriorates until, once more, he poses a danger to himself or others, gets picked up by the police, and gets another ticket to ride the commitment carousel from a judge.

By the time my father took a header into the Willamette River, he had been riding the commitment carousel for many years. I'm guessing he just got tired. By that time, I had seen plenty of untimely deaths and I will never be inured to the sadness. His death was no exception, but I did not feel it as I felt

248

the natural death of my grandfather, who had taken up the role my father abandoned.

Clifford Wayne Teehee certainly did not ask to be schizophrenic. All of his offspring have an interest in how he got that way, because the research suggests there is a genetic component. He sired four sons and two daughters. One of the daughters, Bonnie, was a beautiful young woman who appeared to be headed for a modeling career...had she not been schizophrenic. Bonnie died young of cancer and never had a chance to become a regular rider on the commitment carousel.

The only other evidence I have for a Teehee schizophrenia gene dates from September 4, 1901, at Ft. Gibson, Indian Territory. My great-great grandfather Lee Teehee came to the Dawes Commission to claim his piece of the Cherokee Reservation. A commissioner asked if he was the man listed as "Lee Tehee" on the Prison Roll in the Tahlequah District, 1896. He agreed that was him.

Lee Teehee, fullblood Cherokee, author's great-great-grandfather. Family photo acquired at Teehee family reunion.

He told the commission that his children were being taken care of by a woman named Tennessee Carnes. He was at the time married to a white woman named Virgie. At first, Lee claimed that Lucy Barber, his deceased Cherokee first wife, was the mother of all of his children.

On cross-examination, it came out that Lucy was not the mother of all his children (although she is the mother of my great-grandfather, Henry). Lee had another wife who slipped his mind, a white woman named Clarinda Brannenberg, who was the mother of one of his children. Lee also carried the Teehee smartass gene:

Q: Were you ever divorced from Lucy Barber?
A: No, sir.

Q: You were married to her, weren't you?
A: Yes. I guess we are divorced now; she is dead.

Q: Did you live with her till she died?
A: No, I said another man was living with her.

Q: Well, you and her just separated?
A: Yes, sir.

Q: And then you married this Brannenberg woman?
A: Yes, sir.

Q: But you were never divorced from Lucy?
A: No, didn't need any divorce them days.

The things that leap out from Lee Teehee's testimony—because of what I know of my father's life—is that he got himself incarcerated and that he had many relationships with women but none appeared to last long.

Putting all the evidence together, I was not sure it would be wise of me to pass on all of my genetic material to innocent babies. That's what my brain said. My emotions still told me I wanted a family. As my life unfolded, the dilemma resolved itself. In my personal life as well as my professional life, I cannot deny the role of luck.

The personal and the professional always proceeded on parallel tracks. Sometimes one did better than the other, and that imbalance limited my productivity. Born heterosexual, I needed a woman to be my partner, and my early prospects of finding one were as bleak as my early education.

The recap is not pretty. I never had a serious girlfriend in Bristow or Odessa. In Beaverton, I met Tori Motte and she was delightful...until the day she disappeared from Milwaukee.

At the time Tori disappeared, I was not seeing anyone else. It would not have occurred to me to see anyone else. She was going to have her own radio show and I was going to write the great American novel. We never discussed marriage, but I expected we would be shacked up while we both became rich and famous.

When that bubble burst, I settled back into my first normal dating behavior since the accident destroyed my face in 1966. By the middle of 1968, I had false teeth and the beard to cover up the angry red scars. I did not look like I had before the accident, but I no longer felt like every day was Halloween.

TO MARRY FOR MONEY

My next serious personal relationship—after Tori Motte disappeared and my attempt to marry Kitty Lyons ran aground on the rock of her mother's opposition—happened to me when I wasn't looking. I had my head down and my nose firmly pressed on the academic grindstone when I found a romantic pairing that would eventually resolve the stack pass problem as one of many side benefits.

In the second summer session of 1970, I met Betty Ann White in a course called Psychological Foundations of Secondary Education. She was a working class girl from Ft. Worth, exactly my age, and I took her to be much smarter than I. Later, I learned that we also had in common the Professor Richard Zaner fan club.

She lived in a room with a private bath on 11th Street, a couple of blocks from the Texas Capitol. I began spending so much time in that room after the Wonsley house failed that it made sense to move in with her. Pooling our resources made it two hands to two mouths.

How poor were we? Nothing like we were in my childhood. We always had something to eat. We even briefly had two functional cars, hers a Mercury Comet named Ingmar—after Bergman—and mine a Ford Falcon named Blue, partially for the color but also in the hope he would be faithful as an old bluetick coonhound, something accomplished only with some parts off Ingmar.

I found Betty's habit of not paying the phone bill on time every month un-nerving, but she knew the phone company's habits and the service was never cut.

When we had shacked up long enough to know that we got along well, I mentioned to her that my GI Bill would pay a little bit more if we were married. After some decidedly unromantic discussion, I bought a marriage license and we set out for the Student Health Center, where she knew a counselor who could marry us.

We began with that cold mercenary motive to increase our income, since we were living together anyway. But before we got there, we were holding hands and declaring our feelings for each other.

It was a bit ironic that my first brush with marriage had involved a Jack Catholic—meaning one who maintains the cultural trappings of Catholicism without internalizing all the outlandish beliefs. That is, they don't believe the Pope is infallible when speaking *ex cathedra* in matters of faith and morals or that the only way to approach God is though the offices of the "one true Church" and let's not get started on whether transubstantiation is symbolic cannibalism or real cannibalism. If you narrowed Church doctrine down to birth control, most Catholics have parted company, so for most folks, "Jack Catholic" is a matter of degree.

The irony is that I no longer had a near miss. Betty Ann White had been a nun, but she had been kicked out of the convent, she said, over theological differences. After we got together, she started taking birth control pills, but that did not separate her from most Catholics.

We got in our mailbox *National Catholic Reporter*, an organ of the liberal wing of the Catholic Church. Reading NCR and interrogating Betty disabused me of a lot of stereotypes that I had somehow clung to even after reading Pope John XXIII during my time in the USAF hospital and having my near marriage experience with Kitty Lyons.

Betty and I each had a quality possession that we hung on to through being impoverished students. For me, it was a Goya guitar, an instrument much finer than my playing ever deserved. For her, it was a Leica camera, with which she became a regular contributor of photos to *The Rag*.

She was also a talented writer, but I only know that because I was married to her and observed it over time. Unlike me, she sometimes got blocked. I watched her suffer through the block and stack up incomplete grades because of papers not turned in, but I was not equipped to help her then as I could now. I did not understand the affliction and could only sympathize. With her blocking problem, Betty could only watch me move from a weekly to *The Daily Texan*. Photography remained her primary creative outlet.

She backed me up in my many purposeful trips to jail, but the only one she took was not on purpose. The day of the dedication of the LBJ Library on the UT campus in May of 1971, there was a law enforcement presence the likes of which we had never seen. Also, the university went into federal court in an untimely manner and got a judge to sign an injunction forbidding most activities by those thought to be political ringleaders. Nothing was to pull attention from the planned LBJ worshipping.

I was flattered to be considered one of the ringleaders and therefore worth suing but I did not need a lawyer to tell me the injunction was an unconstitutional piece of nonsense. I would have needed a lawyer to tell me that the university timed the application to prevent a full hearing. They scooted in for a temporary order claiming an emergency, which, if it existed, was of their making. I cannot speak for others, but the impact of this charade on my conduct was zero.

May 22, 1971 was a lively day. I gathered up what I had of my military uniform and marched in formation with the other veterans up to the barricades around the library, where we asked to speak to the ex-president or the current president, Richard

Nixon, who was also attending. Denied that, we chucked our military decorations over the police lines, symbolically returning them to LBJ. My dinky set of chest ribbons was not impressive, but there were some purple hearts and bronze stars, and the throwing took long enough to make great theatre.

After that, I spent the day with everybody else, running around the police lines looking for a way in while the supervisors directed squads of officers in riot gear hither and yon to stay between us and the bigwigs. Had we gotten in, we only planned to have a debate about the war. I was present at most of the uber-secret planning meetings and most of the discussion was about how to generate enough noise to make the attendees pucker and clutch their pearls.

The festivities had pretty well wound down when a group of us repaired to a pizza joint on the first floor of a big parking garage across the street from a dormitory that was repurposed to house some of the lesser dignitaries. We saw a phalanx of police run by the front window and Betty took her camera and followed to see what was going on. I sat tight and waited for the pizza until somebody ran in and told me my wife had gotten arrested.

I got outside in time for her to shout me the short version, that she was being arrested for photographing police misconduct (expressed in more colorful language). As they were loading her on one of the busses on the scene for extra-large paddy wagons and she and I were shouting back and forth, a guy came up to me dressed a bit more formally than anybody else and handed me his card. He told me that he saw the whole thing and if I would notify him of her trial date, he would return to Austin at his own expense to testify.

I thanked the Good Samaritan, stuffed his card in my shirt pocket, and hurried off to see about arranging bail for Betty. I don't remember when I got around to looking at it, but Betty was glad to see she had a willing eyewitness in Bill Moyers, who was an invited guest because of his role as White House Press Secretary from 1965 to 1967.

Betty's story was that she was photographing an officer applying his club to a boy who had either done nothing at all or, at any rate, was helpless at the time. He interrupted the beating to tell another officer to arrest her. The charge was assaulting a police officer, and the officer's story was that she had whacked him in the chest with her camera.

Leaving aside our relationship, I knew that could not have happened because I had seen Betty get knocked to the ground at a demonstration and protect her precious Leica with her own body as she went down. There was no way she would use it to hit somebody.

She did go to trial, but we did not need our celebrity witness. A photographer came forward who had the entire incident on Super 8 film from a vantage point on the second floor of the parking garage. The officer who claimed to have been assaulted with a Leica told his lie. The arresting officer lied for his fellow officer.

Then we showed the judge a movie of the entire event. He had the beating before Betty came into the frame and there was daylight between her and the officer when he gestured toward her with his club and the other officer arrested her. Years later, both of those officers appeared in my court, and I tried my best to disregard my knowledge of their perjury.

It was around this time that we quit paying the telephone service excise tax. Congress had enacted it to fund the Spanish-American War but never got around to repealing it, so it was repurposed to fund the Vietnam War. The amounts of money were trivial, but the IRS had to chase down tax resistance when it had political motivations.

We got over a year reprieve when the postal service mistakenly delivered a card meant for them to our mailbox asking Betty's whereabouts. She checked the box that said "deceased," and that threw them off the scent for a while, but there came a time when the IRS took custody of her entire paycheck. She was working full time then and I was getting part-time gigs, so there was no way we could hold out.

She went to the IRS office in Austin and forked over the sum they demanded...in pennies, except for thirty dimes—thirty pieces of silver. The agent counted out the legal tender and growled that she was a penny short. She whipped out a news magazine cover from reports in fall of 1976 that Lt. William Calley's conviction had been reinstated on appeal. Litigation over the My Lai Massacre had been proceeding for seven years and the last report in 1976 inspired Betty to tape the last penny over Lt. Calley's hat brass. The IRS agent did not share my admiration for her theatrical sensibility.

Betty and I were compatible politically and, I thought, sexually. In particular, there was a time when I was in the Rio Grande Valley working for the farm workers and we were apart for three weeks when she came down to visit. We headed for the bedroom and there was no foreplay whatsoever—the lubrication was practically running down her leg. I would have reason besides the fond memory to recall this later.

Just after I graduated law school but before I got my bar scores back, my younger half-brother Paul had a son. I was unaware that he had gotten married. Our mother called and suggested that Paul and his wife were not capable of taking care of a baby.

Betty and I went to San Antonio and found an underweight baby with a dirty diaper in a crib with older dirty diapers and a nasty cigarette burn on his leg. We visited with Child Welfare, which already had an open file, and were informed that their plan was to teach Paul and his wife Gloria how to be parents so we should butt out.

We didn't have a lot of choice but to butt out while they tried.

Some months later—luckily, after I had passed the bar—I got a call from Child Welfare, and a different person than we had spoken to before had gotten a lot warmer toward the idea of getting a court involved. Red hot, in fact. Social workers were prepared to sign affidavits about imminent danger based on personal knowledge and when we got there they even had an assistant district attorney who had the pleading forms on one of those newfangled word processors.

I had to get the filing fee from my mother, but with a lot of help we were soon at the Bexar County Courthouse to prevail upon Judge Franklin Spears to sign an emergency order granting Betty and me temporary custody.

It was getting late when we located the baby at the home of Gloria's parents. We hoped they would comply with the order because it would have been a miserable time to find a deputy. They complied by handing us the baby with a wet diaper and little else.

We stopped at a store on the way out of town to purchase some diapers, some formula for the baby we had been warned was lactose intolerant, and something for his nasty diaper rash. We had become parents with little warning, and I quickly came to see the value in a nine-month glide path to parental status.

Betty and I were both working full time but I had more flexibility than she did, so the first day I took the baby to work in an ice chest. My co-workers and hers collected all kinds of baby paraphernalia for us. I was quickly bringing him to work in a porta-crib rather than an ice chest.

That did not solve my feeling of incompetence. I remember Paul crying once. I checked his diaper, but it was dry. I offered him a bottle, but he was not hungry. I was holding him close muttering something like, "Nice baby, please tell me what you want," when Bobby Nelson, an experienced lawyer and also an experienced mother, came in and took him. He quieted right down in her arms. I felt like she knew the secret handshake and I did not.

When we were able to find childcare, I was back and forth to San Antonio stalking evidence. Paul and Gloria had been using the baby as a meal ticket, hitting up churches for money and food. None of the ministers I interviewed would help. I subpoenaed one anyway and he disregarded the subpoena.

I was able to prove though social workers that Paul and Gloria believed spanking was appropriate discipline for a child less than 6 months old even when the only offense was crying. I was able to show that another social worker brought them a case of baby food and within days the parents had eaten it.

I visited the clinic where a doctor had turned in a suspected child abuse report. Waiting in Dr. Fernando Guerra's office, I was facing a sign behind his desk suggesting, "The next time you get sick, call a lawyer." When he walked in and saw the look on my face, he laughed and told me his brother was a lawyer. I'm not sure if that made it better or worse, but he gave me an affidavit and assured me he would testify consistent with the affidavit if I subpoenaed him.

The senior partner in the civil rights law firm where I had worked as a clerk during law school and as an associate after I lost my run for Justice of the Peace, Jim Simons, went with us to San Antonio to try the lawsuit to terminate parental rights. I had prepared the case well, including a take-off sheet for Jim on each witness, but I was petrified, probably too scared to be a good advocate.

I had a couple of social workers, the doctor, and the minister if he answered the subpoena, and I intended to put Paul and Gloria on the stand to explain things to the judge. When we attempted to call the birth parents as hostile witnesses, the judge summoned us to the bench and admonished Jim and me not to waste his time because their mental limitations were obvious. That was not why we called them, but when the trial judge tells you to stop, you stop. Also, it deterred their lawyer from trying to call them again.

During the trial, I developed the intent to use the minister no-show to give Jim and me some breathing space if things seemed to be going south. I would request a writ of attachment for the missing witness and that would give us some time while the deputy tried to serve it. My intent never came to fruition because the wind from the bench seemed to be blowing our way.

We won, and I could breathe again, because Betty had told me that if we lost, she was going to take the baby and disappear. I had become attached to the baby, who the birth parents had named Paul. We decided Paul was a perfectly fine name, but he had no middle name. I had intended to call him Paul César—

after César Chávez. When it came time to do the adoption in Austin, I backed off the middle name so as not to saddle a baby with my politics.

I had also become attached to Betty, far beyond what might have been predicted from the way our marriage started. There came a time when a doctor advised she had been on birth control pills too long. How, she wanted to know, would I feel about a vasectomy?

I did not think about being with anyone other than Betty, and so I wanted to do it to protect her. She made it clear she did not want to be pregnant, then or ever. I was traumatized when I got thrown in the deep end with Paul and I could not imagine having another child. Finally, I had begun to get wind of my biological father's further misadventures with women—attracting them easily and then abusing them—and I began to wonder if I might carry a gene related to his mental health issues.

I did make one tiny hedge. I got the kind of operation where they inserted a little spigot that could be opened should I want a reversal. There were mirrors set up in the operating room so I could watch my delicate parts being sliced open. I do not recommend it for the entertainment value, but as long as they were in there anyway, I wanted to see what was going on. I was never tempted to reverse my vasectomy, but some of my reasons for getting it held up better than others.

Paul had come into our lives in 1975, during the time I was running my first electoral campaign in the Democratic Party primary for justice of the peace in the precinct centered around the University of Texas. The race had seemed a slam dunk until Frank Ivy, the students' attorney, got in. It also did not hurt his chances that he outspent me 2:1.

I spent most of the campaign going door to door with Paul on my back in a baby packer. I'm sure some people thought I was displaying the baby for political ends but the truth was Betty had to work and I had to have Paul with me. We could not afford any alternative.

Perhaps my most foolish political decision that year was to refuse to take campaign contributions in excess of $50. Part of the reason it was foolish was nobody cared and part of it was my choice of the limit came from my background. To me, $50 was a serious sum. At the time, the lawyers who were most likely to care about judge races were billing their time at $150 an hour.

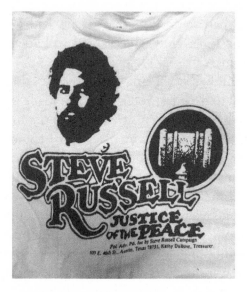

Justice of the Peace campaign T-shirt, 1975. The author's picture came from his column in The Daily Texan—note the United Farm Workers button above the "V." From the collection of Gerilyn Farb Gordon. Used by permission.

I could not afford polling, but I was able to get a question piggybacked on a poll by somebody who could. It showed I was going to lose. This set me to moping, but my campaign manager, Alan Hirst, threatened bodily harm if I did not get my ass back out there knocking on doors. One of my supporters and an old friend, Petra Carey, said that I was not going to lose, but if I did, she would take me to bed as a consolation prize, as long as Betty would not be offended.

I had a conversation about monogamy with Betty back before we even thought about marriage. I thought sexual monogamy was a dumb idea and said so. She did not disagree, and so I told Petra I had no reason to think Betty would be offended.

262

I lost the election, 53% to 47%, which was not bad considering I had filed before my bar scores came back and my opponent had been practicing law for ten years and was not only the students' attorney but was endorsed by *The Daily Texan*. Hirst was right. By continuing to knock on those doors, I had made it close enough that the loss did not mean I could never appear on a ballot again as a serious candidate.

There had always been a lot of sexual tension between Petra and me. It was months later when she delivered my consolation prize on a rainy afternoon. It was delightful but she made it clear it was only once.

When Betty found out—which was no great trick when neither participant was hiding it—she *was* offended. She felt burned and I felt burned that she felt burned. I wanted to stay with her enough that if she was, from my point of view, changing the rules, I would agree to the new rules no matter how goofy I thought they were.

When I lost the election, I had been working for the most visible civil rights law firm in Austin, (Jim) Simons, (Cam) Cunningham, (Brady) Coleman, (Bobby) Nelson, and (John) Howard. They let me stay on as an associate.

Betty should have graduated from UT about the same time I did in 1972, but she had three incompletes in courses where she owed term papers. When she moved enough incompletes to finish her undergraduate degree, she applied to UT law and was accepted. I had finished law school by the time she was in a position to start.

She had worked full time to put me though law school while I had continued with part-time gigs—*The Daily Texan*, grading assistant to a government professor, research assistant to a law professor, law clerk. When she started law school, my goal was to spare her all that part-time work. The law school recommends that students refrain from working at least for the first year, but I could not swing that.

Law school does require more attention than undergraduate school, but Betty flat disappeared, and I was effectively a single dad. That was OK with me. I would have done the same if I could have. I kept my willful blinders on as long as I could, but the affair she was having was just a couple of houses down and the object of her affections was not a law student so the old studying ruse would not work.

By the time we talked about it, she was ready to revise what she had told me about why she got kicked out of the convent. The new story was that she had been caught in *flagrante* with another nun. She has maintained from the time of that conversation that she is gay and was trying to deny it. She said she had not lied about the convent—she had "forgotten," an amnesia brought on by her efforts at denial.

I have chosen to believe her because we had a child to raise and I could see nothing valuable in starting a fight by claiming she lied. I also kept to myself my opinion that she is bisexual, in spite of leaving me for a same-sex relationship. In a way, she proved my point by continuing to have sex with me for months.

During one of those assignations, I was complaining out loud about ever finding another partner. I had by that time become an associate judge on the Austin Municipal Court, and she replied that the black robe would be a splendid aphrodisiac. It was slow happening, but I was able to date again. It was over a year before I got around to filing for divorce because I still didn't want one and I did not care if she had a girlfriend.

I got a good deal in the property settlement. She agreed that I needed the house because I was taking care of Paul, and the house was our only asset. The cash payments I was making to her became compensation for her interest in the house, but they were payments I would have made anyway because in my mind I owed her the same support during law school she had provided me. I did not make enough money to make the house payments, pay her for her half, and cover her law school costs, so she let me slide with two of the three.

Divorce, even a friendly divorce like mine, is a terrible experience I do not recommend. As a lawyer, I've watched unfriendly divorces go by, ugly dances with the darkest devils that can subsist on bile.

Either as a practicing lawyer or as a judge, I would much rather deal with a criminal docket than a divorce docket. Would you rather deal with bad people at their best or good people at their worst?

When I finally overcame my reluctance, Betty Ann White and I got a divorce without showing each other our worst sides.

STEVE RUSSELL

~29~

HURRICANE DONNA

The women who worked on *The Rag* were so talented and so smart and so willing to assume the same of me that I had powerful motivation not to make a fool of myself. Perhaps that was the reason the lady who first captured my attention was all of 5 years old.

A tiny rug rat would often show up on layout night and hang around to make conversation with the adults until she got too tired or the adults got too tiresome and she would fall asleep on one of the old overstuffed chairs.

The Rag's unofficial mascot was named Mary Katherine and I quickly learned that her mother, Donna Mobley, was one of those working far beneath her abilities when she came in to do typing and layout.

When I arrived in 1969 to become a freshman at the University of Texas, I still believed "this is men's work and that is women's work," but nobody tagged me for that sexist attitude because I was a good typist and did not mind typing. I never became skilled at layout, but people did their best to teach me. I just wanted to be a newspaper guy and I was willing to start anywhere.

How late we worked depended on who showed up and how much copy got changed at the last minute for legitimate reasons. There was a continuing problem with illegitimate reasons— "midnight edits"—where there would be a big argument during the copy meeting about some bit of esoterica and the loser would sneak in at some point and change the outcome by replacing a word or a sentence or at most a paragraph, wiping out the result of the argument with a bit of rubber cement.

The change would blend in with all the corrections made in the same manner. At the next copy meeting, the ostensible winner would raise a stink, but not a very big one. There was an unspoken assumption that if you did not want to be victimized by a midnight edit, you needed to put the paper to bed yourself.

The paper usually went to bed too late for Mary Katherine, and it would be necessary to carry her downstairs and put her in a car to go home. Donna must have had a car because this was Texas, but I do not remember one.

I became the usual ride, and it was a good thing there were no car seat requirements for transporting rug rats in those days. Donna would get in my Karmann Ghia on the passenger side, usually with the top down to make the operation easier when I put the still sleeping Mary Katherine in her lap.

When we arrived at their home, the drill reversed. I would peel Mary Katherine off her mother and carry her to the door. More often than not, I would come in to put her to bed and Donna and I would stay up a while longer. I was dazzled by Donna's intellect, even in the context of *The Rag*, where it seemed like half of the women were graduate students.

I came to learn that the woman taking up with the dropout had been the 1959 valedictorian at La Marque High School, a public school of excellent repute. Her husband, Mary Katherine's father, had taken himself out of the picture for reasons unclear to me then. The more I hung out with Donna and Mary Katherine, the crazier I took Jim Mobley to be, although I never met him.

Because sex did not complicate relationships in the university community the way it had everywhere else I had lived, Donna and I moved along toward real intimacy, or so I thought. I quickly came to view Kitty Lyons as a girl and Donna Mobley as a woman, with Mary Katherine as a major fringe benefit of the relationship.

I saw the Tori Motte movie again when Donna didn't show up either at the copy meeting or for layout. Some mutual friends came in late and solved the mystery for me. Donna had gone back to her husband. Out of state.

No explanation, although I suppose she didn't owe me one. But no goodbye, no chance to find Mary Katherine a little gift or ride her on my back one more time. They were both just gone, and I was left replaying everything in my mind over and over.

It was more than a dozen years before we reconnected and immediately fell into a conversation that felt like we had been together just the day before. But I had to ask her.

"Why?"

"I did it for Mary Katherine."

"But Mary Katherine and I were big buddies."

"She didn't need a buddy. She needed a father."

There was not much I could say to that then or at the time Donna left. I had not seen a lot of role models for parenting. Then there was the additional detail that when Donna and I first met, I had just taken the students' vow of poverty.

If we had merged our fortunes, I would have considered making a living to be my responsibility. I could have done it, but only with an about face back into data processing, leaving the promised land of a great university.

Donna and I had working class origins in common. Her father, Wesley Harris, was a union man who risked his health every day in one of the many chemical plants in the Texas City-La Marque area, where the air eats the paint off your car while you wonder what it's doing to your lungs. We were both first generation college students and we both cut unlikely swaths through our respective careers.

Those careers developed separately, and hers was more varied. I stayed in Austin and pursued the law. She followed Jim first to California and then to New York.

Landing an organizing job with the Amalgamated Clothing and Textile Workers, AFL-CIO, Donna was privileged to attend the Highlander Folk School, by then known as the Highlander Research and Education Center after the state of Tennessee shut down the original incarnation because of Highlander's role in the civil rights movement.

In the early '60s, you could see billboards all over Texas with a picture of Martin Luther King, Jr. seated at a school type of desk and captioned "Martin Luther King at Communist Training School." The billboards were funded by the John Birch Society, intellectual forebears of the Tea Party, with seed money out of the same deep pockets. One of the founding members was Fred Koch, father of Charles and David Koch, the infamous "Koch Brothers" who bankroll so much contemporary right-wing politics.

Highlander was certainly a training school for organizers, and the fact that it would not—like the mainstream civil rights movement would not—expose and expel anybody with Communist sympathies was enough to earn the label in the eyes of the Birchers. The picture on the billboards was taken at Highlander Folk School, a seedbed of union and civil rights organizing and the birthplace of the version of "We Shall Overcome" that became a civil rights anthem pulled together from different strands of old spirituals.

Donna's training at Highlander related to her stint as organizer for the union she called "the Amalgamated" all over the Deep South. The fictional character that won an Oscar for Sally Field as _Norma Rae_ was based on the true story of Crystal Lee Sutton, but that was exactly the kind of work Donna did and I've called that part of her life her _Norma Rae_ period to express my pride.

Her organizing experiences led to a job teaching trade union women's studies courses at Cornell University's State School of Industrial and Labor Relations from 1975 to 1977 in spite of having never graduated from the University of Texas. This parallels my own work on many dissertation committees when I had no PhD of my own.

From 1969–1978, Donna went on to several editing gigs in New York City publishing, but her broken marriage never did heal. She told me of nights when Jim was drunk and violent and she rode the subway all night with Mary Katherine to avoid being beaten. This was hard news for me after her judgment that I lacked the skills to be a husband and father when we first met. How much skill does it take, I had to ask myself, to know that a man is not supposed to hit any woman—but particularly the mother of his child?

During her time in New York, Donna underwent a "medical bankruptcy," when she had an infection in her gall bladder that almost killed her and she lacked the funds to pay the doctors and the hospital.

After she recovered her health, if not her credit rating, she was a volunteer on the 1976 presidential campaign of former Oklahoma Sen. Fred Harris, a campaign managed by our mutual friend Jim Hightower. While she was working for Harris in New York, I was working for Harris in Texas. I admired Harris for refusing to dance with the oil companies that were accustomed to getting whatever they wanted from Oklahoma politicians, but I must admit that the prospect of having a Comanche First Lady, LaDonna Harris, was exciting to me as well.

Harris barnstormed the country in a Winnebago with a loudspeaker on top blasting "This Land is Your Land," the Woody Guthrie song I always thought should be the national anthem because, unlike the anthem we have, it's singable by amateurs. When he had to throw in the towel, Harris famously remarked that his campaign for "the little people" failed because they were too little to reach the levers on the voting machines.

About five years later, Donna and I would reconnect at an Austin fundraiser for Jim Hightower, who was making a successful run for Texas Agriculture Commissioner in the 1982 election. I had been single for a couple of years. I was drinking beer at a Hightower gathering in an Austin's Pease Park when I looked up and there she was...almost fifteen years fell away instantly.

When Donna returned to Austin to head Common Cause of Texas, I was an Austin Municipal Court judge, a position that requires two years of law practice. At the time she left, I had no thought of law school. Her return, she said, was also about Mary

Katherine. Donna was concerned that Mary was more interested in being a street musician than in high school. Leaving aside that busking was not a promising career choice, there were more unsavory things on the streets of New York that were best avoided by a return to Texas.

I ventured that since I had become a judge without finishing high school, I couldn't say much to Mary Katherine about dropping out. Donna was already resigned to that and was satisfied that Mary had taken and passed the GED test at age 16—even younger than I had passed it.

New York had taken something out of Donna besides her gall bladder. I could not deny that the surgeon had done a sloppy job of closing her incision, but she was so reluctant to take off her clothes that I thought I had been demoted from lover to acquaintance—that would certainly be up to her but the signals she was sending were otherwise positive.

After we got past that, she demonstrated that she absolutely intended to control the pace of the relationship when she told me marriage was not an option, at least not anytime soon. Still, when the lease was up on her apartment in 1984, she moved in with me, after putting a couple of window air conditioning units on her credit card. I've been an air conditioning wimp ever since Donna did that, but at the time the significance of that expenditure to me was that her reluctance to discuss marriage was not about money.

I never came to understand what her problem was with marriage, but we stayed together from the time she moved in to the end of her life eleven years later. Soon after we got together, we moved up from my little two-bedroom house to another one in the same East Austin neighborhood with three bedrooms, two living areas, a fireplace, and a deck overlooking a creek. The house was big enough that daughter Mary and son Paul could both live with us at once in their own rooms. I never imagined in my life I would live in such a grand place, and we bought it jointly, using both our incomes to qualify for the loan. We were still not married and we were both careful not to say we were, in order to avoid common law marriage.

Son Paul perched over author's shoulder in the courtroom, 1985.
Photo © Suzanne Chesner. Used by permission.

Donna started out running Common Cause of Texas and then had one position after another of statewide import. I moved from the Austin Municipal Court to the Travis County Court at Law. In many of the political functions we attended in Austin, she was known and I was not. The "statewides" in a state the size of Texas were swimming in a bigger pond than county or city politicians. By the time I was Donna's date to her 25th La Marque High School Reunion in 1984, I was used to being Mr. Donna Mobley.

Donna's first move from Common Cause was to direct the Public Servant Standards of Conduct Advisory Commission. The Speaker of the Texas House of Representatives, Billy Wayne Clayton, had gotten swept up by the FBI in one of the Brilab ("bribery-labor") sting operations.

The indictment was for bribery, fraud, and racketeering. The government claimed that the Speaker had agreed to reopen bidding on an insurance contract in return for $5,000 cash down and another $600,000 to follow later from a labor leader who was acting on behalf of a government agent who claimed to work for Prudential Insurance without, it turned out, Prudential's knowledge.

Clayton accepted the $5,000 in cash, put it in an envelope, and stuck the envelope in a credenza in his office, where, he said, it slipped his mind and so he did not report it as a campaign contribution. It probably says something about politics in Texas that thousands of dollars in cash can be so common as to not stick in an office holder's mind, but it may say even more that a jury bought the absentmindedness story and acquitted Speaker Clayton of all charges in 1980.

The Public Servant Standards of Conduct Advisory Commission was Billy Wayne Clayton's brainchild, an interim study of governmental ethics to the end of serving the public while cleaning up the Speaker's reputation. The project would require a director whose ethics were above reproach, and that was what led Clayton to make an offer to poach Donna from Common Cause of Texas.

Donna and I had several long conversations about whether to accept Clayton's stated goals at face value and therefore accept his offer. In addition to the matter of Clayton's sincerity about providing the necessary resources, there was the question whether Donna was being asked to produce a report that would produce a few headlines but no new laws.

The project depended on the Speaker's good faith, and Donna knew him better than I did. She decided to trust him and take the job, which was by its nature temporary.

THE WORST NIGHT OF MY LIFE

I enrolled in graduate school at the University of Nevada-Reno. The program gave me credit for the introduction to being a judge I had already taken, provided I could pass an essay exam on the latest version of the course. After that, the classes were spread out and the only concession to judges having full-time jobs was that the classes met every day instead of two or three times a week. Donna and I drove to Reno for the Fall semester of 1988, the Spring semester of 1989, and the Summer sessions of 1989 and 1990. We made the drive so many times, we spoke of it in terms of the southern route (I-10 through El Paso) or the northern route (I-40 through Albuquerque). She began working on a book about the Donner Party, the pioneers who got snowed in crossing the Sierra Nevadas in 1846 and famously resorted to cannibalism.

Her book was a fictional speculation on the fate of Tamsen Donner, who disappeared without a trace. Tamsen was the wife of family patriarch George Donner, and she declined to leave with one of the last rescue parties because George was dying from an infected wound. She would not leave him to face his fate alone.

The summer of 1991, we headed for Reno early to have time to trace the path of the Donner Party, from George Donner's farm in Illinois to the place where the wagon trains organized themselves in Independence, Missouri, and across the Great

Plains to Ft. Bridger, Wyoming, where the pioneers took the fateful "short cut" south through the Wasatch Mountains and across the Great Salt Desert.

After all of that, the Truckee Meadows—later to become the site of Reno—was a paradise of sweet water and tall grass for the animals. Lingering too long in paradise, the pioneers did not top the Sierras before the first snowstorm. The rest is brutal and gruesome history.

My desire to have a professional life and a personal life firing on all cylinders together was closer to realization than I could ever have imagined. The kids were a challenge, but I don't know anyone who raised preteens and teens with no problems. Looking back, our issues were trivial.

I had agreed to split custody of Paul with his mother once she graduated in the interest of keeping the split amicable. That was certainly convenient for me, but it was not the best thing for Paul. Naturally, he played us off against each other. Naturally, the two households had different rules. This was predictable, but I had my attention so focused on my judicial career and my marriage that was not a marriage that I failed to predict it.

Similarly, everything that happened with Mary was predictable. She did not remember me. I was just her mother's boyfriend but I'm sure she could sense the relationship was not brand new. I still wanted to be her buddy, and that caused some light friction with Donna when Mary got to the age when she needed her own transportation.

Remembering the Silver Pigeon, I thought two wheels would do the job and Mary seemed more levelheaded than I was at that age. We went to the Honda dealer, and I cosigned the loan so Mary could buy a small and basic means of transportation. The Honda Passport was like a moped except without the "ped." It could not be pedaled and 70cc limited it to city streets.

A Honda 450 Nighthawk followed me home as well, the first new bike I owned since selling my off-road Suzuki and my road-conquering BSA to pay for school.

Donna was only a tiny bit worried about the Passport and I had to be the cosigner because we were still in the process of rebuilding Donna's credit from her medical bankruptcy. I hoped the arrangement would recreate some of the esteem I felt from Mary when she was the unofficial mascot of *The Rag.*

Mary would repay the loan from her earnings waiting tables, but I bought her a top quality, Snell Foundation certified, full-face helmet and demanded a blood oath that she would always wear it. Mary's safety was on my mind, but also the fact that the whole two-wheel enterprise was my idea and if Mary suffered any harm Donna would blame my attempt to be a pal rather than a father figure.

Mary's Passport was stolen, and because it was worth more than she owed on it, the insurance settlement left her with enough cash for a down payment on a real motorcycle, moving up from 70 cc to 250 cc.

I cosigned again. Donna was still OK with the transaction, but she was beginning to get nervous about Mary's safety. I explained again about the Snell Foundation and Mary's blood oath.

What happened next was a classic teenage comeuppance to controlling adults. Mary paid off the little commuter bike early. Having paid off two notes, she no longer required a cosigner when she financed a Honda V-45 Magna, a water-cooled four cylinders displacing 750 cc. This veritable crotch rocket was reviewed for the enthusiast press in a category called "muscle bikes."

Even worse, I caught Mary several times riding without that expensive helmet. She always had it with her—just not on her head, and the helmet acquired a strip of black from rubbing against a tire when she rode with the helmet dangling from the hook under the saddle

I started plotting to buy the Magna out from under her. It took some time for her to move on from what she called her biker chick phase, but she did sell it to me and I was able to breathe again. I must also admit it was more fun to ride than the civilized commuter Honda I had bought in that original visit to the dealer.

After some years of living together and after I had pretty much given up, Donna suddenly announced an unforgettable birthday present. We got married on my birthday, February 10, in the middle of an ice storm that had just struck a city that never has ice storms. Everything was closed down and we went to Judge Guy Herman's house. He married us in his living room with only the kids present and gave us a bottle of champagne.

Life was good in both the personal and professional spheres. Even before we married, Donna and I had taken up both sightseeing and camping in the Texas state park system. We had several experiences that made me question whether Donna was some kind of pied piper for cardinals—especially the males, the bright red ones.

Red was Donna's color. It suited her dark hair, and when we acquired the Oldsmobile convertible from the muscle car years she always wanted, I got it painted bright red and the interior done in red velour. It had red fuzzy dice hanging from the rearview mirror and a sound system that would tenderize meat.

She wrote in a red journal, her personal telephone was red, and her favorite attire around the house was a red silk kimono I brought her from Japantown in San Francisco.

Donna's affinity for red was the inspiration for a practice of mine that persisted over years. It was easy before we put our money in the same account; then it got harder. I would put aside a little bit each payday and sneak down to a jeweler, where I always had some loose rubies on layaway—the only way I could afford to buy them.

When the stones were paid for, I would have them made into a piece of jewelry for Donna. I gave her ruby earrings, a necklace, a bracelet. She had a pretty good collection of shiny red rocks before she understood they were real.

Until I got used to Donna's pied piper routine, I had always thought the male cardinals were too aggressive to hang out together, but I saw what I saw. Not just two or three. Many. I did not say it out loud to Donna before we were married, but in some Cherokee lore the redbird is a matchmaker. I did not want her to think I was making up stuff to change her mind. Why should I do something like that when we had been living together and even bought a house together?

Then Donna gave me that amazing birthday present and I had it all, until her health began to break down. At first, it seemed like one little thing after another, but then she was in the hospital for a fairly routine operation on her spine when her heart stopped. The surgeons called Code Blue, flipped her over, and started CPR. Then they brought out the defibrillator and applied electric shock. It took over ten minutes to restart her heart.

When she came around, she was not the same. She was generally more fragile, had gaps in her memory, and—most disturbingly—could no longer read or write. Overnight, we became dependent on my salary alone. Mary moved back in with us to help take care of Donna, who needed care as she slowly came back to normal.

While Mary and I were adjusting to our new realities, the medicos got an echocardiogram on Donna and discovered an aortic aneurysm. Had the aneurysm ruptured, even in the operating room, Donna's chances for survival would have been only about 1 in 5. By leading to the discovery of the bulge in her aorta, the cardiac arrest made repair of the aneurysm possible.

Because of the danger, she was back in the operating room as soon as the doctors judged her able to handle general anesthesia, which was in a matter of weeks. The paddle burns on her chest from having her heart shocked back into rhythm had not healed when she went back to the hospital for round two.

This time, they cracked open her chest, sliced off a section of her aorta on both sides of where the aneurysm had made the deadly little balloon that showed on the echocardiogram. Then they installed an artificial aortic valve. Thanks to that valve, she would be taking a blood thinner for the rest of her life to avoid clotting around the valve and a stroke when the clot broke loose.

The operation went well, but Donna had been seriously whacked, and her recovery was slow. Luckily, I had good health insurance, but good is not perfect. The day I came to take her home, I stopped by the billing office. Her previous hospital stay had taken care of all our deductibles, so I was not expecting much of a bill, but I got a surprise.

Hospital room, covered.

Doctors, covered.

Medicines and lab work, covered.

Artificial heart valve, not covered.

If I ever need another heart valve, I hope I have enough notice that I can try Craigslist, because that little sucker cost several thousand dollars. So it was that I whipped out my Visa card to pay for a heart valve, the most expensive thing I had ever charged at the time. I wondered if, should we not pay the Visa bill, they would come and repossess the valve?

It was good to snuggle with Donna at home that night, and she seemed to think so as well. Then, resting my head on her side, I heard KaKLICK KaKLICK KaKLICK. Her new valve was loud. I had the thought that anybody could check her heart rhythm without a stethoscope. I asked her if she could hear the valve clicking, and she said she could.

While I had not thought about it, seeing that incision down the middle of her chest and hearing that bionic woman noise led me to think the sexual part of our relationship might be gone. I was scared to death of hurting her.

It did not occur to me that she so strongly disliked being treated like a hothouse flower until the night she resolved to do something about it and pulled me on top of her. That KaKLICK that seemed so loud destroyed my erection but, right then, she began to unload on me about how she wanted her normal life back rather than just not being dead.

If the KaKLICK had not been a buzzkill, her tearful rant would have been, but I was able to settle down, reassure her, and start over. When I performed to her satisfaction, I was as relieved as she was. I had been only accepting the end of our sex life if it had to be—not liking it.

Her ability to read and write was also very much a part of her normal life, and it did not reappear right away. The first writing she was able to manage was signing her name and her signature was a thing of beauty. It was the opposite of what happened to my signature when I became a judge and had to sign stacks of documents every day. Her signature got as much better as mine had gotten worse.

Donna had gotten back into recreational reading and she had begun to compose short stories, which she was able to type into a computer. She had, as they said in state government, a "powerful Rolodex," and if she wanted a full-time job, she could get one.

We had—involuntarily—discovered we could live on my income alone, and she had always wanted to be a writer. I could understand that, because I have always been a writer and always wished I could get paid for it directly. In both of my careers, I got paid for it indirectly, but I understood the urge she was feeling. The urge to create was exacerbated by her brush with mortality.

I was so happy to have her back I would not have denied her anything. The next time I went to Reno for graduate school, I dropped off Donna at a writing class offered at the D. H. Lawrence Ranch, a beautiful venue for creativity owned by the University of New Mexico. She came out of the class even more pumped up than when she went in.

She gave me another gift when she started submitting her writings to literary journals signed "D. M. Russell." I had never said a word to her about using my name, but I was touched when she did, particularly in that context.

She was still in the process of collecting rejection slips (of which I and every writer I know have many) when her next health issue important enough for a scalpel came along. This was after many minor issues that came with the diagnosis of Marfan syndrome. She needed a rotator cuff repaired in a shoulder, a surgery that is common and not terribly risky.

After the heart stoppage scare, she and her family had emotionally prepared for her demise to the extent we could. She and I arranged our affairs to avoid probate. Rather than writing a will, we just owned everything jointly with a right of survivorship. The scare was over, but the property preparations remained. The emotional preparations, not so much.

The surgery went well, with no complications. She came home with plans for physical therapy on the shoulder just repaired, as she was able to tolerate it. The shoulder was not a problem, but I came home from work one day to find Donna with a bad headache.

She was not up to cooking—a task that we traded anyway—so I prepared some tortellini in pesto sauce. It's amazing the things you remember. She did not eat and she snapped at me when I urged her.

She had already taken her migraine medications to no avail, and when it got to be bedtime, the headache was still bothering her enough that she asked me to call the Austin Regional Clinic and ask what we should do. She was not up to dealing with it, so I would have to relay information to the nurse on duty.

I made the call and started discussing the pros and cons of heading for the emergency room with the nurse when Donna suddenly screamed. I looked at her, and she was holding her head in both hands and her mouth was still open but the scream had died down.

I hung up on the nurse. Donna had fallen backward on our waterbed still holding her head. She was not responding to me when I said we need to go to the ER, and I put my ear to her chest. I could hear no KaKLICK.

I called 911 and told the story as best I could in my state of panic. The operator dispatched an ambulance and told me to begin CPR. She said that was not going to work on the waterbed, so I had to get Donna on the floor.

Getting her on the floor was easier said than done, and it did my emotional state no good when the words for why I was having trouble flashed in my mind: "*dead* weight." Somehow, I was able to get her over the rail and cradle her head as she fell to the floor. I straightened her out, tilted her head back, held her tongue out of the way with my thumb, and I had just begun to puff when the doorbell rang. I set her head down softly and ran to the front door to let in two EMS techs.

They went to work on her immediately. While one handled oxygen, the other started an IV. He put the bag on one of those holders on wheels and turned to me and asked me to hold it while they worked, as if that were the most important task in the world.

I did what he said, but I was thinking that the IV bag was not going anywhere. *He's giving me something to do so I won't interfere.*

Standing there with the IV pole, I looked down at Donna being manipulated by these well-meaning strangers, completely unresponsive. *She's gone. Why do they bother? She's gone.* I leaned my back against the doorsill to keep from falling.

Next thing I remember, they had her on a gurney and they told me they were headed for the ER at Seton Hospital, the scene of so many of her medical ups and downs. When they left, I took out the home Rolodex and began making calls.

The hardest call first: Mary Katherine. Then I called Donna's siblings, all of whom lived in the Houston area. I told them what I had witnessed and that her condition was extremely critical but I did not express an opinion.

When I had made all the calls that seemed immediately necessary, I slumped down the wall and sat on the floor, crying. The next thing I remember is my dogs, Copper and Nelson, licking my face. We had recently taken in a stray from the neighborhood, who we called Pete. He was too short to reach my face while I was sitting up, but he was pacing nervously.

I got up and walked back to the bedroom. There was some sort of liquid stain on the carpet where her body had been. I could not say if it came from some of the medical stuff or from her. I got myself in a deliberate, one-foot-in-front-of-the-other mode and took a shower. I dressed and got in the truck and drove well under the speed limit to Seton. There was no reason for me to hurry, I thought. The others need to hurry because they don't know yet what I know. *She's gone.*

Time becomes a jumble. I remember that for some reason I called some friends who had put us up in their Manhattan apartment and we had invited them to come stay with us...did I think they were going to take a cab to LaGuardia and hop on an airplane?

I found my way to the room for those waiting for news about loved ones in the ER. I remember Hillary Miller, who was my primary care physician and Donna's, getting there. I remember Donna's brother Gene, who lived in some piney woods outside of Houston, getting there. How long were we in that room?

I can't say how long we were there, but I was still in my uber-practical mode, and I made some notes from which I would compose Donna's obituary. That sounds morbid now, but at the time it just seemed like what I ought to do to make myself useful. When Donna was dying before my eyes, I had not been useful. *Useless as the teats on a boar hog.* It's amazing the things you remember.

I think it was Dr. Miller who brought them the news. I remember Gene letting out an anguished howl. That man did love his sister. How in the world did he get to Austin so quickly?

Dr. Miller was telling me it was a slow bleeding stroke and if I had gotten her to the ER, they could not have saved her. Or was it that they would not have figured it out in time? What difference does it make now? I was on the goddamn telephone dithering over taking her to the ER rather than doing the one thing I could have done for her.

I'm not the only person to have experienced loss on such a scale. I knew even then that there is worse pain but I could not imagine experiencing it or even hearing about it.

It's a common custom to give grieving people some distance, to handle them with care. It's a valuable custom.

All these years later, and knowing people will read this who have been or will be in such pain, I am not here to blow smoke. No, you will never "get over it."

You will, in your own time, learn to park it somewhere that allows you not to trip over it.

~31~

INDIAN MEDICINE

Call him Shotpouch. That's not his name, but I didn't get his permission to write this and the Shotpouch outfit is big enough that no individual is likely to be mistakenly identified. He'll be as safe as I'd be among the Teehees, another big Cherokee outfit.

I first met Shotpouch in the early 70s at a little mom-and-pop in Jay, Cherokee Nation, Oklahoma. It was breakfast time and we got scrunched into the same table because there were more bodies than tables and it was that kind of place.

Shotpouch appeared to be full-blood, which turned out to be true, and of an age that his face no longer reflected any particular age, but you could tell that guy was *old*.

I had some bureaucratic problems with the BIA, and I was whining about them. He chuckled at my rendition, then launched into his BIA story. His complications one-upped mine considerably, and even though he spoke softly in that cadence of people still thinking Cherokee-to-English, by the time he finished his hilarious saga of bureaucratic ineptitude, the normal noises of people eating and chatting had quieted down considerably.

There was virtually complete silence when he finished, followed by a roar of belly laughs, and I knew I had just seen the art of storytelling practiced by a master. He also made me feel better, because my hassle was so trivial by comparison.

We wound up leaving at the same time and, as I got into my Karmann Ghia, he started walking in a direction where I didn't think there was much destination. One look at his gimpy stride led me to offer the old man a lift.

Shotpouch lived up in the hills, without electricity. He had a spring for water and an outhouse prudently downhill from it. His cabin was surrounded by what looked like an amazing vegetable garden...except I did not recognize some of the plants, and he appeared to be cultivating others I thought were weeds. He had chickens and several piglets to whom he spoke in Cherokee.

He was a fascinating man and that tale at the eatery was just a tiny example of what he could do in English. I was dwelling on the thought he must be incredible in Cherokee when a middle-aged couple showed up in a Chevrolet that looked older than they were and started an animated conversation in Cherokee that I had no hope of following.

I excused myself and strolled through his garden for a while. By and by, he came out and went directly to a row and oh-so-carefully removed a couple of green plants, roots and all. He sandwiched the plants between two damp paper napkins and handed them to the woman.

The man reached for his wallet and the conversation smoked me again, but some money changed hands. In spite of my limited Cherokee, I could see that the transaction was routine and both parties were satisfied. Whatever the purpose of the plants, the buyers seemed certain they would work.

My experiences that day led me to look the old man up whenever I drove to Jay from my home in Texas, usually more than once a year. Sometimes I would give him a ride to the store in Jay. Other times, we would just sit on his back porch drinking herbal tea. I was always partial to sassafras.

There came a time when I drove up that gravel path to his house and found his garden in terrible disarray. I drove over to the Seventh Day Adventist Hospital in Jay, where my R.N. aunt worked, and asked after him. I knew the medical community was small enough in Jay that everybody would know. I was told Shotpouch had walked on some months before.

He had a large extended family to mourn him, but he would also be missed by the public generally, or at least the Cherokee part of the public—just under half the population of Jay. Medicine people are an endangered species in Indian country. In some cases, the people who remember the ceremonies have already walked on, but it's more problematic that the young are not willing to devote their lives to learning the practices.

The lack of new blood is not about money. People are willing to do the hard work because they want to heal, but our medicine has proven insufficient shield against foreign diseases. In a world of antibiotics and X-rays, the old ways appear to be nothing more than superstition.

The scientific method is my lodestar for finding the truth and most people consider it the polar opposite of superstition. The only time I question the scientific method is when it fails to explain what I see in front of my face. It is at those times superstition seems to be less of an extra-scientific pejorative term and more of a category for an alternative tool kit.

Thinking of it that way results in equivocations like the absurdity of not "believing in" UFOs. If it's a thing, an object, and it appears to be flying, and I cannot identify it, then it is either a UFO or a failure of the English language to describe reality.

"Unidentified" is a placeholder that might be read as "pending more complete information." "Superstition" might be understood as a philosophical placeholder. In both cases, the fact that I cannot explain it does not prove that it can't be explained.

In the winter of 1990, a team from the Texas A&M University Archeological Research Laboratory was conducting a survey for the purpose of inventorying sites of prehistorical interest on Ft. Hood, the largest U.S. military installation in the world, located in Central Texas equidistant between Austin and

Waco. The Aggies noticed a formation of rocks on the ground obviously arranged by human hands.

Artifact density in the area was only "medium." Ft. Hood is in a rural area with good access to water. It has been suitable for human habitation for long enough that fire pits and arrow points are common. Some farmers who have worked Central Texas land for generations have extensive collections of prehistoric artifacts, principally arrow points.

Dr. Jack Jackson, the Ft. Hood staff archeologist, contacted the wife of the farmer who worked the land before Ft. Hood acquired it in WWII. She knew nothing of the rock formation but expressed the opinion that cultivation would have been limited to the flood plain of the Leon River. The river was close by, but the rocks were on high ground.

Brush was thick around the stones, but an early drawing of what was exposed at first discovery shows an inner and outer circle of rocks and three spokes on the surface. That summer, after some brush clearing exposed more rocks, archeologists began referring to the site as a medicine wheel.

My people are not of the Plains and we did not build medicine wheels, but we would keep a medicine wheel from harm because it is sacred to other peoples. In 1994, the pan-tribal American Indian Resource and Education Coalition (AIREC, of which I was a member) took on a serious cleanup of the site to facilitate further archeological study and to consider whether it was feasible to rebuild the medicine wheel.

Part of the plan was to cut the trees that had grown inside the wheel since it was constructed that would have obviously been in the way had they existed during the building. Most of the trees got cut, but the hazards of Indian volunteer labor were illustrated when the workers refused to cut one tree because it had an active bee hive and another because the branches contained prayer bundles.

AIREC members were allowed to visit the wheel as well as work on it, and apparently some members jumped the gun on using the wheel for its intended purpose. The tree with the prayer bundles was a small juniper that would, if the visible arcs were extended, fall between the inner and outer rings.

The bee tree was a large live oak, and for once Cherokee beliefs dovetailed with Plains Indian beliefs. We consider it bad luck to molest bees, and there is a ceremonial apology due if we enter a hive to take honey.

The work on the medicine wheel was going on after Donna and I were married. She knew about my ethnicity and she knew about the politics of treaty abrogation by the U.S. government and she shared my outrage. However, we never had occasion to delve into sacred matters because Cherokees just don't peddle their beliefs to others, Cherokee Baptists excepted. Donna knew that my great grandfather, Henry Teehee, was a Cherokee Baptist minister and I was a bit sheepish about that.

Donna was a well-known second wave feminist in Austin. Nothing in feminist thought contradicts Cherokee beliefs as I was raised to understand them. Cherokees find it normal for women to hold any position in traditional government, including war chief. It is true that women were more likely to be peace chiefs, but Cherokee warriors have shown themselves willing to accept leadership from a woman.

On the family level, our culture is matrilineal and matrilocal. The children belonged to the mother's clan, and upon divorce the father had to take his personal equipment and leave. I am the product of three generations of exogamy with white women, and I've heard it speculated that some Cherokee men preferred a white wife because Cherokee women possessed a bundle of rights unfamiliar to white women.

I hope that's not true as a matter of Cherokee demography and I particularly hope it's not true in my own family, but it's a common speculation that is not completely outlandish. Before the settlers showed up, Cherokee women expected equality. Plains Indian women, not so much—and there was the rub that concerned me.

Within AIREC, the Plains tribes were taking the lead in rebuilding the medicine wheel. There had already been some grumbling by Cherokee and Choctaw women about the rigidity of sex roles. Women could not go in the medicine wheel and young women having their period could not go anywhere near it. A conspiracy of women had integrated the sweat lodge we built next to the wheel, setting off some men who considered themselves very traditional.

What would happen, I wondered, when a white second wave feminist intellectual was added to this political stew because she was married to me? If there was a rift, which side would I take? I could see no middle ground.

Sounds hard, but it would not be. Just extremely unpleasant. I'm with my wife. As it happened, there was no problem I needed to finesse.

The Army had let us have a couple of empty barracks on Ft. Hood and one of them had a full kitchen suitable for feeding lots of folks. I unloaded our truck because Donna was in no shape for lifting. I got delayed a little bit navigating the boys over here and girls over there routine so I could sleep with my wife. I staked out our space and Donna was nowhere to be seen. I walked the length of the barracks without finding her, so I proceeded to the other building reserved for us, entered, and followed the sound of laughter. I peered through the doorway into the GI kitchen and there were about a dozen women in there, mostly middle-aged, and from their skin tones I would expect that their Indian blood quanta ranged from 4/4 to 0/0. Donna was sitting in the middle of this crew with a knife in her hand cutting up vegetables probably destined for the stew pot already warming on the stove.

I expected to be pretty hungry by the time that stew was done, so I eased out without interrupting anything, made it back to the truck, and drove out to the medicine wheel to get to work.

At the wheel, there was an animated discussion about the rotating cast of characters resting on the bee tree. It had been a colorful day, with appearances by blue jays, cardinals, mockingbirds, and the ever-present shiny black grackles.

Worthy of special notice was the bird the Plains Indians claimed was supervising the whole show. There was a hawk riding the thermal currents over and around the medicine wheel. None of these feathered spectators was at all unusual in Central Texas. I expect the hawk was dining well on the rodents uncovered as we cleared away the brush.

Several weekends at the medicine wheel blend together in my mind. Non-Indian readers need to understand that, because I am Cherokee, the medicine wheel is as foreign to my understanding as it is to theirs; medicine wheels exist outside of Cherokee culture and everything I know I learned as an adult.

My current understanding was formed over many conversations with medicine people from Plains tribes conducted over several years and in many contexts. All the tribal people who informed me seemed to agree on the broad strokes even though I never said a word about what others had told me. My conversations with old people, most of whom are gone now, involved Comanche, Kiowa, Shoshone, Cheyenne, and Lakota.

The medicine wheel is understood to be a portal to the spirit world. The location came as a gift to a tribal person, who would supervise the building in a manner consistent with his vision. These were Plains tribes and these visions came to males. More often than not, unsummoned.

First the land would be cleared. The spot where the man with the vision stood would locate the central cairn and spokes would radiate from there. Sometimes, stones would connect the spokes and give the appearance of a wheel, but sometimes the outer lines between the spokes remained in the minds of the users of the wheel. They existed in a ceremonial sense but were never built on the ground.

The stone cairn that would be built in the center was the spot where important business was done. Approaching it without the proper purification ceremonies would be extremely unwise, all my informants agreed. The least bad consequence would be the portal slamming shut. The worst would be allowing things to enter this world that do not belong here and therefore can only cause trouble.

What about all the handling by the scientists before they turned it over to Indians? None of that mattered. The wheel was dead. No ceremonies had been held there in many years. Some of the stones had even been carted away for use elsewhere. It was nothing but a pile of rocks, but it was located in a place that once held great power and might again.

The place we now call the Leon River Medicine Wheel was located by archeologists traipsing through featureless brush and cedar looking for any evidence of prehistoric human habitation. Sometime earlier, Indians were looking for a place to put a graveyard.

A political fight had been raging for many years that goes on to this day about human remains on this continent that are known not to be the remains of white people, either because they are too old or because of the items interred with the dead. To some, these remains are scientific data and those of us who claim they are human beings are no better than book burners.

This is not the place to have the argument, but only to explain that the federal government came around early and Ft. Hood contains a great geographical area that has been suitable for human habitation for a long time. Therefore, Indian artifacts and human remains are discovered regularly, and that is one reason Ft. Hood had an archeologist on staff.

Ft. Hood made every effort to repatriate human remains to the tribe with most likely cultural affiliation to the burial, usually Comanche. The Army offered an empty area where Indians could construct a cemetery. It would lend digging equipment and provide a fence. Since the place was in a nonpublic area of the military reservation, security would not be a problem

A Comanche medicine man was brought down from Oklahoma to pick a site for the cemetery. He was one of those with whom I subsequently discussed the medicine wheel, but the medicine wheel was not known by him to exist at the time.

The old man was taken out into the area the Army designated. He walked around, chanting softly in the Comanche language. His walking went on long enough to tire some younger people. One of them told me that what made him tired was not so much the distance as that the land the old man was traversing all looked alike. There might be a cedar grove here and a big old stand of prickly pear cactus there, but there would be more just like them over the next hill.

Abruptly, the old man looked right and left as if taking in metes and bounds by sight. Turning back to his escorts, he stated with certainty, "This is where they want it. Right here."

Nobody was certain who he meant by "they," but months later we learned that "right here" was a stone's throw from the Leon River Medicine Wheel. When I tried to engage him in conversation about what happened that day, he skated around the big questions. He was not angry at being cross-examined—I would say he was more amused—but he was not going beyond what he had already said and he remained convinced his choice was "correct" by standards he refused to explain.

Rebuilding the medicine wheel was simple. All we had to do was clear the brush and locate enough matching stones. The stones would not be finally put in place until the hard part, the attempt to renew the wheel.

The ceremonies to renew the medicine wheel, to attempt reopening what by then I understood to be a portal, according to the beliefs of my associates, took place on May 18, 1994. Donna left me the night of May 4, 1994. Her death certificate reads May 5, which if true would have destroyed the Cinco de Mayo holiday for me forever, but regardless of what the certificate says I know what I experienced. She was gone when they took her out of our house and all the disturbance of her body that took the pronouncement of death past midnight was just our modern ritual.

I was brain-dead for a long time after the night of May 4. Vivian Mahlab, who had been my law partner, was my keeper part of that time. My Air Force buddy Lou Axeman showed up as quickly as he could get a flight into Austin. In the Army's official report on the Leon River Medicine Wheel, there is a list of "men who took part in the rebuilding" and their reasons for being there. On that list appears:

"Louis Axeman, Assistant to Steve Russell."

That was a kind way to put it. Lou was my keeper. Even now, it's as if I went to sleep after the conversation with Dr. Miller at Seton Hospital and I woke up being hugged by Lee Lonebear, Cheyenne medicine man, at the medicine wheel.

This man I had never met before walked up to me at the medicine wheel, put his arms around me, pulled me close, and started whispering in my ear about my loss.

How does he know? Lou does not know Lonebear. Maybe the guys who brought the drum to Donna's memorial?

He said that he could see my pain and touching me he could feel it and I must be open to leaving my pain in this sacred place. Lonebear was still whispering to me but I could not make out his words over my sobbing.

Others were present, some of whom I knew and some I did not, but I was not embarrassed. It felt as if Lonebear had reached inside me and pulled out some of the weight I had been bearing.

I thanked him for his concern and concentrated on breathing deeply. To my surprise, there was no longer a catch in my breath.

The other Cheyenne medicine man, the older of the two, was about to speak to the group. William Tallbull was a legend in the repatriation movement, and he went on at some length about the solemn responsibility we were undertaking.

"You must remember," Tallbull said, "that all the relatives that we have are here; and the animal life, all the birds, the insects and all the plant life that's here—those are our relatives. And you treat relatives with respect. You ask them for help when there is a prayer."

Maybe there is not as much distance between Cheyenne beliefs and Cherokee beliefs as I thought.

Those of us selected to physically replace the missing stones in the wheel chose which stones to carry from piles of appropriate color and shape, some of which had come from Montana. Shoshone medicine man Haman Wise admonished us to think of each stone as a person we knew, whether living or walked on, and to meditate on the sufferings of that person as we carried the rock and placed it in the pattern. Each of us placed a final rock in the central cairn.

The final rock was Donna and I only briefly wondered if Lou's final rock was Carmen. He, too, had lost his wife, and that was part of the reason he had come to my aid so quickly.

When the geometrical form of the medicine wheel was complete, we shared prayers and the sacred pipe. I am terribly allergic to commercial cigarette tobacco; my eyes and my nose react instantly. Ceremonial tobacco has never bothered me, and I have always participated in the pipe ceremony, Cherokee or not.

On this occasion with the pipe, I had more emotional focus than I ever had before. Through the smoke, the smoke from my lungs, I saw a bird. There had been no birds during the ceremony, save the hawk high overhead. With over twenty men moving about, most wildlife had left the area.

When we filed out of the medicine wheel to where William Tallbull had prepared the sweet smoke for the final purification, the bird lit on a tree behind Tallbull.

It was a cardinal.

The red bird was a sign or it was hysteria, assuming there is a difference. Nobody who saw me before and after the rebuilding of the Leon River Medicine Wheel would deny that I was better. Not healed, but better. Better enough that I went back to work.

Getting back to work helped get me as close to normal as I was able to get.

STEVE RUSSELL

~32~

TO MARRY FOR GOOD

I thought I knew loneliness before I lost Donna.

Being alone was much worse after not being alone and Donna's years at death's door had imposed a ruthless practicality that taught me I could never be at my best by myself.

I am not wired for solo flight.

As I became able to open my eyes without immediately crying, I eased back into dating. I learned quickly that none of the women who had known me as Mr. Donna Mobley would turn me down. The problem was that Donna was always present.

Donna's death shook my life just as I was crossing between my first career as a judge and what I hoped would be a second career doing what I set out to do in the first place—teaching. I had effectively disengaged from being a judge when I sent back campaign contributions and signaled to the woman who was running anyway that she had a clear runway.

I got short-listed at three schools: California State University at Sacramento, and two University of Texas campuses, Tyler and San Antonio. After the interviews in Texas, I withdrew my application in California, because taking their money for a plane ticket would be wrong when I already had an offer from my first choice, San Antonio.

I had just written a scholarly paper about the fights in Texas over the Native American Graves Protection and Repatriation Act and agreed to read it at the annual meeting of the Law &

Society Association in Phoenix. I revised the paper the very next year, 1995, and it was published in the *American Indian Culture and Research Journal* at UCLA, one of the top three Indian studies journals. It appears in volume 19, dated 1995, but my recollection is that the referee process took longer than that, so I'm guessing the journal was running behind, something I did not yet understand to be common in academia because I was a rookie.

Driving to Phoenix alone in my mental state would have risked winding up in the Pacific Ocean wondering how I got there. Petra Carey agreed to act as relief driver and to be certain I did not forget where I was going.

In Phoenix, I met James Riding In, who would later become the editor of *Wicazo Sa Review*, another of the top three Indian Studies journals. Riding In chaired the panel where I read my paper, a presentation of which Petra gave me a friendly critique the night before.

Between finding a job and reading a paper, my new professional life was going as well as I could expect. My personal life was in a shambles. I was intimate with Petra again on the trip to Phoenix—my first sexual experience since Donna's death— and I had some hopes for when we returned. I gave her a key to my house in Austin.

One night we had an argument about something too trivial to recall, and she left, poking my key back through the mail slot. She thought better of it later, but my fear of abandonment had dialed off the charts. Petra would always be my friend, but not my mate.

I had high hopes for a couple of relationships from before Donna and I got back together, but my excellent taste in women meant that nobody who interested me would be sitting still. Most were paired up in happy relationships.

One had gone to Mexico to write. That sounded romantic, but I still had responsibilities in Austin, promises to keep.

Desperate, I started answering personal ads. Or I tried. There were just not many promising ones. The descriptions of what ladies were seeking usually disqualified me, and there was the further complication that I knew I was damaged goods and it was too soon to fully assess the damage. Then, on July 29, 1994, an ad showed up in the *Austin Chronicle* that appeared written directly to me:

WOODSTOCK REUNION? Are you
A hippie? Successful? Like cars? 40
something? SWF looking for...Call.
NSNDDF.

I still don't know what NSNDDF means, but the ad had a phone number and I understood that. After some telephone tag that only had a felicitous outcome because my son Paul and her daughter-in-law Robin had great tolerance for ambiguity, I invited the ad writer, who gave her name as Tracy Colton, to come to the court and watch me work. I assured her I would not know she was there. She did and I didn't.

When nothing that happened in court scared her away, we met for lunch at a little vegetarian place north of the UT campus.

I brought my resume and several short stories I had written, only one of which had published. I was 47 years old and if anything had fewer social skills than I had at 17, but I was still methodical. Everything I did or said was directed to telling her, truthfully, who I was.

She was driving the red Corvette I always wanted to drive. She had two dogs; I had two dogs (Pete and both of the cats had gone to live with Mary). She had been married twice; I had been married twice. Neither of us had really been at Woodstock. She was beautiful; I was still fat and ugly—there are limits to symmetry.

The lunch was a success in that she agreed to see me again. I was attracted to her, but pessimistic because I was not sure we had enough in common in spite of the apparent symmetry. I had only dated women who were not intellectuals a couple of times and never married one. It was not that she would bore me;

I worried that I would bore her, because I was as into my work as I had always been.

Either I did not bore her, or boredom suited her. Before long, I was living with her in the far away Austin suburb of Wells Branch, which is now practically in downtown Austin. This was because the house in East Austin that made me so proud when Donna and I bought it held so many memories: Mary's wedding party, the ice chests of red snapper we brought home from the trip where Paul failed to catch a shark, the night Davy Rodriguez cut a record album with my court reporter Cecil Caperton as sound man, the hot dog roast I put on for my St. Edward's students, the nights spent pasting mailing labels on political propaganda...all evidence of a life full to the brim, but any thinking of the good times would bring on the night of May 4, 1994.

I could not pay the price of continuing to relive that night.

Tracy and I went out a lot when we lived in Wells Branch in spite of the fact we both worked full time. She worked for the state auditing job-training funds. I think we were out on the town more than normal so I would not sit and get depressed. We also took long drives in the Texas Hill Country.

One night after the fall semester of 1994 would have started, we had been on one of those scenic drives and arranged for it to come out near the UTSA campus, where I would be teaching after I kept my promise to the voters and finished my term, which ran out at the end of the year. As it got dark, we were in Boerne, and I was driving my truck along the river, when we were suddenly surrounded by ducks and geese. Tracy got out of the truck and walked in my headlights, shooing the birds out of the way.

Tracy and I were together all the time for months, and our dogs had easily formed a pack of four. My dogs, Copper and Nelson, had always been outside dogs except when the weather was bad, but they were more than happy to learn to be inside dogs.

Getting married was not a simple decision, but Tracy made it easier. She knew that Donna had been the love of my life and she was OK with that. She once said we might all walk on and she would have to share me in the spirit world. I was gratified that she would think of me in those terms.

We were driving along in the Hill Country one day, talking seriously about my feelings for Donna and how that made Tracy feel. We enjoyed each other's company, but I would have to leave soon for my new job. Was it too soon, I asked?

In the midst of that conversation, a big male cardinal swooped down so close to the windshield I had to tap my brakes. He turned and came back for another pass in front of us. I pulled over.

The cardinal lit on a cedar limb a matter of feet from where I had parked the truck. It was regarding the two of us as if we all needed to discuss something.

I started the truck moving slowly and the red bird chose that moment to fly to the other side of the road.

Tracy had heard my story about what happened at the medicine wheel.

Don't ask me. I don't know. I do know that if Donna were able to speak to me though an animal and Copper the Corgi were not available she would pick a cardinal. Copper never expressed an opinion, but Tracy did. She maintained that Donna had given consent.

Donna gave me permission to remarry before she died as part of the adjustments we made after her cardiac arrest, when we were staring into the dangerous and uncertain black hole of open heart surgery. That I would pair up again was something Donna had practically demanded. Because she had been so clear about her wishes, my major issue was the kids.

Beth had caught on quickly that I was not just a dating interest. Tracy had told me that the ad I answered was composed on the spur of the moment at a party thrown by the *Chronicle* that promised all those who attended free personal ads. But the reason for attending was to grab a free ad *for Beth*. The ad I answered was the result of "Why not? It's free." I've always wondered if Tracy would have reeled me in so easily with an ad composed in advance and carefully thought out.

However that might have gone, the ad written on the fly had resulted in a serious relationship, and Beth seemed to be OK with me. I predicted she would just want her mother happy and she would hate to see a strike three, but subject to that trepidation, she would not object.

Paul was a special case. He had gone back and finished high school because the Marine Corps recruiter made him do it—I lacked the credibility. He had enlisted and had a date to ship out before Tracy and I closed the deal. He had heard of Tracy and talked to her on the phone but had not met her.

I foolishly gave Paul permission to have an unchaperoned going away party at the East Austin house. I was not living there, so if he made a mess, it didn't matter. The whole place would have to be cleaned up before selling it anyway.

Paul's going away party turned into a brawl. Paul sustained a blow to the head from a blunt object and got an ambulance ride to the emergency room. The hospital notified me, and I was with Tracy when I got the word. We hurried over to the ER.

That was how my son first made the acquaintance of my bride-to-be. He was drunk as well as injured and he vomited on her shoes. While she was wearing them.

From outside the family, it might appear that Mary would be a sticking point, but Mary and I had been through the preparations for Donna's death when it didn't happen in the heart surgery. Mary knew that Donna wanted me to remarry and she had no reason to dislike Tracy.

Tracy's son, Mykol, was in Seattle and getting most of his information about me from his mother.

Vivian Mahlab, my ex-law partner and my dear friend, stepped up to marry off her problem child, me. The wedding was at her house with Brady Coleman—who was by that time a recovering lawyer using his Screen Actors Guild card every chance he got—officiating by authority of being ordained a minister by the Universal Life Church.

The Universal Life Church had arisen with the counterculture, occupying a place on the edge of the First Amendment near the Church of the Flying Spaghetti Monster but of more practical use than the Pastafarians. Send in $5 to the Universal Life Church and you would be ordained for life. Unlike the Pastafarians, there was no theology—it was a card in your wallet rather than a colander on your head. I always pictured the founders of the Universal Life Church kicked back on some Caribbean island sucking down those little foo-foo drinks with paper umbrellas in them, because it had been raining $5 bills for a good long time.

For the vows, Tracy and I selected a well-known bit of Apache fakelore, the one with many lines expressing mutual dependence and ending:

"Now you are two persons, but there is only one life before you."

I'm Cherokee, not Apache, so why not an authentic traditional Cherokee wedding? The immediate practical reasons were that it was not deer season and Tracy had not had time to grow the corn even if she had a place for the purpose. On the other hand, there's a lot more Cherokee fakelore than Apache and I could have come up with something if I were willing to give a false impression of Cherokee practices on purpose.

My raising in the Muscogee (Creek) Nation combined with my father's neglect makes me error prone in Cherokee practices, but I would never misrepresent Cherokee ways on purpose. The importance to us was that the faux Apache vows expressed our intent.

I remember holding Tracy in my arms and the electric tingle I felt all over. She was so soft and warm, but it felt kind of strange kissing her with such enthusiasm in front of that many people...however, it would have been completely inappropriate to kiss her *without* enthusiasm.

Tracy looked younger than I, but she turned out to be a couple of years older. Her birthday is February 12; my birthday is February 10. It's handy, because I will never forget the anniversary of our marriage on February 11, 1995.

Tracy's background was a bit more prosperous than mine. Her dad worked on the line at General Motors; her mother was an executive who hit the glass ceiling at Avon. Like Donna, she came to me a bankrupt—hers a divorce bankruptcy rather than a medical one.

She has some college credits from Southern Illinois University and St. Edward's, but no degree. She had a real estate license, but it was inactive at the time we married. Raised Protestant, Tracy converted to Judaism before we met, a conversion that requires enough study to command respect. She did not keep kosher, but if she had it would have been OK with me because I am long weaned from Granma's habit of cooking everything in bacon fat.

Tracy backed me up through the years of sweat to earn tenure twice, first at UTSA and then at Indiana University in Bloomington, a pleasant little college town in Southern Indiana. Writing requires solitude—or mine does—and that means, for married candidates, an understanding spouse. This is the meaning of "publish or perish" to the family lives of professors.

Our married life began in an ancient two-bedroom mobile home situated on an acre of rural land. One weekend, I dropped by my office at UTSA, where I had high speed Internet rather than the dial-up situation in our trailer. While I worked, Tracy picked up a San Antonio newspaper to kill time. It wasn't long before she was reading me something that sounded impossible. A 250-year-old log cabin was for sale equidistant between the UTSA campuses. It was a humongous 3,400 square feet and the asking price was far below what we understood to be the going prices in San Antonio.

"It has to be a misprint," I said.

Tracy suggested that such a blazing bargain was at least worth a phone call and she asked me if I was up for looking at the house right then if the ad was correct. I was, but it didn't seem likely. Within the hour, we were on our way to look at the house, which turned out to be one of a kind. Love it or hate it—neutrality seemed unlikely.

We loved it, as did the owner. He was a graduating student at the UTSA School of Medicine and sale of the house was interfering with a lucrative move to a new job. His asking price was less than he owed. I had never before seen a real estate closing where both parties were paying the bank. Another thing we had in common with the new doctor was that we were in love with a strange house that had been built in Virginia, taken apart, and shipped by rail to Texas.

The walls were over a foot thick. The floors were stone and Saltillo tile. The roof was metal, with the added on central air conditioning stuffed up under the added-on metal roof. One of the oddest of many oddities was the front door, which came from a jail. It was about six inches thick and it came with one key, longer than six inches and weighing over a pound. It was too big for my pocket and the weight would have torn my pants. Tracy could lug it in her purse.

Two bathrooms has been added on, since the house had been built before indoor plumbing, like the house where I grew up. Downstairs, the toilet and sink were in a little room created by walling off a corner of the living room. But the shower—oh my! It was a fiberglass modular shower behind a door that opened directly into the living room. There was no room to get dressed and nowhere to hang a robe, so using that shower was a family-only deal.

We quickly came to understand that we needed working cats if we did not wish to share our unique home with rodents. We got Fox and Dana from a no-kill shelter; they were allegedly littermates, but Fox was a big white polydactyl cat and Dana was a small Siamese. The others were feral cats Tracy spent months civilizing: Emily and Samantha and a big old Maine Coon cat named Walter who was FIV+ and so lived in my office to keep him away from the others.

At the other end of the house was a room bigger than our entire mobile home with stone floors and a high ceiling with fans. There were two rooms between the living room with the jail door and what we thought of as the "party room," though we could never afford to throw a party in it. One was a bedroom and the other held a hot tub big enough for eight people and four dog crates for our pack.

Komar's Wolfgang Jazz was the only one who came from a breeder and we never did that again. We have always had at least two dogs and they have all been rescues. Still, Jazz was special: a big apricot Afghan hound, perfect enough to show if we were into that.

Jazz came to my family with a shiny black female Afghan we called Odessa because, Tracy's dad said, she was bow-legged and therefore had to be from West Texas. The real reason she was bow-legged was that, when Tracy adopted her, she was the sickliest of a malnourished basket of puppies considered worthless because the father was unknown. It was not certain they would be Afghans, and that story was my first notice that an Afghan puppy does not have the trademark long schnoz. They look like any other puppy when they are tiny. When Tracy got her treated for worms and started feeding her right, Odessa blossomed into a beautiful black Afghan hound, albeit without papers. Odessa was the only one who had but one name.

The brains of my two was Copper Rain, an imperfect Cardigan Welsh corgi, adopted during a visit to an outdoor sculpture exhibit. When I picked her up, she was sitting on a plaque naming the artist: Copper Rain.

I first learned she was a corgi from my vet. The other kind of corgi, the Pembroke, does not have a tail, and Copper did. She was light brown with black accents and personality to spare.

Finally, I had a black dog who was descended from two dogs with papers. Unfortunately, they were not the same breed. Nelson Mandela was the offspring of a fence-jumping operation, and his parents were known: a cocker spaniel and a black Labrador retriever.

You have to understand the status of dogs in our family to know that picking a human namesake was an honor to the human. Nelson was the sweetest dog you would ever meet, but he was dumb as a box of rocks. He was the only one of the four who never got the hang of walking on a leash.

Tracy's government auditing job was easily transferable to San Antonio, but in 1997 it got to be more trouble than it was worth. She mentioned that her new boss ran the office differently than the Austin office ran it ways that made it less transparent. I wrote it off to the difference between Austin—

where public service means living in a glass house—and San Antonio, where even newspapers have to report in the world of open records requests. I wrote it off until the day Tracy was abruptly fired.

The alleged reason was "losing" a file, which made no sense because of the limited number of places a file could be within the office. A misfile could be tracked down by looking next to every other file Tracy had handled. I didn't worry too much about the merits of the reason, because Tracy had been given zero due process. Texas is an "at will" employment state, but she was a public employee with many years in and the government owed her at least notice and a hearing.

I made a list of state laws and federal laws I felt were violated and got an appointment with the agency's lawyer. When I made the offhand remark that Tracy thought the job had become more trouble than it was worth, the lawyer folded like a cheap suit and Tracy got out with a clean employment history and a lump sum settlement for back pay. I was entitled to attorney's fees, but I did not insist because I was still getting used to what I could and could not do as a retired judge still available for assignment.

Tracy and I were both rendered dazed and confused, unsure of exactly what had happened and why. The firing was plainly on a pretext, but what was the motive? A year or so later, we read in the newspaper that the person behind the firing had been indicted over the disappearance of some public money. The indictment might have suggested why getting rid of an auditor with differing ideas about transparency made sense, but we just chuckled briefly.

Tracy had become a reservation agent for Southwest Airlines. She got a quota of free passes and I was allowed to use them. Daughter Beth graduated from St. Edward's University and briefly came back to live with us in the log cabin. Before long, she got a job as a flight attendant for Delta Airlines.

Beth, too, had a quota of free passes that her parents could share. She could have chosen her biological father or me to share her flying benefits. She chose me, and my feelings about her choice are as much about Beth's acceptance of me as they are about the professional advantage her choice conferred.

The ability to attend conferences on the cheap was invaluable to my tenure pursuit, and the companionship side of our marriage was enhanced because Tracy and I were able to travel together on both Southwest and Delta. We both have passports and we've used them in Europe, Canada, Mexico, the Bahamas, and Central America.

Twenty five years later, my third wife is living here in Sun City with her third husband and we have sufficient income for a middle-class retirement, although this is the United States and so that can be wiped out overnight by the wrong kind of illness. We faced plenty of challenges in a quarter century together and that was enough to put some punch behind my remark when I got my cancer diagnosis and realized I had to write this book now or never: *We had a helluva run!*

~33~

PATHS NOT TAKEN

If the song is correct and I'm entitled to one life for myself and one for my dreams, I am doubly blessed because the two lives are one.

I was born poor and I did not enjoy that. I did not become wealthy, but that was my choice. I chose it first when I quit the best job I ever had to enter the University of Texas. I chose it again when I graduated from a top tier law school and did not even interview for the jobs leading to wealth. That was not why I came to law school and I already knew I was not going to be poor again.

I did not get where I would have preferred in either of my professions, but—in both cases—there was a clear path from where I was and I did not doubt my ability to walk it. From my last year of law school, when it became clear there was no path to be a civil rights lawyer and get my school loans paid on time, I wanted to be a judge. That caused a spike in my grades towards the end, but I'm not sure my grades mattered because I knew I would have to start at the bottom as a justice of the peace or municipal court judge. Statewide, only a tiny minority of judges on those limited jurisdiction courts were lawyers but Austin had plenty of lawyers to fill the lower courts.

To start in the general jurisdiction court—the district court—you generally needed to be appointed by the governor. Governors favor lawyers from firms that have raised lots of political money for them. Those firms had offices in bank towers with glass walls and deep pile carpets. We ordinary mortals, who billed our time at less than half what those firms charged, called them "rug lawyers."

I caught the lower rung of the career ladder on the second try. In my dream of dreams, I would be an appellate judge, because I always understood myself to be a writer, no matter what I had to do to feed my family. Writing is important to a trial court judge, but appellate courts do all their business in writing.

Author, on the bench, 1987, © Alan Pogue.
Used by permission.

The place I wanted to be was the court of appeals, an intermediate appellate court, because that's where most cases end. Courts of last resort are picky about what they hear, and when people vow to "take it to the Supreme Court," they usually don't understand that how far you take it is up to the Supreme Court. A well-crafted dissenting opinion in an intermediate appellate court can have as much impact on the law as being in the minority on the court of last resort.

To judges on the highest courts, we who labor on the lower rungs of the system sometimes say, "You're not correct; you're just last." To sit on an appellate court is to be a public part of the ongoing conversation that determines what the law is when the legislature is ambiguous. In that conversation, I would expect to be part of a minority more often than not.

The path to an appellate bench was wide open for me. All I had to do was run my trial court for the benefit of the bar rather than in the public interest. That meant I should always continue a criminal case "to locate the missing witness, Mr. Green," and I should abandon my practice of sharply cross-examining lawyers against whom I found myself about to rule.

In the former case, I could not comply because—for an innocent person or a victim—justice delayed is justice denied. For a guilty person, the longer the time between the bad conduct and the punishment, the weaker the link between the two. The minority of cases that need a trial get harder to try as they get older. Memories fade and some witnesses just disappear. There is simply no public interest in delaying a criminal case for the lawyer to get his fee.

Having been in the defense lawyer role with Russell & Mahlab and also with Simons, Cunningham, I understand that whatever part of the fee you have gotten when the case is disposed of is all of the fee you are going to get. I understand the problem, but I could not discover a solution that did not prefer the bar's interests over the public interest.

The other problem, the colloquy with lawyers appearing to be on the short end of a decision, I will cheerfully admit is one of my own making. I have a perhaps excessive fondness for making correct decisions and I have more confidence in a decision I have talked though. A lesser consideration is that when I was practicing law, I hated to be blindsided by a judge...but I recognize that's just me.

An easy path to the Third Court of Appeals depended on adjusting those two policies. I had still determined to make a run for it and I was serious enough to live at the edge of the Austin court's appellate district in Comal County rather than where my UTSA teaching job was located in Bexar County.

My plan to make the run was a political Rube Goldberg machine that sputtered and died when the Republican Party took over. By the time partisan politics blocked me, I had been ignoring an open glide path for years. It was my choices that kept me from reaching an appellate bench—not the circumstances of my birth.

As a university professor, I would, in my dream of dreams, retire as full professor. Once more, the path to that end was clear if I chose to walk it. All I had to do was, in the words a superior at the University of Texas, "lay off the Indian stuff."

Even at Indiana University, it was clear that what I brought to the department was not that I was Cherokee but that I was a judge. It's true that there is plenty of research to be done in the nascent field called "judicial studies," and that I have a graduate degree in that field. Also, I remained a judge available for assignment while teaching at IU and I did hear a few cases.

When picking my research topics, I decided that Indians needed me more than judges needed me, and I picked accordingly. Once more, the path to my dream of dreams, full professor, was open to me and I knew what I had to do. As in the matter of reaching an appellate court, I decided with my eyes open.

If the paths to the Austin Court of Appeals or to a full professorship had been blocked by matters beyond my control, I would feel that fate shortchanged me. As it was, I was not shortchanged at all.

I had the education and experience to be, as a poet wrote, "the master of my fate" and "the captain of my soul." More than that would require a sense of entitlement reserved for people born wealthy. My prospects were meager, but I've been blessed beyond any rational expectations.

As I've aged, I've come to understand what most women understand much sooner. My real legacy is my children. I have enjoyed plenty of sex but to my knowledge I've never impregnated anyone. The schizophrenia gene has ruined enough lives in my family. So, I have four children, none of them children of my body unless you count my heart.

My four kids have given me nine grandkids. I can't "know" it's the same as if I were the sperm donor, but when my cancer was diagnosed, all four of them were there for me. To my children's children, I've always been a grandparent.

Appointed and elected and tenured all had their place, and they all rebut the evaluation I had put in my face as a boy. But at the other end of my life it's my family that convinces me I am not useless as the teats on a boar hog.

STEVE RUSSELL

~34~

BIRTH FAMILY

I owe the taxpayers of Texas more for my education than anyone in my family. For most of that first rate education I was paying $50 per semester. Let me say it again: not per semester hour, but per semester, without regard for how many hours I took. When I got to law school, I paid no tuition at all, because Texas does not charge tuition to veterans after their GI Bill runs out.

That tuition scheme birthed a practice that would be impossible today for any student not wealthy. I would sign up for eighteen or even twenty-one hours, attend all the classes for a couple of weeks, and then drop down to twelve or fifteen hours. Sometimes I missed the free drop date and so the courses are listed on my transcript, indicating that I had to take one exam and show I was passing.

The low tuition and free tuition for veterans were important when I had no family support. My grandmother encouraged me, but she had no money to offer.

My mother did not encourage me and she was not impressed when I graduated. She never had any respect for credentials of any kind, so my law license was no big deal. She was a bookkeeper for most of her adult life but she never considered becoming a Certified Public Accountant. While she would have made more money, she would have lost the pleasure she derived from expounding about what idiots CPAs are.

Texas judges are elected and I never got a campaign contribution from anybody in my birth family. In my first race, I would not take a contribution in excess of $50, so it's not like supporting me would have been terribly expensive.

By the time Tracy and I were married, I was done standing for election. My adoption of Paul had left me permanently estranged from Paul's biological father (my half-brother), who drove a cab in San Antonio and slandered me whenever he had a fare who identified as an Austin lawyer. I know because the Austin lawyers would tell me.

When I got hired by Indiana University in 2001, Tracy and I took on moving not just our stuff, but four dogs and five cats. We rented a van just for dogs and cats and daughter Beth went with Tracy as relief driver. I drove a rental truck with our car towed behind. I had the FIV+ cat and my half-brother Robert went along as relief driver.

Robert had dropped out of high school and served a hitch in the Coast Guard. When he got out, he went to work for Dow Chemical in a plant on the Texas Gulf Coast. He's still with Dow, and he would be more prosperous than I am except that he lost a lot of money and retirement funds on two very bad marriages.

His first wife got arrested for theft back in 1977 when I was practicing law and I agreed to represent her. She lied to me and did not come down off her lie until I was ready to pick a jury. From that time, I wanted nothing to do with her, so I had little to do with Robert until she cleaned out his bank account and left him.

I discovered two things about Robert when he was helping me move. One was that he lived within the right-wing media bubble where facts don't matter and the other was that he is an alcoholic. I hadn't had beer for breakfast since I was a teenager but he started drinking early every day. At my insistence, he drove early and then I would take over as he became less sober.

Because my mother changed jobs and never paid into a retirement account, she had nowhere to go and no income but Social Security when she got old. Her son Paul could not help her and Robert, for reasons unclear to me, refused to help her. My home in Bloomington had an apartment in the basement and I let her live there.

She was driving a fairly new Kia, and my son Paul drove her to Bloomington in her car. The part of her golden years I saw in Bloomington was spent playing bingo and Texas hold 'em poker. By and by, she pestered me to check her into a nursing home, but she could not afford one. I was pleasantly surprised that she understood when age rendered her unsafe on the road and she had me sell her Kia; I had thought I would have to pry the car keys from her cold, dead fingers.

When I decided to retire back in Texas, I got her into low income housing in Georgetown because she claimed she "would rather die" than live in Sun City "with all those rich people." I had picked Georgetown because we could no longer afford Austin and Georgetown was the closest city we could afford. Tracy picked Sun City.

As my mother's health deteriorated, I made a Medicaid application for her. On the second try, it was approved, and in 2015 I got her into the same nursing home where Tracy's mother was a private pay patient. At one point, we had them in same room, but they both zoned off into dementia.

Tracy's mother claimed my mother had a gun. My mother claimed that little people were invading her room through the ventilation spaces and that there was a dormitory for undocumented workers on the third floor. There was no third floor. One of the nurses was a German immigrant with a thick accent, and she accused him many times of assaulting her, even after management banned him from her room. When my mother got on the telephone and arranged her own transfer to the nursing home in South Texas where her last husband had died, the Georgetown nursing home was ecstatic, because each false report required an investigation and a copy of the file to the state agency that regulated nursing homes.

My mother's last marriage, which probably happened in 1968 when I was in Milwaukee, was to Coleman Pady, an Anglicization of "Padier," which he claimed was "coonass."

317

She thought Coleman's family would visit her when she moved, but that did not happen, and so she asked me to get her back in a Georgetown nursing home. The one she had moved herself out of would not take her back, and two others refused her based on her record of making frivolous complaints to which they would have to respond. The last one in Georgetown took her, and I moved her back in 2016.

From the time of my cancer diagnosis in December of 2017 and the various infirmities cancer brought along, I expected my mother would outlive me. That did not happen. When her cancer returned for a third time, she refused treatment and went into hospice, from which she walked on December 11, 2019.

When my health took a dive, but before my mother's did, I contacted Robert to ask for backup. His response was to say that I was a fool to involve myself with her and she was my problem. She had been my problem, and Tracy had agreed to watch out for her upon my demise. My last service to my mother, if you don't count cremation, was sitting in her hospice room as often as I could manage.

This dispatch began from my mother's hospice room, and I'm going to report from that night in my voice that night. The flashback digressions and digressions within digressions will be confusing, but they were confusing to me as well. My mind would wander, leading to dozing off and then being jolted awake by the least disturbance and taking too long, I thought, to orient myself to time and place.

One day the first week in December, 2019, my mother told my wife that she expected to walk on in the next twenty-four hours and she would like somebody to sit with her. So my wife took the first shift and I showed up that evening for the second.

It was a small room. I was sitting in her wheelchair and my laptop was resting on my walker. I plugged it in over next to the oxygen port, where the red plug normally supporting oxygen was not in use. My battery was charged up but I'm one of those paranoid souls who always plugs in when possible.

I woke her when I came in—not on purpose—but in no time she was resting with her eyes closed, either back asleep or about to be. She did not appear to be having any pain.

Just after Thanksgiving, she had given me a quiet chuckle when she made a complaint I had already made *in the same words* at her last care meeting. Her chart contained two pain medications to be dispensed on request: Tylenol and morphine.

I had complained that the former was too little and latter was too much. When I say the same words, I mean "too little" and "too much." My mother would never say "former" and "latter."

On my next visit in November, she related having had some pain after I had made that complaint and the nurse only offered Tylenol or morphine and so she just remained in pain.

"Why didn't you take the morphine?" I asked. "It might be overkill, but you would be out of pain and I could chase the doctor and get the order changed."

She told me why she refused the morphine: "It's *addictive.*"

It's not my custom to argue with somebody on her deathbed, but I was thinking that the government has won some hearts and minds for the so-called war on drugs when a patient will refuse a pain medication for fear of addiction at the very end of her life.

I went directly to the nurse's station for a look at her chart, and it turned out the doctor *had* dealt with my complaint. He had prescribed Tramadol—a mild opioid—and when the nurse made the offer, my mother heard "Tylenol" because she was used to hearing it.

I got the failure to communicate straightened out and then suggested to my mother that, if the Tramadol did not do the job, she should take the morphine and we would worry about any side effects later. I don't know if I convinced her. She didn't want to die a junkie dope fiend.

The last time we talked about pain, she said she only gets it when she eats certain kinds of foods—those being pretty much everything she likes.

The hospice nurse came along while I was still chuckling for the purpose of "taking vitals" and asking her directly about pain. She said she had none. I was glad she told others what she told me. I had been in so much pain for so many months that I would have traded being in hospice for the good drugs.

I had been taking opioids for about fifteen years. I had quit cold turkey three times, the last time a couple of months before my mother went into hospice. I had no symptoms of withdrawal. The last time, I was experimenting with weighing my pain against the petty humiliations I must endure to get the opioids. If I still knew the illicit drug market in Austin, I would get my drugs there, where nobody is going to count the pills or have me pee in a cup. I lasted a couple of weeks with no opioids and no withdrawal sickness, but I finally decided that I would have to suppress the pain or I would get no work done.

The nurse left and my mother was asleep before he hit the door. He told me she was wrong about walking on within twenty-four hours. I didn't know if he was correct but I was solid certain that he was telling the truth as he believed it to be rather than blowing smoke.

My mother awoke briefly and I told her what I wrote above. She just smiled. She, too, was telling the truth, not crying out for attention. I did not know who got it right until the next day.

I was pretty sure I wouldn't last that long. Not that I was going to die, but I was likely to wimp out. On that famous 1-10 pain scale, I was at 11 after doubling my allowed opioid dosage. And I was hot because my mother was always cold and they maxed out the heat for her. There was no way to get comfortable.

I can't help but wonder if I would feel differently—less of a wimp—if this woman had raised me? Or contributed anything to any of my political races? Or my university education? Or even, just once, told me she was proud of anything I ever did?

My earliest memory of my absentee mother was being beaten with a belt at age 3, when she had taken me along on her life in the oil patch of Pampa, Texas. When I was older, I watched her deal with the younger ones, Robert and Paul, the same way. I got no more belting, and I've had the cockamamie thought that might have been her way of showing affection.

There was certainly no other way.

On her fourth try, my mother had married a man who did not abuse her, Coleman Pady. While no abuse was something to celebrate, Coleman did have some downsides. He was a beer for breakfast alcoholic. Luckily, a mellow drunk rather than a mean one. He was illiterate. Totally. He was scared of road trips because he could not read maps or traffic signs that offered directions. He had memorized the safety ones to give verbal answers on his driver's license test. He would get irritated when other people read books in his presence, so she quit. She used to read trash, but she read lots of it, and when she visited Bristow—most often when one of her parents was in the hospital—I would score a couple of hours of entertainment from her castoff paperback mystery novels.

Coleman made his living by day labor—he was very good at carpentry and roofing—and he preferred to be paid in cash, because he could not read checks. Because he preferred cash, he did not pay as much as he might have into the Social Security system.

He was much older than my mother. All either one of them had was Social Security. When he walked on, it only took her a few months of watching her cash flow to realize she was bleeding.

They owned a home he had cobbled together when he bought a kit house, assembled it, and then expanded it on several acres of cheap land south of San Antonio.

She sold it to an undocumented Mexican on a contract for deed, since there was no way an undocumented person could get a mortgage. He paid her like clockwork. Getting paid was not her problem, because the man was hardworking and honest, as are virtually all of the undocumented immigrants I've known. Her problem was where to live.

By the time my mother sold out, my wife and I had a home in Bloomington, Indiana, with a basement built out into an apartment. The only part of the basement I used was the living room, where my desktop computer lived surrounded by bookcases. I offered her the use of the rest of it.

Why did I do that? Because I was presented with an elderly person who had no place to live when I had more space than I needed. I can see now I had an ulterior motive to learn more about myself. I always intended to write this memoir, with the major purpose to offer hope to other dropouts.

I knew that my relationship with both my parents had been cold and distant but I could not account for why. It's not that the account I had was unsatisfying. Rather, it was that I had none.

A couple of years after she came to Indiana, my mother could no longer drive, so when I put her Kia up on Craigslist for sale I quickly learned that contemporary students do not know what a "stick shift" is, much less how to operate one. Great hilarity ensued when they actually got in the car, but I learned quickly to screen the calls.

It was in Bloomington that my mother expanded her gambling from bingo to Texas hold 'em poker. I learned to play because she needed a ride once a week and I got tired of sitting off to one side reading a book.

I got to be pretty good when I could keep my head in the game. By that time, I had been a judge for twenty years and therefore had twenty years practiced at reading people. Hold 'em, I quickly decided, is not about your cards. It's about your opponents.

Over those years in Bloomington, I had many private conversations with my mother, ranging miles wide but only inches deep. The excuses she offered for not having me to burden her were so thin they did not even convince her, so we seldom talked about what her absence meant to me.

It was during this time I learned that she never had a ceremonial marriage to the man with whom she had two children and created a middle-class life for herself in the Permian Basin. I would not learn of the existence of my half-brother Douglas until I was retired and back in Texas.

She had given Douglas up in an open adoption, so finding him was no great trick in the age of Internet. In 2011, I drove her to Florida to meet him.

He appeared more mentally healthy than any of her other offspring, me included. He had some physical health challenges that led to a serious problem with short-term memory loss, but I could tell what kind of man he was by his wife and children. He was retired from a technical career and it appeared that his kids had launched successfully.

Meeting our mother took up a lot of emotional space for him. Our mother, not so much. She was not nasty but also not greatly interested. The road trip to Florida was an opportunity to hit several casinos and see the Redneck Riviera.

I slipped into reminiscing rather than focusing on my situation in a dark room that was uncomfortably hot watching a 91-year-old woman sleep. The pain in my back kept dialing higher and I knew I was not going to make it an all-nighter.

I understood wanting somebody to sit with her. I felt the same way when cancer came calling. It felt good to be visited by all four of my kids, but I came to know that dying is something you do by yourself. That is so even if there is someone literally holding your hand.

I would, of course, have taken her hand if that's what she wanted. But that gesture would lack authenticity. It struck me that we never shared a hug—not once, not ever. Still, I was willing to pretend. I suppose I was, in some sense, making myself available for confession. To the extent I could offer absolution, I would.

And it would have to be me. She had four sons. I was number one.

Number two, Douglas—the one I learned about in 2011—was supposed to rest quietly after surgery for an aneurysm. He was in no condition to travel.

Number three, Robert, after many days finally answered my text messages from a hospital in Houston. He had just had surgery for the same cancer I had, my grandmother had, and which was then killing my mother on the third try. Her experience is why I tell people I am a cancer survivor "so far."

Number four, Paul, was missing from the streets of San Antonio. My mother requested that I make an effort to track him down and tell him she died. Then I was to give him $500 and tell him he inherited it. I would provide the $500. I was fortunate that our mother figured that $500 was the maximum amount of money he could handle without danger of overdose.

This last part, starting with the accounting for my half-siblings, was written from my home, where I was slightly overdosed on opioids and looking forward to my bed that raises my legs and eases the pain.

She woke up as I was trying to escape. I told her, "I'm sorry if this will convince you I'm a bad person, but I can't do this. The pain is too much. I'll be back in the morning."

I didn't tell her that my conversation with the hospice nurse convinced me she was not going to die that night. She did not believe in professional expertise. Not the nurse's, not mine, not anybody's.

I resolved to get some rest as soon as the pain pills kicked in, but I found myself wishing I had more professional expertise than I did. I know little about hearing a confession and less about absolution.

Within two weeks after my futile attempt at an all-nighter, she did walk on. The hospice nurse called and said she kept trying to get out of bed. I knew the cancer had taken too much of her energy for that to be possible, so I asked if he thought that was the night. He said he did not think so. I thanked him for calling and said I would be along in the morning. He was wrong.

Absolution never became an issue, but now I find myself moved to offer a short sermon. The text from my half-brother Robert had said he just had most of his colon removed. I texted back:

"Cancer?"

When he responded, "Maybe," I could hear his voice with the undercurrent of "I don't have to admit you were right!" Yet.

We were both remembering the years I had pestered him about getting a colonoscopy and he would never tell me whether he had.

When the lab report came back, I thought it probable he had not, because his cancer was much more advanced than mine. It was bad enough that he had a colostomy bag, but the cancer had already spread to other organs.

My primary care doctor, Hillary Miller, had taken on fighting with my insurance company so I could start getting colonoscopies in my forties. I always tried to cut a deal with the anesthesiologist that he or she would not put me out unless I gave the high sign that meant I was having discomfort.

That agreement secured, I would then importune the surgeon to put the screen where I could see it. I've seen most of my colonoscopies because there was never the least twinge of pain and so I never gave the high sign.

It seemed like I always had polyps, which are where cancer is likely to start. They look like mushrooms, and the doctor lassos them with a thread and cuts the "stem." The first time I witnessed a polyp removal, I could not suppress, "Wow, that's a big one."

There was a pause, and the surgeon spoke up, "You do understand that this picture is greatly magnified?" Of course I did, but I was still impressed with all that activity going on inside me and I could not feel a thing.

Cancer, on the other hand, hurts like the very dickens. Mine was caught early. Robert's was caught late, perhaps too late. It is not irrational to fear cancer. It will hurt you and then it will kill you. It is irrational to fear a colonoscopy. I had no modesty issue because of my hospitalization as a teenager. I left every shred of modesty I ever had in that hospital. But if modesty is an issue for you, the anesthesiologist will be happy to put you out during the procedure—I always had to talk them out of it and sometimes they put me out anyway.

My mother has now walked on without having told me anything useful about how it was I had to make my own way. My father's header into the Willamette River removed him as a possible source, although I can imagine him protesting that he did his best to teach me how to set terrazzo. My half-siblings on my father's side are cordial enough, but none of them identify as Cherokee.

My grandparents gave me the only help I got from my birth family in launching out of Bristow. My grandmother walked on in my first year of law school, the spring semester of 1973. I hitchhiked up to Jay, Oklahoma, a small town in the Cherokee Nation where my Aunt Eleanor was watching over Granma's last illness. I stayed with her until she could no longer recognize me, and then hitched back to Austin.

The first year of law school is an intellectual boot camp, and most people who are going to flunk out do so in the first year. Dean of Students T.J. Gibson called all of my profs, smoothed over my absences, arranged for me to make up work, and arranged an untimely withdrawal from the only course for which make up work was impossible. Without the man the students called "T.J.," my attempt to chase a law degree would have ended the first year. T.J. joined Mr. Back, Mr. Gay, Sgt. Treviño, and Professor Sweeney among the pantheon of persons who extended opportunity to me with acts of kindness. None were relatives; none were Cherokee.

Bessie Russell was my mother to the extent I had one. She had expected to be gone before my education was complete, but she did not expect getting educated would take me so long. Jud Russell, my father surrogate, died in November of 1961, when I was 14. With both of them gone, having a family required my own acts of creation.

JUDSON GEORGE RUSSELL

Fathers matter, and the fact that our nation is peopled from coast to coast with single mothers and most of them have found ways to take up the slack does not make fatherhood as optional as many young men treat it. Writing about the death of my second wife was hard; writing about my father was harder.

Barbara Teehee, like so many single mothers, found ways to take up the slack. Her sons are responsible fathers.

My own situation was more complicated because I lacked even one responsible parent, but my grandparents worked wonders. In particular, they built a protective shell around my young ego, a belief in my human worth that could be damaged but not destroyed.

I'm more elderly now than I ever expected to be and I cannot claim that my father's opinion did not matter. Of course it mattered, but I was able to push back against the hurt. He was wrong about me. He had to be wrong about me.

Both of my sons are responsible fathers, but one of them was on that path before I entered his life. My wife Tracy was a single mother who took up the slack.

I try to be a responsible father. It's tempting to say that I only know what that is by knowing what it's not. I would never tell a child of mine that his or her talents are unfit for an adult man or woman. It's easy to see that is wrong, but how did I ever get a clue to what is right?

If I have a clue how to be a responsible father, if I've been able to keep a fire, most of the credit goes to a man who was 72 years old in 1947, the year I was born.

I told him I wanted to be like Mickey Mantle,
who escaped the poverty of rural Oklahoma,
and appeared to own New York City.

Mickey Mantle got to play in the World Series every year,
which I took to be annual games
between the New York Yankees and the Brooklyn Dodgers
to determine possession of New York.

"What position do you want to play?"

"Just like Mickey Mantle. Batter!"

Grampa laughed and laughed
until the laughs found the smoke in his lungs
and turned to coughs.

Grampa always wore a suit and tie to town.

He would walk to the post office, check box 384, and head for the Playmor pool hall. This was a men's place and Granma did not approve.

It was cool and dark. If I was with Grampa, and if I was quiet, I could watch the elders play dominoes around cigarette-burned tables with brass spittoons at the corners.

I often lost track of who won among the tall stories of the oil boom days and it took a long time for me to realize that the elders lost track of who won, too.

I learned to play dominoes and to lose track of who won at Grampa's elbow, sipping my Grapette,

uninterested in the stink of his Falstaff,
and oblivious to the clouds from his Pall Malls.

November 11, 1961 from the VA hospital in Muskogee
Grampa walked on, leaving

Memory:

Rainwater stained the wallpaper in the middle bedroom

where we kept Granma's glass jars,
evidence of her habit from the Depression:
pickled watermelon rind, green beans from the garden
peaches put up just in time from an overripe bushel
pears from a good year of the tree in the back yard

where we kept an old trunk
full to the brim with years and years of Reader's Digests

where I learned that Queen Elizabeth liked to drive
one of those English roadsters
on the left side of twisty rural roads
and her security detail complained.

where I learned that hurricanes
and giant fires and floods
broken dams and all manner of disasters
killed or did not kill
people who chose poorly or well
bad people and good people.

where I learned that Einstein might be correct
that the speed of light is a universal constant
but he's also incorrect:
God *does* play dice with the universe.

where I learned that a condensed book
is to a book
as condensed soup is to soup.

To protect the sustenance
for the body and the mind
Grampa and I, he too old and I too young
climbed the roof without shingles
and covered the leak with an asphalt sheet.

Memory:

The water quit coming through the roof
and then quit coming through the faucets.

Grampa had been trying to patch the hole
in the bathroom floor that made an icy draft
between the toilet and the bathtub
but he used the claw hammer to remove the patch
and expanded the hole big enough for a fat kid
to descend with a propane torch
crawl through the icy mud
and thaw the pipes.

Memory:

Loud mouthed Baptists at the door
invited themselves in
and invited themselves to pray
for Grampa's salvation

I learned loud nonsense is still nonsense
lengthy nonsense is still nonsense

The fools went on and on
and rather than interrupt the nonsense
Grampa peed on himself

when he should have peed on them.

Memories:

I still cannot tie a necktie, Grampa,
but I have taken your name.

I remember you blowing Pall Mall smoke in my ear
to soothe an earache.

I remember how you walked an Indian child down Main
Street,
not hearing that which should not be spoken.

And I want you to know

I am still playing batter.

~36~

DYING CHEROKEE

The cancer that seems wired directly to my childhood memory of my grandmother's cancer is, as I write, under control. It left me some gifts that complicate my life and cause pain every day, but I have won the race to finish this story before my biological finish.

While I hope to entertain, I was in a hurry to present my story to kids born to dire circumstances and to those who work with those kids. A close perusal of my story offers little hacks that got me through the university, but the broad strokes of my life offer advice not particularly profound:

Never give up.

Be willing to accept blows before you betray your most important values. Give thought to what those values are before walking into conflict.

If conflict walks into you, try to display the courage of the people you come from. Always have a plan...and a plan B, C, and D.

I was born Cherokee and I knew it, but I had to discover that I am Indian, descendant of those who survived the waves of death that depopulated the Western Hemisphere.

I first learned I was an "Oklahoma Indian" when I was introduced as such by a Paiute speaking to another Paiute. He did not mean it as a pejorative but just a fact. I learned later it is sometimes meant as a pejorative. As best I can tell, that is a legacy of the intertribal melting pot, which dilutes culture as much as intermarrying with white or black people.

When the U.S. was pursuing the "one big reservation" idea, it was still against the law in many states for Indians and white people to marry. Tribal laws did not usually reciprocate, but they did sometimes treat marry-ins differently, as in the Cherokee law limiting white men to one wife, a rule that did not apply to Cherokee men.

This law addressed a serious problem of white men marrying in to take themselves out of the "intruder" category and then marrying a white woman. The Cherokee wife would then become the cleaning lady while the white wife took on the social role and the white children were preferred to the Indian children.

Some tribal laws—to our eternal shame—did ape the colonial ban on intermarriage with black people, a ban that was often disregarded.

Both of my non-Indian grandparents had vivid memories of Indian Territory that they shared with me. The white folks who came to Indian Territory not on government business did not mind mixing with Indians because they really needed work or because the opportunity to swindle Indians outweighed any distaste for socializing with them.

My grandfather had mustered out of the army and needed work; my grandmother was brought to Indian Territory by her father and abandoned there as a teenager. They explain the most recent of three generations of exogamy by Cherokee men that produced me. In the two prior generations, I only know a bit about the Cherokee men. Of the white women they married, I only have their names.

The existence of my Cherokee citizenship represents a cultural dilution from after the Cherokee Nation became a constitutional republic. Before then, I would get my clan identity and therefore my citizenship from my Cherokee mother or not at all.

My raising among the Creeks did not give me any feel for the Muscogee language—I actually heard Cherokee more often—

but I did acquire some historical Creek heroes like Opothle Yahola (Laughing Fox), a war chief in the Seminole wars who then stood against slavery in the Civil War. More recently, both the white and Cherokee sides of my family told tales of Chitto Harjo (Crazy Snake), leader of the so-called Snake Rebellion against allotment of the Creek Reservation.

I took Harjo to be the Creek analog to Redbird Smith, who led the Cherokee resistance, and I took the Red Stick Creeks to be a Creek analog to the Nighthawk Keetoowah Society. The important thing to my growing up was to know that there was resistance to the destruction of the reservations in both tribes— the tribe of my blood and the tribe of my residence.

My early understandings may offend historians. I don't know how many Creeks the Snakes whipped for accepting allotments and I don't know if Redbird Smith really vandalized allotment records. The general narrative I internalized and later related to the African-American civil rights movement was historically accurate:

Both the Cherokees and the Creeks were evicted from their homelands under cover of bogus treaties, but those bogus treaties stipulated that the land in Indian Territory would never become part of a state without tribal consent.

I grew up with respect for Creek resistance and Creek ceremonies. The first stomp ground I attended was Creek rather than Cherokee but I always knew I was a guest. When I grew up and acquired a car, Cherokee ceremonies would not be so far away.

The Cherokee purification ceremony translates "going to water." That's all a non-Cherokee needs to know, and the only reason a non-Cherokee needs to know that is because sometimes when there is a public hearing over polluting a river, you may hear unusually passionate pleas from uneducated Cherokees who appear out of place in a discussion of parts per million of substances for which there is no word in Cherokee.

I can only write as who I am, and I have trouble separating the mundane from the sacred when I object to pollution of a river, be it in the Cherokee Nation or the Creek Nation or off somewhere claimed to have been nobody's property before the settlers showed up. A river is a river, and bits of ceremony cling to me that I have no desire to shed after all these years.

They lead me to tell those of you kind enough to read to the end why you may see an exhortation in my writings and those of other Cherokees: *keep a fire!* It sometimes ends important speeches and writings, a reference to the Cherokee Sacred Fire, a symbol of our survival as a people, burning from time immemorial. To lay a ceremonial fire, the first logs are aligned to the cardinal directions. The fuel is built up from there and is, if at all possible, fed by seven particular woods and lit by coals from the Sacred Fire. In modern times, through triumphs and tragedies, the Cherokee people have kept a fire.

Indians have bought a lot of nonsense from the settlers about the inferiority of all Indian cultures. At first, Indians paid for their shortcomings with land. They continue to pay when they accept the false but relentless claim that Indians are useless, vestiges of a time long gone. The epic scam that built the USA continues, the scam that claims a nation was made wealthy by stolen African-American labor bringing crops from stolen Indian land but nobody who lives today profited from theft.

Challenging that scam requires education and education requires that our kids understand that knowing a bit of our tribal teachings will make them welcome at many fires. That's the reason I wanted to write about my life.

As a child, I wanted to be like Will Rogers, the Cherokee who showed me what Cherokees can do and so perhaps what I could do. As an adult, I want to defy cancer like the great Ojibwe poet, Jim Northrup, defied cancer. And like some ladies named Harjo—the most famous being Suzan and Joy—I want to add another story of strength with roots in the Muscogee (Creek) Nation, another story that shows kids indigenous blood is a blessing if you reject the spirit-killing garbage we all had to traverse on the journey to discovering our inherent value.

Every story on that journey is another rebuttal to the calumny that Indians are on the brink of extinction. If you will have me, I'd like to add my story to many.

It's not up to me to say if it's wisdom.
Keep a fire!

STEVE RUSSELL

ABOUT THE AUTHOR

Steve Russell is enrolled Cherokee but born and raised in the Muscogee (Creek) Nation. He dropped out of Bristow, Oklahoma High School after the 9th grade.

After serving in the U.S. Air Force from 1964 to 1968, Russell acquired undergraduate and law degrees from the University of Texas at Austin and a graduate degree from the University of Nevada at Reno. He is retired from a first career as a trial court judge in Texas and a second career as a professor. His second career started at the University of Texas at San Antonio and ended with *emeritus* status from the flagship campus of Indiana University at Bloomington.

His first book of six, *Sequoyah Rising: Problems in Post-Colonial Tribal Governance*, was published in 2010 by Carolina Academic Press. His poetry book, *Wicked Dew*, was the winner of the Native Writers Circle of the Americas First Book Award in 2008.

His academic publications span thirty articles and fifteen book chapters in nine academic disciplines and have appeared in the United Kingdom, Sweden, Canada, India, and the Netherlands.

His popular publications include a cover story on the relationship between Texans and their guns for the December 15, 2017 issue of *Newsweek*, and his work for Indian Country Media Network included a series on tribal disenrollments, a biography of Will Rogers, a series on investing in the stock market, and several columns on academic pretendians. He was recognized by the Native American Journalists Association for best column in 2009, for best op-ed in 2013 and 2014, and first place for best on line editorial and second place for best on line column in 2016.

He lives in Georgetown, Texas with his wife Tracy, various four-legged friends, and a realization awakened by this book:

I pass on some useful hacks, but I'm not as important as I thought I was to the outcome. While I knew I had luck on the level of being struck by lightning now and then, I did not realize how many times others picked me up and carried me in the same way I have tried to carry my students. Looking at the number of smart people who took me on as a project, it becomes harder to see my tale inspiring others to the degree I thought it would. I persevered in the hope that the value lost in my faulty memory will be made up by the value found in the kindnesses done for me and that kind behavior will be passed on to create more of the magic that was my life.

Made in the USA
Las Vegas, NV
13 January 2021